English Words

This new edition is concerned primarily with the learned vocabulary of English – the words borrowed from the classical languages. It surveys the historical events that define the layers of vocabulary in English, introduces some of the basic principles of linguistic analysis, and is a helpful manual for vocabulary discernment and enrichment. An online workbook contains readings, exercises, and root lists accompanying each chapter to strengthen knowledge acquired in the classroom.

New to this edition:

- Updated with a discussion of the most recent trends of blending and shortening associated with texting and other forms of electronic communication.
- Includes a new classification of the types of allomorphy.
- Discusses important topics such as segment sonority and the historical shifting of long vowels in English.
- Includes a new section on Grimm's Law, explaining some of the more obscure links between Germanic and classical cognates.

DONKA MINKOVA is Professor of English in the Department of English at the University of California, Los Angeles.

ROBERT STOCKWELL is Professor Emeritus in the Department of Linguistics at the University of California, Los Angeles.

English Words

History and Structure

DONKA MINKOVA

AND

ROBERT STOCKWELL

CAMBRIDGE UNIVERSITY PRESS

Cambridge, New York, Melbourne, Madrid, Cape Town, Singapore, São Paulo, Delhi

Cambridge University Press
The Edinburgh Building, Cambridge CB2 8RU, UK

Published in the United States of America by Cambridge University Press, New York

www.cambridge.org
Information on this title: www.cambridge.org/9780521709170

First published 2001
Sixth printing 2006
Second edition 2009

Printed in the United Kingdom at the University Press, Cambridge

A catalogue record for this publication is available from the British Library

ISBN 978-0-521-88258-3 hardback
ISBN 978-0-521-70917-0 paperback

Wittgenstein: "The limits of my language are the limits of my world."

Contents

Preface to the second edition and acknowledgements

This is a completely revised version of *English Words*. We reorganized and expanded the material on word-origins in Chapter 1, updating it with references to the most recent trends of blending and shortening associated with texting and other forms of electronic communication. Our chapters on the morphological composition and phonetic structure of English are also rewritten and updated, and now include a new classification of the types of allomorphy, as well as discussions of important topics such as segment sonority and the historical shifting of long vowels in English. Revisions in Chapters 6 and 7 will provide more information and clarify obscure points concerning the word-formation rules. Chapter 8 has a new section on Grimm's Law, explaining some of the deep historical allomorphic links between Germanic and Latinate cognates. Our discussion of semantic change, in Chapter 9, was reorganized and significantly enriched. Chapter 10 contains new sections on syllable division and syllable weight, leading to a more principled account of the stress-rules of the loan vocabulary of English. The Appendix, which contains all root morphemes from the Workbook and the affixes in Chapter 5, has been thoroughly revised.

This second edition is also accompanied by a Workbook arranged to correspond to the chapters in the textbook. All Workbook exercises and root lists have been revised and updated; many new exercises have been added. The link to the Workbook includes a special chapter on recently borrowed words from both ancient and modern languages, and one on technical vocabulary in law and medicine. The Workbook is available on the Cambridge University Press website.

Since the appearance of the first edition in 2001, we have had the benefit of comments and suggestions by many colleagues and reviewers, for which we are very grateful. Henry Ansgar (Andy) Kelly returned our present (a copy of the book) with extensive corrections throughout. Among the colleagues who used the book and wrote back to us, we want to thank Thomas Cobb, Karl Hagen, Anahita Jamshidi, and especially Barbara Blankenship. Philip Durkin generously shared his research with us. Jared Klein's detailed criticism of the book made us much more aware of the potential for errors – we hope that all of the ones that he pointed out have now been eliminated. At UCLA several generations of TAs have helped us identify obscure passages and shortcomings. For this we thank Helen Choi, Mac Harris, Jesse Johnson, Dorothy Kim, Meg Lamont, Tom O'Donnell, Emily Runde, Jennifer Smith. Sherrylyn Branchaw helped greatly by both sharing her classroom experiences and by working with us on extensive corrections in the Morpheme Appendix and the Workbook exercises. We also gratefully acknowledge the support of the UCLA Research Council for facilitating the work that led to the inclusion of new material in the second edition. At Cambridge University Press we owe special thanks to Kate Brett who initiated both editions and to Helen Barton whose help with the current project we appreciate greatly.

Donka Minkova
Robert Stockwell
March 31, 2008

An introduction to the textbook

This book is about the sources of English words, about their etymology and history, about their sound-structure, and about some formal properties of English word-formation rules. It is important to realize, however, that it is not about *all* possible origins, it is not about *all* the ways in which English has introduced new words into the language, but rather it is primarily about a particular subset, that portion of the vocabulary which is borrowed from the classical languages (Latin and Greek) either directly, or indirectly through French.

This (very large) portion of our vocabulary is a familiar subject. Greek and Latin roots in the English language have been studied and have been part of the core educational curriculum at least since the Renaissance. Departments of Classical Languages traditionally offer courses under titles like "Classical Roots in English," and in the past a decent education necessarily included a full program in the classics. In the twenty-first century, however, it is extremely rare for students entering college to have a clear idea even of what Latin is – some ancient language, perhaps –, or whether English is derived from it or not, and even what it means for a language to be "derived," in any sense, from another. The word *cognate* is not only generally unknown to undergraduate students, it often remains conceptually obscure, because it is simply not one of the topics we grow up with these days.

We take the view that people cannot call themselves "educated" who do not have a minimal acquaintance with the history and structure of the words in their own language. It doesn't take much: if you are a word-lover and use a dictionary a lot, you will probably find much that is familiar in this book. But people don't usually use a dictionary to do more than settle an argument about spelling, pronunciation, or origin. It should be used for *much* more. Learning to appreciate those additional uses is one of the benefits we hope to provide to our readers.

Another benefit is learning to appreciate relationships between words that even the best dictionaries don't always make clear. These relationships are part of what linguists call *morphology*. Morphology, which addresses the patterns of word-formation and change, is not a very "regular" part of language. The forms that words take is largely the legacy of history, whereas both the sound structure of language and its syntactic organization are probably innate, for the most part.

A question which everyone wonders about, and often asks of instructors, is "How many words does English have?" And even more commonly, "How many words does the typical educated person know, approximately?" There is no verifiable answer to this question. We can tell you how many headwords a given dictionary has (or claims to have), or how many words Shakespeare used in his plays (because it is a closed corpus of texts, and we can count the number of different words – about 21,000 if you count *play, plays, playing, played* as a single word, and all similar cases, almost 30,000 if you don't). A very generous estimate of the vocabulary of a really well-educated adult is that it may reach up to 100,000 words, but this is a wildly unverifiable estimate. We can quote the *Oxford English Dictionary*'s statistics on the number of main entries: 231,100 (http://dictionary.oed.com/about/facts.html), but that figure is not particularly meaningful because it includes ancient as well as modern words, and most of the ancient words are unknown to us. They are obsolete and of antiquarian interest only.

One thing is certain: well over 80 percent of the total vocabulary of English is borrowed. The more we know about the sources and processes of linguistic borrowing, the better our chances of coping with technical vocabulary and educated usage in general.

An introduction to dictionaries

To use this book, one must have easy access to a good dictionary. Let us therefore start by asking, what makes a dictionary good? This prompts further questions: how did such books come into being? How do we get the most out of them?

All the major dictionaries of English are available in electronic form. The advantage of an electronic version is that it can be updated frequently, it allows easy cross-referencing, it allows complex searches on dates, etymology, author(s) of citations, it allows audio links to the pronunciation, etc. Beware: the electronic Thesaurus included in word-processing programs does not and cannot stand in for a dictionary which contains a full array of information relevant to the origins, the history, and the forms of words. Such electronic applications are primarily for spelling and for finding synonyms.

English dictionaries are a recent invention. Curiously, in Britain they started as an accidental by-product of ignorance. Anglo-Saxon monks often did not know Latin very well. Most of the texts they were copying were written in Latin, so they jogged their memories as any elementary language student might do today by writing translations ("glosses") between the lines. By the beginning of the eighth century the first lists of Latin-to-English glosses appeared, organized either by topic or alphabetically. Such lists are known as *glossaries*. The earliest known glossary arranged in alphabetical sequence not by the Latin, but by the English word, was produced in the thirteenth century. These were, however, only bilingual aids. It took another three centuries before someone realized there might be money to be made by publishing lists of English hard words with explanations of their meanings also in English. The first such publication appeared at the beginning of the seventeenth century. The first moderately complete English dictionary was another 150 years later: *A Dictionary of the English Language* in two volumes, by Samuel Johnson, published in 1755. Modern lexicography is therefore less than 300 years old.

The making of dictionaries has been a major scholarly occupation and a flourishing business enterprise for publishers in the last two centuries. In the twenty-first century electronic versions of the printed dictionaries have become an essential teaching and research tool. Since availability and access varies, here we will introduce three sources without which the exercises in the online Workbook accompanying this textbook cannot be completed.

The **Oxford English Dictionary** (**OED**) (http://dictionary.oed.com/) will be your primary reference aid. The *OED* online is unsurpassed in the richness and flexibility of use of its database. The wealth of information and search options available on the website can, however, be intimidating. For the college or university student unfamiliar with the organization of the entries, the website provides a helpful guide; we recommend also the very useful article entitled "Working with the online version of the Oxford English Dictionary" by T. T. L. Davidson (http://dictionary.oed.com/learning/university/worksheet.html). The article offers easy-to-follow step-by-step advice on searches with the following sample aims (we cite):

- Look up the meanings of a word and how they have developed.
- Look up when words and meanings were first used.
- Find out the etymological source of a word.
- Find parts of words (e.g. the uses of prefixes such as *pre-*, *arch-*, or *peri-*, or suffixes such as *-ology, -nik*, or *-ate*) and generally to investigate word-formation in English.
- Find out how far the *OED* systematically records relationships between words such as synonyms (e.g. the relevant senses of *reel* and *spool*).
- Secure some support for the ideas that speakers have about likely collocations of words (e.g. that we can say *notable collector* and *distinguished collector*, but only *notable frequency* and not **distinguished frequency*).
- Examine the details of processes in English such as the emergence of "zero-derivation" forms such as when *paper* started being used as a verb, presumably having been around for some time as a noun.
- Dig out meanings of words which poets might have been using when the poem was written but which have since disappeared.
- Try to recreate the vocabulary "fields" of political and social discourses of the past.
- Find out what contribution particular writers have made to the development of new words and meanings.

The American Heritage Dictionary of the English Language (*AHD*) is another important source of information related to the contents of this book.

Its fourth edition (Boston: Houghton Mifflin, 2000) is available at www.bartleby.com/61/. Although it does not have dates or citations, the *AHD* has many additional valuable features. The main entries are accompanied by sound-files, so the student can hear the word pronounced. Many items have links to color illustrations of the word, so one can actually *see* what a *pricket*, a *quoin*, or a *rabbet* looks like. Entries can be accompanied by notes on regional usage, current recommended usage, synonyms, and word-histories. Most importantly for the student interested in the earliest word-connections, the *AHD* provides links to Indo-European roots for words whose etymologies can be traced all the way back to reconstructed proto-forms. There is also an online article on Indo-European and the Indo-Europeans by Calvert Watkins, Indo-European sound correspondences, and a searchable appendix of Indo-European roots. Since the *OED* policy is not to provide reconstructed Indo-European forms, the *AHD* will be indispensable to the user of this book for mastering the material in Chapter 8.

Webster's Third New International Dictionary, Unabridged, is found at http://unabridged.merriam-webster.com/. The (current) electronic version carries a 2002 copyright. It is a fully searchable version which contains over 450,000 vocabulary definitions, each with etymological and phonological information, and very extensive usage examples. The *Webster's Third* provides some dates of the appearance of new senses; it allows searches of authors cited, and in addition to the usual types of searches it has the potential to search for rhymes, homophones, cryptograms.

We have only mentioned three online resources here – we believe that between them anyone using the book will be sufficiently well served. They have "aged" well, if a decade is enough for that qualification. This is not to say that there are no other good resources on the web – the electronic-based records of language are constantly growing, but we have no doubt that the *OED*, the *AHD*, and *Webster's Third* will continue to provide most reliable scholarly lexicographical information.

1   Word-origins

The two general themes of this book are the origins and the structure of English words. Our word-stock is huge. It is useful to divide it up between words that belong to the common language that everybody knows from an early age and words that are learned in the course of our education. The former, the core vocabulary, is nearly the same for everyone. The latter, the learned vocabulary, is peripheral and certainly not shared by everyone. The core vocabulary is not an area where we need special instruction – the core vocabulary is acquired at a pre-educational stage. Our learned vocabulary is a different matter. It varies greatly in size and composition from one individual to another, depending on education and fields of specialization. No single individual ever controls more than a fraction of the learned vocabulary. Often the extent of one's vocabulary becomes a measure of intellect. Knowledge about the history and structure of our words – both the core and the learned vocabulary – is a valuable asset.

The vocabulary of English is not an unchanging list of words. New words enter the language every day, words acquire or lose meanings, and words cease to be used. The online *Oxford English Dictionary* (*OED*) is updated quarterly with at least 1,000 new and revised entries; this is a fair measure of how dynamic our vocabulary is. The two sources of new words are borrowing and word-creation. In fields of higher learning, like the life sciences, physical sciences, medicine, law, the fine arts, and the social sciences, English has usually borrowed words from other languages to get new words to cover new concepts or new material or abstract phenomena. Words referring to notions and objects specific to other cultures are often borrowed wholesale. We may borrow a word as a whole, or just its central parts (the roots). We have borrowed mainly from Latin, Greek, and French. The discussion of borrowing will be a central theme in later chapters; in this chapter, we focus on the patterns of vocabulary innovation – the creation of new words – that occur within English. Before we identify the many ways of vocabulary enrichment, however, we want to address briefly the whole notion of lexical heritage.

1   Lexical heritage

Our lexical heritage consists of all those words which we as speakers receive from our predecessors when we acquire our native language. These inherited words in turn have originated, one generation, or many, back from the present, through borrowing or any of the types of word creativity listed below. The inherited words divide into **core** vs. **periphery**. For the most part, the core vocabulary has been part of English for many centuries, passed down with minor changes. Much of it is shared with closely related languages like Dutch, the Scandinavian languages, and the classical languages Latin and Greek. The notion of what it means to be a closely related language is the topic of Chapter 2. For the moment the notion of relationship can be understood in a pre-scientific sense, as in "family relationship."

The core vocabulary includes all of the common prepositions (*by, for, to, on, in, of, with, over, among*, etc.). They are learned well before the age of five, and so are conjunctions like *and, but, or*. They are an essential part of the glue that holds sentences together. Other core words are the auxiliary and linking verbs (*be, is, was, were, are, am, have, can, could, may, might, will, would, shall, should, must, ought to*) and many common verbs having to do with perception and the senses (*feel, think, dream, touch, hear, see*) and common names of everyday essentials and properties, body parts, kinship, colors (*food, drink, water, bread, mouth, eyes, hand, foot, leg, mother, father, brother, sister, black, white, green*). If we look just at the 1,000 most common words of English, over 800 of them are of this type. Many of them can be traced back as far as language history allows us to go – at most about 6,000 years before the present time. Among the top ten most frequent nouns identified by researchers at Oxford University Press: *time, person, year, way, day, thing, man, world, life, hand*,[1] only *person* is a historically borrowed word, and it has been in the language for over seven centuries. All five most frequent verbs in the language: *be, know, say, make, get* have existed in English as long as the language itself, and are shared with genetically related languages. Some of the other words have popped up in the language during more recent times – the last two or three millennia – and though more recent, in many instances their origins remain mysterious. For instance, the base of the word *penny*, which has been around for as long as English has existed, since early Old English, is completely unknown, *brunt* as in 'to take the brunt of the attack,' has been in the language since 1325, but it remains of unknown origin; *blear(y)*, from the fourteenth century, origin also unknown; *duds*, as in 'to wear fancy duds,' from the middle of the fifteenth century, also unknown. Closer to our times, *copacetic, posh* are from the beginning of the twentieth century; their etymology is unknown.[2] *Snazzy* is from the first Roosevelt administration starting in 1933, but no one knows its ancestry. Even words first recorded within our own lifetimes: *wazoo* (1961), *glitch* (1962), *ditsy* (1978), *full monty* (1985), *wazzock* (1984) have unknown or highly speculative etymologies.

---

[1] The information is found on the BBC News website: http://news.bbc.co.uk/2/hi/uk_news/5104778.stm.

[2] *Posh*, it should be pointed out, has been mistakenly claimed to be a blend of 'Port Out, Starboard Home,' the wealthy way to travel on a Mediterranean cruise, to avoid having the sun in your porthole. The *Oxford English Dictionary* considers this etymology to be without foundation.

In addition to its core vocabulary, English has a rich supply of learned words (*learned*, in this meaning, is pronounced as two syllables). The learned vocabulary is different from the core vocabulary in that most of it is acquired through literacy and education. It tends to be associated with technical knowledge and professional skills, though there is also a large part of it which is associated with humanistic education, with literature and the arts. Vocabulary enrichment in all of those areas has drawn heavily on borrowed words and roots. We return to the notions of core and periphery in Chapter 3, Section 3, when we will know more about the entry of borrowed words into English. Indeed, most of the rest of this book is devoted to finding out when and how the learned vocabulary came into English. But first we need to examine the sources of other words, words that are not part of the inherited core vocabulary and that are not directly drawn from the classical languages. These are words which are created by inventive minds, and they follow a small number of patterns. The next sections in this chapter address this topic: where do our new words originate? How do they get created and integrated into the language? The two general headings under which the specific types of new words can be grouped are "Regular word-formation" and "New word creation."

2　Regular word-formation

2.1　Derivation by affixation

Unlike the coining of new words which are not immediately transparent to the native speaker, discussed below in Section 3, deriving new words by affixation is usually completely transparent. This way of generating new lexical items is "regular" in the sense that it relies on pre-existing and recyclable language units that are familiar to any native or fairly proficient speaker of the language. The processes under the umbrella of regular word-formation, jointly known also as **derivational morphology** are, in many instances, so obvious that significant numbers of derivations are not even treated by dictionaries as separate entries. Since most of this book is about the complexities of derivational morphology, we do not want to anticipate details here. Roughly, by way of introduction, derivation by affixation consists in making up new words by adding affixes, or endings, to more basic forms of the word. Mostly these derivations require no special definition or explanation because they follow regular rules. For example, from the *Chambers Dictionary*, under the headword *active*, we find these derived words: *activate, activation, actively, activeness, activity, activism, activist*. Four of them are given no further explanation at all, two of them are given only the very briefest explanation because the meaning has become slightly specialized, and one – *activate* – is treated at more length because it has a technical sense that requires explanation. The question is, when is a derived form merely that, predictable and comprehensible by general rules of the language, and when does the derived form require treatment as a separate word? The line is not really clear, and different dictionaries make different decisions. But the basic principle is this: if the new word can be fully comprehended given a knowledge of the meaning of the base and also of the endings, then it is not a new word and should not receive independent dictionary treatment, because just by knowing the parts you also know the whole. But if the new word is not transparent in that way, then it requires full definition. Examine each of these pairs of words. The members of each pair obviously have a historically based derivational relationship:

graceful	disgraceful	spectacle	spectacles
hard	hardly	late	latter
new	news	custom	customs
civic	civics	sweat	sweater

The one on the right comes from the one on the left, but the relationship is obscured because some sort of change has occurred in the meaning of the derived form (on the right) which cannot be understood by general rules of the language. Under these conditions we must then say that the derived form is a new word (in the new meaning).

2.2   Derivation without affixation

Consider the following pairs of sentences in which the same words appear in different functions (e.g. as a noun and as a verb):

This is a **major** oversight.
She graduated with a **major** in geography.
She **majored** in geography.

My **account** is overdrawn.
I can't **account** for where the money went.

They weighed **anchor** at 6:00 a.m.
Tom Brokaw **anchored** the news at 6:00 p.m.

They wanted to **green** the neighborhood.
They were given a **green** light.
The kid pushed aside the **greens** on the plate.

We don't have any **doubt** it's correct.
We don't **doubt** that it's correct.

It's no **trouble** at all.
Don't **trouble** yourself.

In all these cases the verb or adjective and noun look alike and sound alike. There is reason to believe that the verbs are derived from the nouns. They are called "denominal verbs" for that reason, and they are said to be derived by a process of **conversion** – the noun is converted into a verb. In one sense such converted words are not new items in the lexicon. They are already there in another function (they are nouns, in these cases; but there are also adjective/adverb–verb pairs like *near*, *idle*, *clear*, *smooth*, *obscure*, and many more). Since this process allows one word to acquire a new function, we can also think of it as *functional extension*, or *functional shift*.

The process of conversion is extremely productive today: we can *chair a meeting, mask our intentions, air our opinions, panel the walls, stage a protest, weather the storm, storm the gates, e-mail the students, floor our enemies, polish the car, fish in troubled waters*, and so on. Conversions that have been around long enough are normally shown with a single entry in many dictionaries, with the identification n., a., v., meaning that the form occurs as noun, adjective, and verb all three. Recent, or surprising, conversions often get separate entries in the dictionaries. Like other word-formation patterns, conversion may produce short-lived or nonce words: *to history, to beetle* (both found in Shakespeare), *to conversation, to dead, to ditty, to maid, to nighthawk, to perhaps, to proverb, to wool, to word*, and even *to Devonshire* (1607) 'to clear or improve land by paring off turf, stubble, weeds, etc., burning them, and spreading the ashes on the land' (*OED*).

A relatively recent pattern of derivation without suffixation, which preserves the sounds, but changes the stress, of verbs vs. nouns and adjectives, is typified by pairs such as *convict, present, refuse, torment*, in which the last syllable is stressed in the verbs, but the stress shifts to the initial syllable in the other forms. Such words are known as *diatonic words*. Only two words showed such stress shifting before 1570, *rebel* and *record*, but the number of words, mostly borrowed, that have undergone such shifting in the last three centuries has been growing steadily.

2.3   Compounding

This is a very large, and therefore very important, source of new words. To produce new words by compounding, what we do is put together two words in a perfectly transparent way, and then various changes take place which may cause the compound to lose its transparency. A clear example from very early English is the word *Lord*, which is an opaque form of *loaf* 'bread' (you can see the *l* and the *o* still), and *ward* 'guardian' (you can see the *rd* still). A less extreme example, without the phonetic complication, is a word like *hoe-down* 'noisy dance associated with harvests and weddings in the old South and West.' The *OED* gives it as the equivalent of an earlier sense of *breakdown*, now obsolete in the relevant meaning. In neither case can one infer the meaning from knowing the meanings of the constituent parts. It is therefore an opaque compound. Other examples of the "Lord" type which were once compounds and are now recognizable only as fully assimilated single words include *woman* from *wife* + *mon* 'female' + 'person,' *good-bye* from *God be with you*, *holiday* from *holy day*, *bonfire* from *bone fire*, *hussy* from *house wife*, *nothing* from *no thing*.

A full description of compounds is far beyond our scope, but because it is the largest and most important source of new words in the English vocabulary, outside of borrowing, we shall try to convey some sense of the variety of words that have come into English through the process of compounding. We will not include those compounds that are now totally opaque, like *Lord* – which of course is no longer felt to be a compound at all – but will include examples of those that are transparently composed of two familiar elements that have taken on a unique new meaning that cannot be inferred totally from the meaning of the elements, like *airship* or *frogman* or *icebox* or *hovercraft*. By unique new meaning we mean that *airships* are not ships, *frogmen* are not frogs, an *icebox* is not a box made of ice, a *nightcap* as a drink or in baseball is not a wearable object, and *hovercrafts* do not hover.

We begin by distinguishing between *syntactic compounds* and *lexical compounds*.[3] One can always figure out what a syntactic compound means. Such compounds are formed by regular rules of grammar, like sentences, and they are not, therefore, listed in a dictionary. So if someone were to say,

> Playing quartets is fun.

We know, just from the rules of grammar, that they could also say,

> Quartet playing is fun.

Quartet playing is therefore a syntactic compound. Other transparent syntactic compounds are *birthplace* (a place of birth), *bookkeeper* (someone keeps the books in order), *washing machine* (we wash things with the machine), *moonlight* (light provided by the moon), *sunrise* (the rising of the sun), *policymaker* (someone who devises policies). In fact the majority of compounds we use on a daily basis are the transparent syntactic ones.

On the other hand, we cannot figure out what *ice cream* or *iced cream* means just from the rules of grammar. We cannot compute the sense of *ice cream* from something like,

> *They iced the cream.*

Therefore *ice cream* is a lexical compound which (if we don't know the meaning already) has to be looked up in a dictionary like a totally novel word. *Crybaby* must also be treated as a lexical compound, because it refers not to babies that cry but to people who act like babies that cry, i.e. who complain when anything makes them unhappy. Similarly, *girl friend* is not just a girl who is a friend, nor is *boy friend* just a boy who is a friend. Both of these compounds actually can mean what they appear to mean on the surface, but usually they mean more than that. A *bread-crumb* is a piece of bread, but a *bread-winner* does not win bread (or *just* the bread), and a *breadhead* is neither a head nor a bread. A *blue-collar* worker may wear a black shirt. *Sweetheart* is not a 'sweet heart,' whatever that would be, but it

---

[3] Students interested in finding out more about this topic should consult a truly great piece of scholarship, Hans Marchand, *The Categories and Types of Present-Day English Word-Formation*, 2nd edn (Munich: Beck, 1969).

is an opaque compound that has been in the language since the thirteenth century. *Highlight*, as in 'the highlight of my day,' is opaque from the seventeenth century. One can see how such a compound becomes opaque: it starts its life as a transparent description of lighting which causes some object to stand out, and then it is generalized or extended to refer to anything which stands out in one's memory or experience. As soon as this extension of the meaning is taken, then – at least in this meaning – the compound is opaque. *Bull's-eye*, which most speakers of modern English would associate with the center of a target as the primary sense, originally referred to the central protuberance formed in making a sheet of blown glass. Its earliest occurrence is a slang name for a British coin, the crown, from the beginning of the eighteenth century. The transfer of meaning to 'center of a target' is simply an extension of the notion 'center' which is a function of the way glass is blown, starting as a hot glob and gradually expanding outward in all directions from the center.

All of the compounds exemplified above have two parts, and their meaning is a function of the interaction of these parts plus the context of use that may gradually change them from transparent to opaque. Are there also phrasal compounds made up of more than two words? Is *maid of honor* or *good-for-nothing* or *man of the world* or *jack-of-all-trades* a phrase or a compound, and do we care? There is, unfortunately, no easy answer. Where the meaning is not obviously computable, some dictionaries list them as lexical compounds: e.g. the *Oxford English Dictionary* does not list *jack-of-all-trades*, but the much smaller *Webster's Collegiate* does. *Maid of honor* is listed by both, whereas *good-for-nothing* is not listed by any, nor is *man of the world*, though in both these instances there would seem to be good reason to single them out as having special properties: one can know about men and about the world without knowing what man of the world really means, and *good-for-nothing* refers to a special kind of worthlessness, usually laziness. The structure of these compounds replicates syntax, but creates a novel idea; on this basis some linguists put them in a special category labeled ***phrasal words***.[4] While non-phrasal compounds, both syntactic and lexical, may exhibit rather complex internal relationships, in phrasal words the syntax is that of a clause or phrase: a *devil-may-care* attitude, a *dyed-in-the-wool* scoundrel.

3   New word creation

We now turn to some processes which generate new words in more unexpected and, arguably, more creative ways. The main difference between the types of word-formation discussed below and the "regular" types in Section 2 is that "word-creation" can be a highly individual, personal matter. Also, the

[4] See Andrew Carstairs-McCarthy, *An Introduction to English Morphology* (Edinburgh University Press, 2002).

components of the new items are not easily recognizable or predictable. Dictionaries list these words as separate entries.

New words are coined every day – within families, within peer groups on campus, within professional groups, within same-gender or same-race groups, within geographical regions. Although most patterns of word-creation are subject to the normal constraints on sound-sequencing in the language, that is, they are phonetically *well-formed*, their birth, survival, and integration into the language are not guaranteed: whether a newly created underived word is successful or not can be a matter of cultural, economic, or political accident.

3.1   Creation *de novo*[5]

Though one might think it an easy matter to create a new word (without basing it on some pre-existing word or part of a word) for some new idea or new artifact, such creations are rare. Among the earlier such creations are *flabbergast* (1772), *fandangle* (1835), *hanky-panky* (1841), *flamdoodle* (1888). *Blurb* is another such a word, created in 1907 to refer to the embellished descriptions on the jackets of books. *Ditsy/ditzy*, an adjective of unknown origin, currently in wide use in American English, was first recorded in 1978. Other recent new, or "arbitrary" formations, as the *OED* labels these words, are *gizmo* (1943), *blik* (1950), *grok* 'to understand by empathy' (1961), *byte* (1964), *grungy* (1965), *Muppet* (1970), *dongle* (1982) 'a software protection device.'

Completely new words often start as trade-marks. *Kodak* was created and registered as a proprietary name in 1888 by George Eastman, founder of the camera company that bears his name. Of the word itself, Eastman is reported to have said that it was "a purely arbitrary combination of letters, not derived in whole or in part from any existing word."[6] *Nylon, Orlon, Dacron, Kevlar*, and *Teflon* are others, invented by wordsmiths within the companies that manufacture these products. Probably except for *nylon* these are not part of the core vocabulary. Even the *-on* ending of these words is obviously by analogy with words like *electron* and therefore, unlike *Kodak*, these words are not completely made up from scratch. Another word like *Kodak* is *quark*, which first appears in James Joyce's *Finnegans Wake* in the phrase "Three Quarks for Muster Mark," taken over by physicists to mean "Any of a group of sub-atomic particles (originally three in number) conceived of as having a fractional electric charge and making up in different combinations the hadrons, but not detected in the free state" (*OED*). In

---

[5] *De novo* refers to words created entirely from scratch, a process known also as *word-manufacture*; see Laurie Bauer in Bas Aarts and April McMahon (eds.), *A Handbook of English Linguistics* (Oxford: Blackwell Publishers, 2006), p. 498. In some sources the term *neologism* includes both *de novo* formations and *any* coinage of new words and phrases.

[6] The original source of this quotation appears to have been in a letter quoted in a biography of Eastman by Carl W. Ackerman (*George Eastman*, New York, 1930). It was picked up by H. L. Mencken, the great Baltimore journalist whose major contributions to scholarship were his monumental studies of the distinctive words and phrases of American English (*The American Language* and two *Supplements*, New York, 1936 [4th edn, the supplements in 1945 and 1948]).

the world of marketing, such creations are generally the result of massive commercial research efforts to find a combination of sounds that does not suggest something they do not want to suggest, words that have a pleasant ring to them and that are easy to pronounce. But most of the new words that even advertising experts come up with are derived from old words. For instance, the pain medication *Aleve* is clearly intended to suggest *alleviate*. The skin cream called *Lubriderm* is intended to suggest lubricating the *derm*, which suggests skin because of its occurrence in familiar forms like *dermatology, epidermis, dermatitis*. *Travelocity*, technically a blend, is also a new creation for the name of a corporation which assists with and speeds up travel planning. On the other hand other famous remedies, *Tylenol* (1956), *Prozak* (1985), *Viagra* (1996), are like *Kodak*, created *de novo*. *Frigidaire* is a clever coinage for a particular brand of refrigerating device. *Kleenex* is a similarly catching proprietary commercial name based on clean and the pseudo-scientific suffix *-ex*. Among the recent new creations with enormous popularity, the verb *to google* is a conversion of a proprietary name for an internet search engine launched in 1998. The *OED* suggests that "The name of the search engine was perhaps conceived as an alteration *googol* n., with allusion to the large amount of information contained on the Internet." The word *googol* itself, meaning 'ten raised to the hundredth power' was coined *de novo* in 1940. One can predict that *Skype*, the name of the software that allows direct voice transmission over the internet, will soon be making its way into the *OED* as a new entry, based on sentences such as "*Skype* me." or "Have you been *Skyped/skyped* yet?"

3.2 Blending

Creations by blending are also called *portmanteau words*, following Lewis Carroll (Charles L. Dodgson), the author of *Through the Looking Glass* (1871). He wrote:

> Well, 'slithy' means 'lithe and slimy' … You see it's like a portmanteau – there are two meanings packed up into one word … 'Mimsy' is 'flimsy and miserable' (there's another portmanteau).

Of course, to appreciate what Carroll was saying, you have to realize that portmanteau itself is a rather old-fashioned word for "suitcase," originally designed for carrying on horseback. Other examples of blends created by him are *chortle*, from *chuckle* and *snort*; and *galumph*, from *gallop* and *triumph*. In blending, parts of two familiar words are yoked together (usually the first part of one word and the second part of the other) to produce a word which combines the meanings and sound of the old ones. Successful examples, in addition to Lewis Carroll's whimsical literary examples above, are *smog*, a blend of *smoke* and *fog, motel* from *motor* and *hotel, heliport* from *helicopter* and *airport, brunch* from *breakfast* and *lunch, flurry* from *flutter* and *hurry, flush* from *flash* and *gush, sunbrella* from *sun* and *umbrella* (2006). *Blog*, first recorded in 1999, has quickly become an everyday noun and verb used with great frequency – it is unusual in this group because it uses only the last sound of the first word, while the normal pattern is for the beginning of the first word to be preserved.

Sometimes we lose track of the components of the new blend. The origin of the word is then no longer transparent. *Vaseline* is such a word. It was based on German *Wasser* 'water' and Greek *elaion* 'oil.' It was made up in 1872 by the man who owned the company that produced it. It is still a proprietary term (as *Kodak* and *Tylenol* and the other commercial terms above are), that is, it is trademarked and owned by the company that manufactures it. It is not uncommon for new technical terms to be created by blending. *Medicare*, the Social Security term covering medical care for the elderly in the United States, is now totally established, though it dates from as recently as 1965. *Medicaid* is the same sort of blend. In medical practice, a term like *urinalysis*, obviously from *urine* plus *analysis*, is so transparent in its derivation that one hardly notices that it is a separate blended word. In the field of chemistry, developing rapidly in the nineteenth century, new compounds and chemical substances required new names, which were chiefly blends: *acetal* (*acetic alcohol*), *alkargen* (*alkarsin* and *oxygen*), *carborundum* (*carbon* and *corundum*), *chloral* (*chlorine* and *alcohol*), *phospham* (*phosphorous ammonia*), and many more. Blending is an area of word-formation where cleverness can be rewarded by instant popularity: *sexploitation* (coined in the forties but common from the seventies), *Spanglish* (coined in 1954 as *Espanglish* and appearing in English since the late sixties), *sitcom* (1964) have general currency now. On a lighter note, the reward can even be amusement: unpleasant as the phenomena they describe are, the words *guesstimate*, *testilying*, *globesity*, *spamouflage*, *compfusion*, *pagejacking*, and *explornography* will probably elicit a smile.[7] It is no surprise that journalists delight in such blends: *nonsensory (overload)*, *examnesia*, *factigue*, *misleducation* were all gleaned from a single magazine article.[8]

3.3   Clipping

One of the many ways in which speakers shorten their words or phrases is by clipping off some part of a word, and throwing away the rest, like *quiz* from *inquisitive*, *phone* from *telephone*, *plane* from *airplane*, *flu* from *influenza*. The process often applies not just to an existing word, but to a whole phrase. Thus *mob* is shortened from *mobile vulgus* 'fickle commoners.' *Zoo* is from *zoological gardens*. *Ad* and British *advert* are transparently based on

---

[7] *Pagejacking* is an internet scam by which web porn operators clone legitimate web pages. The last three words are from the list of new words attested as available on the web page of the *American Dialect Society*: www.americandialect.org/adsl.shtml. They are defined as follows: *spamouflage* as "the non-spam-like header on a spam email message," *compfusion* as "confusion over computers," and *explornography* as "tourism in exotic and dangerous places."

[8] These are from the essay "Word fugitives" by Barbara Wallraff in *The Atlantic Monthly*, Dec. 2003, p. 180.

advertisement. In many cases it is apparent that they are deliberate shortenings to save time and space; such clippings are, technically speaking, not "new" words, but stylistic variants of existing words, so *copter, gas, tater, sci-fi, poly-sci, math, rep*. Many shortenings have entered the language and speakers have lost track of where they came from. How many people would recognize *gin* as in *gin and tonic* as coming from *Geneva*, *gin* as in *cotton gin* coming from *engine*, or *perk* as coming from *perquisite*? Look up *whiskey* to discover what it is shortened from: the form will probably be completely unfamiliar to you.

In "pure" clippings only one word is shortened, as in *chimp, prom, prof, lit*. In "pure" blends the two parts typically leave a trace which is recognizable as the shared portion of the two words, as in *mo-**t**-el, sm-**o**-g, chu-**nnel**, br-**o**-ast, Reag-an-omics, gl-**ob**-esity, ex-**am**-nesia, non-**sens**-ory, misl-**ed**-ucation, **fa**-ctigue*. Clipping can be combined with compounding, as in *norovirus* (Norwalk + virus), *humnet* (Humanities net), *Eurovision, sitcom*, producing words whose derivational history involves both clipping and blending. It would therefore be proper to classify these words as belonging to both types.

3.4   Back-formation

Sometimes the part of the word that is clipped off is a recognizable affix. The word *edit* is often cited as an example of this process, known as **back-formation**. The *American Heritage Dictionary* has the following felicitous discussion of this topic:

> *Edit* is not the source of *editor*, as *dive* is of *diver*, the expected derivational pattern; rather, the reverse is the case. *Edit* in the sense 'to prepare for publication,' first recorded in 1793, comes from *editor*, first recorded in 1712 in the sense 'one who edits.' There is more to the story, however. *Edit* also comes partly from the French word *éditer*, 'to publish, edit,' first recorded in 1784. In the case of *edit*, two processes, borrowing and back-formation, occurred either independently or together, perhaps one person originally taking *edit* from French, another from *editor*, and yet a third from both.

To *burgle* (1872), from *burglar*, is formed in the same way. Most examples of back-formations are no longer transparent. One does not ordinarily realize, for instance, that *cherry* is a back-formation from *cherise*, with the final *-s* having been wrongly analyzed as a plural suffix. The verb *grovel* is a misanalysis of *groveling*, which was originally *grufe* 'face down' plus *-ling* 'one who.' There are not many of these, and except for very recent ones like *burgle* they are opaque. They came into the language, after all, because the form they came from was itself opaque and open to analysis based on analogy with existing models of derivation. Transparent cases of back-formation by analogy are *to harbinge, to type-write, to baby-sit, to house-sit*, from the respective nouns in *-er*, and *to conversate, to orientate* from the nouns in *-ion*.

3.5   Abbreviations: acronyms and initialisms

3.5.1   Acronyms

Acronyms (*acr-o* 'tip, point' + *onym* 'name') are a special type of shortening. A typical acronym takes the first sound from each of several words and makes a new word from those initial sounds. If the resulting word is pronounced like any other word it is a true acronym. True acronyms are, for example: *ASCII* (pronounced [ass-key]) (American Standard Code for Information Interchange), *NASA* (National Aeronautics and Space Administration), *WAC* (Women's Army Corps, pronounced to rhyme with *lack, sack, Mac*), *SHAPE* (Supreme Headquarters Allied Powers Europe), *NATO* (North Atlantic Treaty Organization, pronounced to rhyme with Cato). *Qantas* stands for *Queensland and Northern Territory Aerial Services* and *FOLDOC* is a *Free Online Dictionary of Computing. Laser* stands for Light Amplification by Stimulated Emission of Radiation. Some of the most famous acronyms of World War II included *FU-*, as in *fubar* (F***ed Up Beyond All Recognition), and the GI favorite *snafu* (Situation Normal All F***ed Up). Often, however, to make an acronym pronounceable, we take not just the initial sounds but, for example, the first consonant and the first vowel together. Thus *radar* comes from *radio detecting and ranging. Sonar* is from *sound navigation* (and) *ranging*, where the first two letters of each of the first two words form the basis of the acronym. Few of us realize that the now very common noun *modem* was similarly formed from *modulator–demodulator*. Sometimes acronyms are based on even larger chunks of the words they abbreviate, e.g. *Comecon* (Council for Mutual Economic Assistance – the organization of the pre-1990 East European counterpart to the Common Market). A similar formation is the name of the computer language *FORTRAN* (Formula Translation). The conventions on capitalization vary. These are half-way between blends, clippings, and acronyms. When an acronym becomes fully accepted as a word, it often comes to be spelled with lower-case letters, like other words: *modem, radar* came to be treated that way, as well as *okay*; and indeed in the case of *snafu* some young people may not even realize that it disguises an obscenity.

3.5.2   Initialisms

If the letters which make up the acronym are individually pronounced, like *COD*, such acronyms are called *initialisms*. The word *initialism* meaning 'a significative group of initial letters' goes back to 1899 (*OED*). America seems to have been the great breeding ground of initialisms. They are rare in English before the twentieth century (*GOP* and *OK* are early examples, both dating from the middle of the nineteenth century). *TNT* (trinitrotoluene) dates from just before World War I. That war produced only a smallish number of acronyms – for example *WAAC* (Women's Army Auxiliary Corps) and *WREN* (Women's Royal Naval [Service]). It was during the first administration of Franklin Delano Roosevelt, starting in 1933, and then during World War II, that the fashion for acronyms and initialisms really got moving. The name for American soldiers was

GIs (for *General Issue*), and the vehicle they drove, the Jeep, was a pronuncia-tion of *GP* – General Purpose (vehicle). Roosevelt created many new government agencies, nearly all of which were referred to by initialisms (*WPA* Works Progress Administration, *NRA* National Recovery Administration, *CCC* Civilian Conservation Corps, *FCC* Federal Communications Commission, *FTC* Federal Trade Commission), to the point where the practice became respectable and started a trend that is now enormously productive in all areas of life. In the US, we pay taxes to the *IRS* (Internal Revenue Service), our driver's licenses are issued by the *DMV* (Division of Motor Vehicles), we watch *NBC* (National Broadcasting Company), *ABC* (American Broadcasting Company), and *CBS* (Columbia Broadcasting System). It would be unfair any longer to think of the trend for shortenings as American: the *BBC* (British Broadcasting Corporation) can be heard all over the world, the *ICA* (Institute of Contemporary Art) Café in London is known to locals and visitors alike, and Dubliners ride their acronymic *DART*, while the people in Berkeley and San Francisco ride their *BART* (Bay Area Rapid Transit).

Classifying a new form as either an acronym or an initialism is not always easy or possible. The words *CD-ROM* (compact disk read-only memory) or *JPEG* (Joint Photographic Experts Group) are initialism–acronym hybrids. Sometimes one and the same word can be pronounced either as an initialism or as an acronym – this is the case with *FAQ* (frequently asked questions), *SAT* (scholastic aptitude test). Yet another mixed pattern of shortening words involves the use of numbers in the writing of the word as in *Y2K* (year 2,000), *3D* (three-dimensional), or in their pronunciation, as in *AAA* ("triple-ey," the American Automobile Association).

In more recent times, the proliferation of initialisms and acronyms has been much aggravated by the ubiquity of computer abbreviations: e.g. *HTTP* Hypertext Transfer Protocol, *DRAM* dynamic random-access memory, *CPU* Central processing unit, as well as further government agency naming (*DOD* Department of Defense, *DOE* Department of Energy, *HEW* Health Education and Welfare). The word acronym itself came into being in 1943, near the end of FDR's life. Al Smith, the New York City mayor who ran for president in 1928 with FDR as his vice-presidential candidate, referred to the trend to create more and more initialisms as "making alphabet soup." Al Smith could not have known it, but in the Gale *Dictionary of Acronyms, Initialisms & Abbreviations*, the initialism *AAAAAA* is recorded as the name of an organization the Mayor would have joined: The Association for the Alleviation of Asinine Abbreviations and Absurd Acronyms. (This is also an example of a reverse acronym: see below.)

3.5.3   Imitative acronyms

An interesting phenomenon in recent years, a sort of political off-shoot of normal acronymic coinage, has been the rise of reverse acronyms – the creators start with a word they want as their name, say, for example, *CORE*, and then they work from those four letters to find four words which represent something like the idea they want to be associated with. *CORE* is the acronym for Congress of Racial Equality, *NOW* is the acronym of the National Organization of Women, *MADD* is the acronym of Mothers Against Drunk Drivers, *CARE* is the acronym for Cooperative for American Remittances to Europe. Organization names such as *AID* (Agency for International Development), *AIM* (American Indian Movement), *HOPE* (Health Opportunity for People Everywhere), PUSH (People United to Serve Humanity) have instant appeal and are easy to remember. A rather nice case of the opposite motivation, namely to poke fun at oneself, appears in the acronym of an investment group which is called the University Park Investment Group – *UPIG*, naturally. A similar jest, which at the same time pokes fun at a super-secret agency of the Federal government, is to be heard in the phrase "A *CYA* operation." A small hint: the first two words are "Cover Your ..."

The frequency of alphabet soup over the last decades is such as to justify the production of numerous editions of the *Acronyms, Initialisms & Abbreviations Dictionary* published by Thomson Gale. In its 11th edition (1987) it already listed over 400,000 entries. The 40th edition, released in August 2008, has at least a million entries; its shipping weight is 21.65 lb and it will carry a price tag of US $1190.00. The equally impressive 41st edition is expected to appear in April 2009. The online *Abbreviations and Acronym Finder* (www.acronymfinder.com/) boasts over 4,195,000 definitions in its database.

On the other hand, alphabet soup easily and quickly disappears from the language: among the many examples above, it is a fairly good bet that not every reader knew *NRA* (as National Recovery Administration), *WPA*, or *CCC*, and those who are not into computers would have been unfamiliar with several more of the above examples. Of the nearly a million items in Gale's *Dictionary*, an ordinary person would be unlikely to know more than two or three hundred. Very large numbers of them are abbreviations for technical terms. For instance, no one but a medical expert would be likely to recognize *TMJ* as an initialism for temporomandibular joint. *NRA* would have been familiar to most readers in reference only to the National Rifle Association, which illustrates another potential problem of acronyms: the likelihood that a sequence of three letters may be used in multiple ways. The 36th edition (2005) of the *Dictionary* lists 221 *AAA* abbreviations: from *Abdominal Aortic Aneurysm* and *Accumulated Adjustments Account* to *Auxiliary Array Antenna* and *Awaiting Aircraft Availability*.

3.5.4   Abbreviations in electronic communication

Another widespread recent phenomenon is abbreviations based simply on some very common phrase. People can produce acronyms or initialisms from any phrase and from just about any string of words. A popular restaurant chain on the West Coast of the US calls itself *TGIF* (Thank God it's Friday), memos start with *FYI* (for your information), individuals are referred to as *DEWMs* pronounced [DOOMs] (dead European white males). This practice did not originate in electronic communication, but now the fast-growing model of replacing words by single letters or digits has become a hallmark of text-messaging, also known as SMS (short service message) language. Some commonly used acronyms on texting are:

adn: Any day now   *lmao*: Laughing my ass off
b4: before
bfd: Big fucking deal   *lol*: Laughing out loud
brb: Be right back   *rofl*: Rolling on the floor laughing
gr8: great
gtg or *g2g*: Got to go   *ruok*: Are you ok?
idk: I don't know   *ttyl*: Talk to you later

3.6   Eponyms

These are new words based on names (*epi-* 'upon' *onym* 'name'). All eponyms necessarily involve some degree of change in the meaning of the word: *watt*, for example, refers to a unit of power, usually electrical, not to the individual named James Watt (1736–1819) who invented the steam engine. The number of new words of this type in fields like biology, physics, and medicine is very large, since new discoveries are very often named for their discoverers. In chemistry, newly discovered elements are often named after prominent researchers or places of research: *Einsteinium* (Es), *Mendelevium* (Md), *Nobelium* (No), *Berkelium* (Bk). Quite often we take the name of an individual, a character familiar from mythology, history, or folklore, a place name, a brand name, etc., and extend its scope beyond the original individual reference, thereby turning what is called a *proper* noun, i.e. somebody's name, into a *common* noun, i.e. a word like *boy*, *doctor*, *house*, *town* that does not refer to a particular individual but to a class of individuals sharing relevant defining properties. Even proper nouns, of course, can be of several types: those which are associated with real people, those that are associated with imaginary creatures or mythological figures, those that are associated with places. All three types have provided words in English based on their names. Some examples:

Based on personal names
boycott (Charles Boycott, an English land agent in Ireland)
dahlia (developed by Anders Dahl, a Swedish botanist)
cardigan (Earl of Cardigan, nineteenth century; a style of waistcoat that he favored)
derrick (the name of a hangman at a London prison in the time of Shakespeare and Queen Elizabeth I)
guy (in Britain, Guy Fawkes Day, November 5; for the Catholic conspirator, member of the Gunpowder Plot in Great Britain, 1606. Since he was held up to ridicule, the word had a common nineteenth-century meaning 'a person of odd or grotesque appearance.' It is apparent that Present-Day English has generalized and neutralized the word.)
lynch (Capt. William Lynch, a planter in colonial Virginia, originated lynch law in 1780)

nicotine (Jacques Nicot introduced tobacco into France in 1560)

ohm (unit of electrical resistance, named for nineteenth-century German physicist, Georg Simon Ohm)

sadistic (eighteenth-century Marquis de Sade, infamous for crimes of sexual perversion)

sandwich (eighteenth-century British nobleman, the Earl of Sandwich, who brought bread and meat together to the gambling table to provide sustenance for himself, and started the fast food industry)

Based on geographical names

bikini (the islands where an atom bomb was tested in 1946; presumably gets its meaning from the shock that the minimal beach-wear originally produced)

cheddar (a village in Somerset whence the cheese first came)

china (short for chinaware, from china-clay, employed in the manufacture of porcelain, originally made in China)

denim (cotton cloth now, originally serge, made in the town of Nîmes, southern France, hence *serge de Nîmes*)

hamburger (the word is an Americanism; from Hamburg steak, some form of pounded beef, found in Hamburg in the nineteenth century and brought to the US by German immigrants, though the word and specific concept of the hamburger originated in the US)

jean (from the Italian city of Genoa, where the cloth was first made, as in blue jeans)

port (a sweet fortified wine, shortened from Oporto, the chief port for exporting wines from Portugal)

sardonic (should be sardinic, coming from the island of Sardinia; the vowel change is based on the Greek form; refers to a type of sarcastic laughter supposed to resemble the grotesque effects of eating a certain Sardinian plant)

sherry (a white wine from, originally, Xeres, now Jerez de la Frontera, in Spain; the final <s> was deleted on the mistaken view that it was the plural suffix, an instance of what is known as morphological reanalysis)

spartan (from the ancient Doric state of Laconia, in the south of Greece; the meaning comes from their chosen lifestyle, which eschewed luxuries)

turkey (an American bird, confused in America at first with an African Guinea-bird, brought into Europe through Turkey, whence the name: but certainly a confusing sequence of borrowing and renaming!!!)

Based on names from literature, folklore, and mythology

atlas (he was condemned by Zeus, the leader of the Greek gods [called Jupiter by the Romans], to support the earth and heavens on his shoulders; the name was assigned by an imaginative early anatomist to the top vertebra of the neck, the one which supports the head; it came to refer to a collection of maps because many early publications of world geography showed drawings of Atlas holding the world up on his shoulders) *casanova* (Giovanni Jacopo Casanova de Seingalt. He wrote vividly about his sexual adventures throughout most of Europe)

chimera (a mythological Greek monster, purely a creature of the imagination)

morphine (Morpheus in Latin literature was the Greek god of sleep and of dreams, who could take on the *form* of anyone he chose: thus, *morphing* from one form to another)

nemesis (after the name of a Greek goddess who punished violations of all forms of rightful order and proper behavior)

panic (noises which caused fear in the flocks by night were attributed in ancient Greece to Pan, who was the God of misdeeds; panic is irrational behavior in the herd)

platonic (Plato was an early Greek philosopher; the word originally referred to the kind of interest in young men that Socrates, the first great Greek philosopher, is supposed to have had. As originally used, it had no reference to women, though now its main reference is to a non-sexual relationship between men and women)

saturnine (as the *OED* says, "sluggish, cold, and gloomy in temperament"; one wonders why a car should be named after it. Presumably the sense of saturnine is based on the fact that Saturn was the most remote of the seven planets known to ancient astronomers)

satirical (a satyr was a creature with a mixture of human and animal properties, and supposed to be gifted with a prodigious sexual appetite; the word satire refers originally to theatrical pieces which hold these qualities, and others, up to ridicule)

Based on commercial brand names

Band-aid® is commonly generalized to refer to any small bandage for a cut or scratch, and it has moved out into general use in metaphors like "The IRS needs major reforms; we've had enough of these taxation band-aids!"

Google® was an internet search engine registered and launched in 1998; the verb *to google* has been in use since 1999.

Jello® a particular brand of jellied emulsion, is generalized to refer to any edible substance of the same type.

Levis® a brand of canvas trousers, now refers to any denim-like, rough and ready, trousers.

Photoshop® to edit a photographic image digitally; used as a verb since 1992.

Skype® as a verb, means to use the special software, launched in 2003, for transmitting voice over the internet.

Sunbrella®, defines a type of fade-proof fabric, first registered in 2006.

Tampax® is one of many brands of feminine hygiene devices, generalized to them all.

Xerox® especially as a verb ("to xerox something"), has come to mean 'to copy by any dry process.'

Zipper®, based on the echoic word (see below) *zip*, which imitates the sound of speeding objects. The verb is from 1852, the noun 1926.

3.7   Other sources

It is part of the common mythology about language that many words must have come from efforts to imitate the sounds that the words represent. There are in fact only very few legitimate instances of this sort, and they are called **echoic** or **onomatopoeic** words. Leonard Bloomfield[9] distinguished between those words that are actually imitative, like *oh!, ah!, ouch!*, those that are coined to sound like a noise made by some object or creature, such as *bang, blah, buzz, burp, splash, tinkle, ping, cock-doodle-doo, meow, moo, baa, cuckoo, bob-white, whip-poor-will*, and those that have the property that "to the speaker it seems as if the sounds were especially suited to the meaning." His examples are *flip, flap, flop, flitter, flimmer, flicker, flutter, flash, flush, flare, glare, glitter, flow, gloat, glimmer, bang, bump, lump, thump, thwack, whack, sniff, sniffle, snuff, sizzle, wheeze*. The total number of any of these types of words that may be called roughly echoic is very small, in English or any other language. It is not a major resource for expanding the vocabulary.

Another rather unimportant, though often amusing, resource for expanding the vocabulary is through a process called **reduplication**, in which part or all of a word is repeated. The repetition can be of the complete word, or of part of the word. The words *itsy-bitsy, hoity-toity, helter-skelter* are based on rhyming, while other reduplicative words can alliterate, i.e. start with the same sound: *mish-mash, flim-flam, shilly-shally, tip-top*. Only a few of these examples are more than trivial expansions of the vocabulary: *dum-dum* (type of bullet), *bonbon, ping-pong, itty-bitty, hip-hop, fifty-fifty, hula-hula, so-so, boob tube, brain drain*.

4   Word-obsolescence and word-death

The previous sections surveyed the ways of introducing new words into English without borrowing them. Since well over 70 percent of the total vocabulary of English is borrowed, the rest of the book addresses mainly the composition and pronunciation of borrowed words in English. Before we go on to the discussion of loanwords, however, we need to add one more dimension to the "growth" of the English vocabulary: word-obsolescence and word-death. Cultural and social changes, or simply the "fashion" of word-choices can make some words obsolete: they will now be recoverable only in the historical dictionaries – they are found only in older texts. Some examples of such words, all of them recorded in the *OED*, are:

barm 'bosom, lap'	*hight* 'is called'
fain 'with pleasure'	*niman* 'to take'
here 'army'	*shaw* 'a thicket, a small grove'

[9] Leonard Bloomfield's book *Language* (New York: Henry Holt, 1933) was the most influential work on the subject in the first half of the twentieth century. It remains to this day a "must-read" for serious students of linguistics.

There is no clear reason for the abandonment of these words, except, perhaps, the coexistence of a word with a similar meaning in the language, as is the case with *here* 'army.' Indeed, a common trigger of lexical loss is the replacement of a native word by borrowings from other languages, primarily Latin or French:

blee 'color, appearance'	*ferd* (military) 'expedition'
dight 'compose, direct'	*fremede* 'strange, foreign'
rede 'advice, to be glad, to rejoice'	*tweon* 'doubt, hesitation'

Some words survived, but are restricted to dialectal use:

atter 'poison'	*busk* 'prepare, get ready'
bairn 'a child'	*emmet* 'ant'
besom 'broom'	*mere* 'marsh, fen'

Words can also disappear because the notions they covered were no longer needed:

fleam 'a surgical instrument for bleeding horses'
heriot 'feudal service/military equipment'
mesne (lord) 'an intermediate lord between a higher lord and a tenant'
sart 'a payment made by tenants for the right of taking brushwood from land'
sparth 'a broad-bladed battle-axe used in Ireland until the sixteenth century'
thane 'a military attendant, follower, or retainer'
wimple 'a type of head-covering for women'

These are words that can be encountered only in specialized historical contexts; they would not be recognized by most speakers of English, for whom they are recoverable only through the good historical coverage of the *OED*.

We can also talk of loss of meaning, when in the process of borrowing one or more of the meanings of the original word is taken over by the borrowing, as in

craft, originally also 'art'
haven, originally also 'harbor'
cynn 'kin,' originally also 'species'
idle, originally also 'empty'

All of these "losses" were amply offset by the adoption of words from the languages with which English came into contact. We now turn to the historical and cultural facts and factors that determine the growth and composition of the Present-day English (PDE) word-stock.

2   The background of English

A quick scan of a couple of pages in a dictionary that records the origin of our vocabulary reveals that many entries in it are historically "un-English." This is not surprising; languages travel with the people who speak them. No language in the world today uses vocabulary which is entirely free of foreign influence, just as no country's population can remain completely indigenous. A genetically "pure" language is as hard to imagine as a genetically "pure" population. Like the society we live in, the language we speak is a product of history. Like nations and governments, languages differ in their attitude and adaptability to external pressure. Periods of hostility, isolation, self-sufficiency, follow upon periods of openness, constructive interaction, and peaceful coexistence with the outside world. The overall inventory of words used in a language is the outcome of millennia of cultural, political, and intellectual history. In many ways our vocabulary mirrors the events which have taken place in the history of English-speaking peoples. The purpose of this chapter is to highlight the important socio-historical events and circumstances which have shaped our vocabulary. We start with some basic notions and facts about the place of English within the enormously broad picture of languages of the world.

1   The family history of English

Language families. The "family tree" is a commonly used metaphor in the classification of languages. Like human families, some language families are larger than others, some families stick together for long periods of time, while others drift apart, some families are mobile, others stay put. The parallel between the genetic relatedness of languages and the human family, or any minimal social unit which produces offspring, is scientifically imperfect, but it is still a helpful way of thinking about language in its historical context. The analogy with the family tree allows us to talk about "parent" languages evolving into "daughter" languages, about the splitting of families into branches of languages, about the maintenance and severance of family ties and the continuity of shared characteristics.

In terms of its ancestry, English comes from a large and mobile family whose daughter languages have developed considerable independence. Without specialized knowledge, the genetic similarities between English and the languages related to it are not immediately obvious. One way of establishing the historical links between languages is by looking into their vocabularies. As will be shown in this chapter, the English vocabulary today is stratified into layers of words that correspond to its family history. Some of these words are shared with languages from which English has been separated for millennia; only a trained philologist can detect their common traits. Sometimes, however, genetic relatedness is recognizable, either because of the "sameness" it involves, or because genetic history has been enhanced by external history. Our first step will be to identify the parent family and the family branches and smaller groups from which English originates. As we describe the family and its branches, we will evaluate the strength of the genetic and social links of English to the other daughter languages.

Indo-European. The family of languages to which English belongs is called *Indo-European*, a name which derives from the geographical range over which these languages were spoken before some of them spread to the New World: roughly from India to Iceland. *Indo-* refers to the fact that many of the daughter languages from earliest recorded times were spoken on the Indian subcontinent, and *European* refers to the fact that from equally early times most of the languages of Europe are descended from that common ancestor also. The term is strictly historical; in the twenty-first century descendants of Indo-European languages are spoken across the globe, in many countries on the continents of Africa, Australia, the Americas. Not all European languages are Indo-European in origin, however. Hungarian, Estonian, and Finnish belong to a language family called *Finno-Ugric*; Basque (in the northwest corner of the Iberian peninsula) is not known to be related to any other language of which we have any record. In India, the southern one-third of the subcontinent is occupied by speakers of a family of languages that are not related to Indo-European. The family is called *Dravidian*. It includes languages like Telugu and Tamil. The name for the ancient language from which the later individual Indo-European languages are descended, is *Proto-Indo-European*. *Proto-* means 'first, earliest form of.' In the context of language study, *Proto-* means that we have no actual records of this language but that scholars have been able to reconstruct in considerable detail what the earliest form of the language was like.

Indo-European is only one of perhaps as many as 120 language families that are not demonstrably related to one another.[1] Ultimately, the number of the "originary" human languages must be much smaller; indeed, it is commonly believed that there was only one human community where genetic evolution led to the emergence of human language because all languages are designed along basically similar lines. However, we have no idea, other than speculation based on modern languages, what the earliest languages were like. Our knowledge of specific languages goes back only about 7,000 years, whereas human languages have existed in forms probably not very different from modern languages for as much as a million years, quite probably a lot longer in some more primitive form. Our direct access to ancient languages begins only when systems of writing were invented and preserved on clay tablets, the earliest ones in the Indo-European family dating from the middle of

---

[1] Our statement is based on Raymond G. Gordon, Jr. (ed.), *Ethnologue: Languages of the World*, 15th edn (Dallas, TX: SIL International, 2005), online version: www.ethnologue.com/.

the second millennium BC, i.e. around 3,500 years ago. (In other language families of the Near East, where writing was first invented, the clay tablets date from about 5,000 or 6,000 years ago.) Our indirect access to the earliest forms of Indo-European, through comparison of ancient recorded languages with each other, allows us to establish fairly reliable reconstructions of Indo-European as it existed, probably in an area north of the Caspian Sea, about 5,500 years ago. This date, as the etymology editor of the third edition of the *American Heritage Dictionary*, Calvert Watkins, writes, is "the latest possible date for the community of Proto-Indo-European proper" (p. 2088). This is also the approximate date archaeologists have established for the spread of the wheel through Europe. Though we cannot prove there was a connection between the spread of the wheel and the spread of the Indo-European languages, speculation along these lines seems reasonable.

The chart below represents, in a very simplified form, the way in which various Indo-European languages "branched off" from the proto-language. The time line is an approximation. For obvious reasons we have included only branches which have living descendants.[2]

Retreat of glaciers in northern Europe
8000 BC
*Proto-Indo-European (c. 4,500 -3,000 BC)
|
*Indo-Iranian[3]-----------**Greek/Hellenic**
|
Celtic[4]---------------------Later European – I ------------------ **Italic/Romance**[5]
|
Balto-Slavic ------------------   Later European – II ----------**Northwest European**

The IE family of languages

---

[2] Indo-European languages of which there are no living descendants are Illyrian, Thracian, Phrygian, Anatolian, and Tocharian. The dagger, †, marks "dead" languages. Sanskrit is included in the chart because of its importance for reconstructing Indo-European. Our time-depth calculations are intended to approximate the dates at which each of the older languages were still more or less cohesive units, at least linguistically. These estimates are based on opinions cited in Calvert Watkins' essay on "Indo-European and the Indo-Europeans," which precedes the Root Appendix in the *American Heritage Dictionary*, 3rd edn (1992), pp. 2081–89, the opinions of various contributors to Bernard Comrie (ed.), *The World's Major Languages*, (Oxford University Press, 1987), and the opinion of Leonard Bloomfield as expressed in *Language*, ch. 4 "The languages of the world."

[3] Indo-Iranian is the (reconstructed) ancestor of two major subgroups, Indic and Iranian. The Indic group is huge, including many of the languages of India and Pakistan (e.g. †Sanskrit, Gujerati, Hindi-Urdu, Bengali, Rajasthani, Panjabi, Romany). The Iranian group includes Persian, Kurdish, and Pashto (Afghan). The oldest documents are in Old Persian; they date from the sixth century BC.

[4] Celtic branches into: *Brythonic* (†Cornish, Welsh, and Breton, spoken in Brittany in northwestern France) and *Goidelic* (†Manx, †Old Irish, Irish, Scottish Gaelic).

[5] The group includes †Latin, French, Spanish, Portuguese, Catalan (spoken in eastern and north-eastern Spain, chiefly in Catalonia and Valencia, also spoken in the Roussillon region of France, in Andorra, and in the Balearic Isles), Italian, Romanian, Sardinian (a Romance language spoken on the island of Sardinia; it is most similar to Popular Latin of all the modern Romance languages), Provençal (spoken in east-central France in a region roughly corresponding to Burgundy and in adjacent areas of Italy and Switzerland).

The Indo-European family is among the most studied of all language families, though other families such as Semitic, to which Arabic and Hebrew belong, and Finno-Ugric, to which Hungarian, Finnish, and Estonian belong, have also been deeply studied, to say nothing of the ancient linguistic traditions of China.[6] The twentieth century was a time of unprecedented interest in the structure and history of previously undescribed language families, from Austronesian and Bantu, to Yupik (spoken in Alaska and Siberia) and Zaparoan (spoken in Peru).

The discovery that some geographically widely separated languages, such as Hindi, Greek, and English, belong to the same family, was made by a British judge, Sir William Jones. He was stationed in India, and his interest in and knowledge of many tongues led him to notice that words in Sanskrit, Greek, and Latin showed similarities that could not be accidental. In 1786 he announced that these languages must have "sprung from a common source, which, perhaps, no longer exists," laying the foundations of a scientific field called comparative-historical Indo-European linguistics. Intense research over the last 200 years has produced many important insights into the relationship, history, and structure of the Indo-European languages. Indeed, understanding the structure of the present-day English vocabulary would be impossible without the enlightening results of Indo-European scholarship.

The chart above includes the "productive" branches of Indo-European. Not all branches are equally important for English. The boldfaced groups (Celtic, Hellenic, Italic) have had the strongest influence on our vocabulary, either because of territorial overlap or proximity, or for historical, social, and cultural reasons. Occasional contacts with other languages in the chart, such as Hindi, Persian, and Russian, have also left some traces, but their effect on English is not due to shared origin. The contribution of these languages to our vocabulary is similar to the contribution from unrelated languages like Japanese, various American Indian languages, or Maori. We start with some information on the branches of Indo-European whose relationship to English is evident only in more recent borrowings.

1.1 Indo-European

Indo-Iranian. Indic is the source of the languages spoken by the descendants of a huge migration into the Indian subcontinent from the Indo-European homeland. Most of the languages of northern and central India and Pakistan, among them *Hindi*, *Urdu*, *Bengali*, and *Gujerati*, are descendants of Indic. Among the earliest texts of any surviving Indo-European language are the hymns which form the basic part of the scriptures of the Brahmin religion, the

---

[6] Mandarin Chinese is by far the most broadly used language in a single country, with nearly 900 million speakers. The three runners-up happen to be Indo-European: English, with between 325 and 450 million native speakers (and an additional 150 million second-language speakers), Spanish and Hindi with over 300 million speakers each. The accuracy of these statistics is debatable – there are significant differences in the available sources, and naturally the numbers are always in flux.

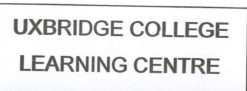

composition known as the *Rig-Veda*, dating from about 1200 BC; this is known to us through much later documents. *Sanskrit* is the classical language of the texts of the Brahmin religion as it was formalized and codified in the fourth century BC. The other branch of this family, the Iranian branch represented earliest by *Avestan*, is the ancestor of modern *Kurdish* and modern *Persian*, which is an Indo-European language even though, under the influence of Islam, it is written in the Arabic alphabet.

Armenian and Albanian are the ancestors of those two modern languages, respectively, and are generally viewed as independent non-branching lineages, though Armenian has two major dialects (East and West).

Balto-Slavic, includes the Baltic languages (Lithuanian and Latvian, though not Estonian, which is a Finno-Ugric language) and the Slavic languages. The ancestor of all Slavic languages is *Old Church Slavonic*. The *Cyrillic* alphabet, now the most widely used non-Roman alphabet in Europe, was devised during the ninth century in the course of translating the Scriptures into Old Church Slavonic. The Slavic languages are *Russian*, *Ukrainian*, and *Byelorussian* to the east, *Bulgarian*, *Macedonian*, *Serbo-Croatian*, and *Slovene* to the south, and *Polish*, *Czech*, *Slovak*, and *Sorbian* to the west.

The Indo-European branches and their daughter languages which are more directly responsible for the shape of our modern vocabulary are Celtic, Hellenic, and Italic.

The Celtic languages.[7] Celtic languages were once spread over most of western Europe, especially along the coastal areas and certainly throughout the British Isles. Celtic is the oldest language group of record in the geographical territory which later became Ireland and Great Britain. The Celts were in Britain when the Romans first arrived in the time of Julius Caesar, in 55 BC. After the Romans left, between AD. 400 and 410, the Celts who remained in southern England were left to their own resources; the traditional story is that their leader was responsible for inviting mercenary warriors from across the North Sea: that was the first-known contact between Celtic-speaking and Germanic-speaking peoples documented in writing. The idea of hiring mercenaries did not work out well for the Celts: the Germanic warriors soon took over, and much of the Celtic population was either assimilated, killed, or pushed to the outlying areas of the British Isles: Scotland, Ireland, Cornwall to the southwest, Wales, the Isle of Man.

The daughter languages of the Celtic group are: Irish, Welsh, Scottish Gaelic, and Breton, all of which are still used, as well as †Cornish and the now virtually extinct †Manx. Irish (also known as Irish Gaelic) is spoken to some extent by about 1.43 million people in the Republic of Ireland and has been taught in school there for a number of years even though English remains the main

---

[7] The first letter of the *Celtic* language group is pronounced [k], unlike the name of the Boston professional basketball team, which begins with [s].

language. It is also used by about 170,000 people in Northern Ireland, and by about 60,000 people in Britain. A 2001 census in Wales showed that 583,000 people, or 20.8 percent of the population, were able to speak Welsh. The number of people speaking Scottish Gaelic in Britain is just under 60,000. However, Gaelic has recently been given a measure of official status in Scotland through the Gaelic Language (Scotland) Act of 2005, facilitating the expansion of Gaelic-medium education and Gaelic learning throughout Scotland. The last speaker whose mother tongue was Cornish reportedly died in 1777, and today the language is familiar to fewer than 200 people in Britain. Breton, which was transplanted into western France by Celtic speakers fleeing from the fifth-century Germanic invaders of Britain, is spoken by some 270,000 people.[8]

Hellenic. The oldest Homeric poems are thought to date back at least to 800 BC, and records of ancient Greek dialects exist from the twelfth century BC. Athenian (Attic) Greek, also called *Classical Greek*, was spoken in Athens between the fifth and the fourth centuries BC, after which it was gradually replaced by *koiné*, the variety of Greek that was spoken between the fourth century BC and the sixth century AD; it is a mixed, de-regionalized language which is the direct ancestor of Modern Greek. It is of interest also because it is the language of St. Paul, whose epistles in the New Testament were written in koiné. It rivals Latin in its importance as a source of influence on the English vocabulary. The Romans adopted and modified many Greek words and roots. In English, Greek vocabulary comes both directly from the Hellenic source, and much more often indirectly, through Latin. As we shall see, the influence is entirely through higher education and scholarship, especially in the life sciences, which tend to use Greek as their main source of technical coinages.

Italic. This is the branch of Indo-European whose daughter languages have had the most pervasive and lasting effect on the composition of the English vocabulary. The group includes †Latin, French, Spanish, Portuguese, Catalan, Italian, Romanian, Sardinian, and Rhaeto-Romance.

Latin is attested since the sixth century BC. It started out simply as the language of ancient Rome, and it was just one of a number of Italic languages. The economic, military, and cultural success of the Romans secured a dominant position for Latin. That language soon swamped all others in the family, as well as non-Indo-European languages like Etruscan that were at one time spoken on the Italian peninsula. The use of Latin by the Roman Catholic Church later played a major role in the spread and continuity of the Latin language, throughout the

---

[8] Fot updates on the state of these languages in Europe the reader should consult the website of EBLUL (European Bureau for Lesser Used Languages (www.eblul.org/), from where our information was collected. Data on Breton are difficult to access because the French state does not recognize the language and therefore does not collect census data on Breton; the information we cite is from the EBLUL link to the Office of the Breton Language.

Middle Ages and indeed to the present day. All the modern Italic languages listed above, also commonly referred to as the *Romance* languages, are simply what Latin became in different parts of the Roman Empire. Thus, Modern Italian is the direct descendant of Latin in Italy; Modern Spanish is one of the direct descendants of Latin on the Iberian peninsula, Modern French is a development of the speech of Romans living in France and so on. Technically speaking, the language differentiation that produced the various branches of Italic meant that Latin "died" as a language acquired naturally and effortlessly by children at home. However, Latin had such enormous cultural prestige that during the Middle Ages and the Renaissance, it continued to be the language of scholars throughout western Europe, and it was studied by educated English speakers throughout the last century. Thus, Latin is a dead language as no one learns it natively, but it has been and is very much of a "living" dead language in the sense that it is still used in the liturgy by the Roman Catholic Church. It is still spoken in the priesthood and in certain scholarly circles.

The various stages of Latin are often referred to by different names:[9]

Ages of Latin

−75 BC	*75 BC–200*	*300–1300*	*1300–1600*	*1600–1900*	*1900–*
Old Latin	*Classical* Latin	*Medieval* Latin	*Renaissance* Latin	*New* Latin	*Recent* Latin

In addition to these chronological stages of Latin, we can also differentiate between *Classical* Latin and *Vulgar* Latin, where *Vulgar* is ultimately derived from the noun *vulgus* 'the common people.' The designation is necessary because between the first and the sixth century AD the ordinary speech of the common people, the vernaculars used in the different parts of the Roman Empire, were gradually moving further and further away from the literary forms of Classical Latin, eventually evolving into the new daughter languages, known as the Romance languages today.

Italian is the national language of Italy, standardized on the basis of the literary language of Tuscany (Florence) that developed during the early Renaissance, with substantial influence from Rome in modern times.

Spanish is the national language of Spain and its former colonies throughout the Americas, including most of South and Central America except Brazil.

Portuguese is the national language of Portugal and Brazil.

French. The modern standard language is based on the variety spoken in Paris, the seat of French government and culture. Although this variety has had much influence on English in relatively recent times, in earlier history the French of Normandy (northern France), which was imported into England with William the Conqueror and his soldiers in 1066, was the source of thousands of words borrowed from French into English.

---

[9] The chart is based on Frederic Wheelock, *Latin: An Introduction*, 6th edn (Glasgow: Collins, 2005).

Other Romance languages include *Catalan*, spoken in Barcelona and surrounding areas, *Sardinian*, *Romanian*, and *Rhaeto-Romance*, the latter spoken in Switzerland. These languages have had no contact with English, hence no influence.

1.2   The Germanic branch

The closest relatives of English are the languages belonging to the *Germanic* branch of Indo-European. "Germanic" is not to be confused with "German." German is the name of the modern language spoken in Germany. Like English, Danish, Dutch, etc., it is one of the descendants of a common Germanic ancestor spoken between 2,200 and 2,000 years ago.

Germanic is further divided into two subgroups with living descendants, *North Germanic* and *West Germanic*. A third group, *East Germanic*, has died out completely. East Germanic is historically important because much of our earliest information about the Germanic languages comes from an East Germanic language called *Gothic*, the language of the Visigoths. Gothic has been extinct since the Middle Ages; one major manuscript, a translation of the Greek New Testament, dates from the middle of the fourth century AD, when a Christian bishop Wulfila (c. 311–c. 382) put together a new, Gothic, alphabet and used it in producing the first known translation from Greek into a Germanic language.

The chart below shows the North-West Germanic divisions of the Germanic branch of Indo-European as they are known today.

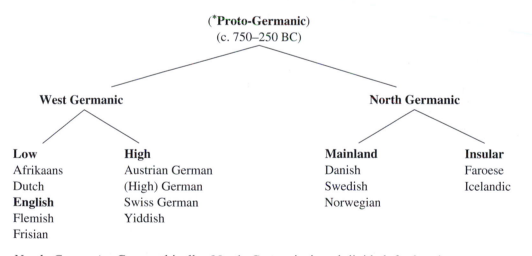

(*__Proto-Germanic__)
(c. 750–250 BC)

West Germanic		North Germanic	
Low	**High**	**Mainland**	**Insular**
Afrikaans	Austrian German	Danish	Faroese
Dutch	(High) German	Swedish	Icelandic
English	Swiss German	Norwegian	
Flemish	Yiddish		
Frisian			

North Germanic. Geographically, North Germanic is subdivided further into *East Nordic*, including *Swedish* and *Danish*, and *West Nordic*, including *Norwegian*, *Icelandic*, and *Faroese*. Swedish is spoken mainly in Sweden, and to some considerable extent also in Finland. Danish is spoken mainly in Denmark. Both Swedish and Danish, though they are distinct languages, can be used as a "common currency" by most Scandinavians. Norwegian has two major varieties spoken in Norway. Icelandic is the language of the oldest Scandinavian documents, except for inscriptions on stones found mainly in Sweden; these documents survive in Icelandic from the twelfth century AD. Faroese, closely similar to Icelandic, is spoken in the Faroe Islands in the North Atlantic Ocean.

The distinction between East and West Nordic is primarily of historical settlement interest, since Iceland and the Faroe Islands were settled mainly from Norway. In modern times, the relevant distinction is between *Mainland Nordic*, spoken by about 15,000,000 people and *Insular Nordic*, spoken by about 350,000 people. An educated Scandinavian from any of the mainland areas finds it fairly easy to get along linguistically with any other mainland speaker, but not at all with insular speakers. What has happened to the Scandinavian languages – a major re-grouping – is an interesting example of how historical linguistic boundaries may become blurred and replaced through long periods of trade, population movements, and shared government.

West Germanic. The languages in this group, listed alphabetically on the chart, can be divided according to historical geographical criteria into *Low Germanic* and *High Germanic.* Low Germanic comprises *Frisian, Dutch, Afrikaans, Flemish,* and *English,* while High Germanic includes *High German* (or simply *German*), *Austrian* and *Swiss German,* and *Yiddish.*

The designations "high" and "low" in the classification of the West Germanic languages should be taken quite literally, in their topographical sense, and not as value judgments. *Low* refers to all the Germanic languages of the flat lowlands of northern Germany and the Netherlands and their descendants. *High* refers to all the Germanic languages of the mountainous southern parts of the area, i.e. the Alps and the hills north of them. The standard language of modern Germany is called High German because it is historically based on the southern varieties, though it is now a standardized school language, not fully identical with any of the native varieties.

Frisian is spoken on the coast and coastal islands of the Netherlands along the north coast almost over to Denmark; of all the Germanic languages, this language is most similar to English. *Flemish* is one of the two official languages of Belgium. *Dutch* is spoken in the Netherlands, and *Afrikaans* is the offspring of Dutch spoken in South Africa after the seventeenth century. *(High) German* is used in government, and institutionalized in grammars and dictionaries of "standard" German. *Austrian* and *Swiss German* are the national varieties used in those two countries. The three languages are as mutually intelligible, or unintelligible, as are the varieties of English spoken in different geographical regions, from Scotland to Alabama, and from New Zealand to New York. Taken together, Austrian German, Swiss German, and German, represent the second most widely spoken Germanic language in the world, used natively by about 98 million speakers.

The "youngest" language within High Germanic is Yiddish, though its "youth" is relative: Old Yiddish goes back to at least 1250. During the Middle Ages, High German expanded vigorously into Poland, the Baltic countries, and Russia, though it did not replace the local languages. At that time there were very large numbers of Jews in this area who learned High German and modified it with loanwords from the Slavic languages and Hebrew; they carried this language with them to western Europe and to America. The name "Yiddish" is from *jüdisch*, from German *Jude* 'a Jew.'

1.3 English

Our earliest records of how Germanic-speaking people invaded the British Isles and settled there come from brief remarks made by continental historians. From an anonymous fifth-century chronicler we learn that in 441–42 the Germanic tribe of the Saxons conquered Britain after prolonged harassment.[10] No other contemporary documentation of these early events exists. About a century later, the Celtic preacher and chronicler Gildas told a somewhat more elaborate story of the conquest. According to him, the Saxons were invited to Britain to help protect the island from an invasion from the north. In return for their military services, the Saxons were given land and were allowed to settle in the eastern parts of Britain. According to an entry for the year **449** in the authoritative *Ecclesiastical History of the English People*, written in Latin by the English cleric Bede in 731, the first Germanic settlers migrated to Britain within the next seven years. 449, however, is the date commonly associated with the beginning of Old English; this is the date that histories of English usually identify as the year of birth of *The English Language*. Obviously, the useful metaphor does not tell the whole story: it took many successive waves of new settlers and at least another hundred years before the demographic and linguistic character of Britain was changed. Moreover, according to some sources, members of Germanic tribes had probably lived in the British Isles since the second century.[11]

As noted earlier, the Celts were the first Indo-European occupants of Britain. The southern British Celts had been first subdued and thereafter ruled and sheltered by the Romans. Julius Caesar's attempt at an early invasion in 55–54 BC did not result in occupation, unlike the results elsewhere in the Roman Empire, in particular Gaul (where the Latin spoken by Caesar's legions became, ultimately, Modern French). It was during the rule of the emperor Claudius (from AD 43) that the Roman invasion was followed by a more permanent occupation and military control. For about 400 years thereafter, Britain was a province of the Roman Empire. By the beginning of the fifth century, however, maintaining occupation forces in that outlying territory became too costly for the Romans, who were constantly subjected to the attacks of the belligerent Germanic tribes on the continent. A highly simplified version of the events that followed is that when

---

[10] For more information on the early records of the Germanic conquest of Britain, see Jacek Fisiak, *An Outline History of English*, vol. 1 (Poznan: SAWW, 1995), pp. 31–41. Richard Hogg covers the Germanic occupation of Britain and cites the relevant passage from Bede's history in *The Cambridge History of the English Language*, vol. 1: *The Beginnings to 1066* (Cambridge University Press, 1992), pp. 1–3.

[11] See Martyn Wakelin, *The Archeology of English* (Totowa, NJ: Barnes and Noble, 1988), p. 18.

the Romans pulled out, with all of them gone by AD 410, the Celts in the south of the island were relatively defenseless. It was then that they invited Germanic mercenary soldiers to come over from northern Europe and protect them from invading Vikings, as well as from marauding Celts from the north and from Ireland (the Scots and the Picts). The mercenaries came mainly from three tribes, the *Angles*, the *Saxons*, and the *Jutes*. The language takes its name from the Angles: *Angle-ish*. The name of the country *England* comes from *Angle-land*.

The entire documentation concerning the early history of English is in Latin. Most of it is heavily "recycled" long after the time of the first invasions and settlements. The Germanic tribes, pagan and illiterate, left no records of their first exploits across the English Channel, though some of the early heroic poetry preserved in Anglo-Saxon may reflect details of their customs and traditions. The archaeological evidence, too, is scanty at best. Place names are of some help: since -*ing* is a Germanic ending, meaning 'belonging to, of the kind of,' it is assumed that place names such as *Harting*, *Hastings*, *Reading*, *Woking* testify to early Germanic presence in these locations. Similarly, place names ending in -*ham* meaning 'settlement, home,' as in *Birmingham*, *Durham*, *Grantham*, *Nottingham*, *Oakham*, probably also indicate early settlement in the respective places, but scholars working with this kind of evidence call for extreme caution.[12] Combining the various sources of information, historians are confident, however, that the language was indeed brought to Britain from the territory of what is northwestern Germany today around the middle of the fifth century. There is also agreement that at least some of the ships of Germanic mercenaries arrived at the invitation of the Celts in southern Britain, after the Romans had withdrawn their military forces to protect Rome from barbaric invasions.

The demographic balance immediately after the Germanic invasion was in favor of the indigenous Celts, who outnumbered the conquerors by a considerable measure. The (approximate) number of settlers participating in the Germanic diaspora ranges between as little as 10,000 and up to 200,000. In some estimates, most of the 3.5 million speakers of Celtic survived the initial conquest.[13] However, the Celts had limited military experience or organization to resist the incursions for more than half a century and by about 550 larger and larger groups of Germanic-speaking peoples moved in, pushing the Celts away – those whom they did not kill or enslave – from the central part of the country west and south towards Cornwall, Wales, and north to the Lothian region. By the end of the sixth century the dominant language spoken on the British Isles was no

---

[12] For those interested in the subject, we recommend the excellent surveys of these issues in Cecily Clark's chapter "Onomastics" in vol. 1 of *The Cambridge History of the English Language* and in Richard Coates' chapter "Names" in Richard Hogg and David Denison (eds.), *A History of the English Language* (Cambridge University Press, 2006).

[13] The distribution of Celtic speakers in the different regions was uneven, with the south more heavily Germanic than the north, where the ratio of Celts to immigrants may have been as high as 50:1. These figures are cited in Hildegard Tristram's study "Attrition of inflections in English and Welsh" in Markku Filppula, Juhani Klemola, and Heli Pitkänen (eds.), *The Celtic Roots of English* (Joensuu: Joensuun Yliopistopiano, 2002), pp. 111–49.

longer Celtic. English had "begun." The subsequent history of rapid expansion of the Germanic-speaking population and the formation of English kingdoms on previously Celtic lands leaves no doubt that the invasion resulted in gradual, but relentless, expulsion of the Celtic speakers from the central parts of the island. Though the earliest preserved written records of the language did not appear until about the first quarter of the eighth century, we can assume that the beginnings of *Old English* go back to the middle of the fifth century.

2   Historical influences on the early vocabulary of English

Territorial proximity and a shared genetic source can account only partially for the degree of closeness between English and its sister languages. Genetic similarities are obscured or even completely disguised by time, cultural, economic, and demographic factors. Indeed, for the structure of the vocabulary, nothing is as important as the historical context in which the language evolved. *All* aspects of language are constantly changing, but vocabulary is the part that reacts most readily and rapidly to external influences. As shown below, English has changed its vocabulary so dramatically that in terms of word-stock it can no longer be considered a Germanic language. This section looks into the historical and cultural factors that defined the composition of the early vocabulary of English; it also covers the events and circumstances that led to its "hybridization."

The history of the English language is traditionally divided into:

Old English (c. 450–1066)
Middle English (1066–1476)
Early Modern English (1476–1776)
Modern English (1776–present)

The historical period during which Old English was spoken is known as Anglo-Saxon. We talk of Anglo-Saxon literature, the *Anglo-Saxon Poetic Records*, Anglo-Saxon religion, law, and culture. The end of Old English/the beginning of Middle English is dated at 1066 to coincide with the *Norman Conquest*. Clearly, a single historical event cannot cause the language to change overnight; the cut-off date is a convenience. In some of its features Old English was still Old English until the end of the eleventh century and beyond, and characteristic traits of Middle English had started to develop before 1066. The same principle holds for the time-span of the other periods.

2.1   The indigenous vocabulary of Old English

The pre-Germanic words. Many words used in Old English, and surviving to this day, can be traced back to the Indo-European parent language. Such words have been in the language, essentially unchanged except for some aspects of their pronunciation, for perhaps 5,000–7,000 years. We assume that the Indo-European language family began, at least in Europe, not long after the end of the last Ice Age, when the glaciers covering all of Europe north of the Alps gradually melted and opened up huge territories where humankind had not lived before, or at least had left no archeologically recognizable remains. Surviving from this earliest period are words denoting natural phenomena, plants, animals, kinship terms, verbs for basic human activities, adjectives for essential qualities, numerals, pronouns: *moon, tree, brother, mother, do, be, new, long, that, me, two, mine.*

Early Germanic words. When Germanic became an independent branch of the Indo-European family about 2,200 years ago, many new words came into existence. Again, these are words which refer to everyday life, natural phenomena, land and sea: *sand, earth, starve, make, fox, find.* Other uniquely Germanic items are *boat, broad, drink, drive, fowl, hold, house, meat, rain, sail, storm, thief, wife, winter.* There are also some suffixes which are not found outside the Germanic linguistic branch: *-dom* (as in *freedom, kingdom, stardom, bugdom*) and *-ship* (as in *friendship, lordship, kinship, stewardship*) are typical examples. Later still, when English was separated from its continental relatives in the fifth century, some words not found elsewhere in Germanic appeared in Old English: *bird, woman, lord, lady, sheriff.*

2.1.1   Earliest loanwords

The vocabulary of Old English, estimated roughly at about 25,000–30,000 words, was mostly homogeneous in origin. Yet even at this early stage in the language, contacts with other peoples brought in *some* foreign words. There are three major sources of "outside" vocabulary in Old English: Celtic, Latin, and Scandinavian.

Celtic. The demographic history of the British Isles prior to the Germanic invasions and settlements might lead us to expect traces of Celtic vocabulary in Old English. Such traces are not abundant, however. The newcomers gradually drove the indigenous Celts to the periphery of the country, or assimilated them. The end of the Celtic territorial and political dominance also determined the direction and the scope of the linguistic influence of Celtic on English: lack of contact, and presumably socio-economic differences, had the effect of isolating Celtic from Old English. Consequently, the Celtic languages were not a significant source of new words, except for a few everyday words.

Borrowings from Celtic dating back to the first centuries of contact between the Celts and the Anglo-Saxons are of two types: place names and some common words. Among the place names and place-name elements borrowed from the Celts are: *Kent, Dover, York, London* (perhaps), *Thames, Esk, Avon, -combe* 'valley,' *-torr* 'rock, peak.' There are also some hybrid place names: **York**shire, **Devon**shire, **Canterbury**. A relatively small number of common nouns were also borrowed from Celtic: *brat* 'cloth, cloak' (obsolete/dialectal), possibly *bin,* arguably also *cradle, dun, crag, curse, reel-(dance)*, *wan* 'pallid,' *loch, cross, anchor(ite)* 'hermit.' This is a near-exhaustive list of the borrowed words that have survived into Present-Day English. The list of Celtic loanwords in Old English can be extended to include military terms from Brittonic and ecclesiastical words resulting from seventh-century contacts between Irish monks and Old English speakers in the northern parts of the country.[14] Among these "lost" borrowings are:

OE *lærig* 'shield rim'	OE *dry* 'magician, druid'
OE *syrce* 'coat of mail'	OE *sacerd* 'priest'
OE *truma* 'host'	OE *lorh* 'pole, distaff'

Latin. About 3 percent of the Old English word-stock comes from Latin, or in some cases, from Greek through Latin. Manuscript writing in Anglo-Saxon times was done primarily in the monasteries, where monks and scribes who were educated in Latin, and often fluent in it, practiced their craft. Many of the surviving Anglo-Saxon records where the Latin loanwords appear are translations of religious or scholarly material; it is therefore difficult to estimate the extent to which the "ordinary" speaker of Old English was familiar with these non-Germanic words. The passage of time has made these very early borrowings from Latin an integral part of our language and has obscured the difference between their points of entry. Still, based on various philological criteria, we can identify two main groups of Latin words recorded in extant Old English texts.

Continental borrowings. Before they invaded the British Isles in the fifth century, the Anglo-Saxon tribes had been in contact with Latin speakers on the continent. The first set of Latin loanwords in Old English is therefore shared with other branches of Germanic. Many words, reflecting the military, administrative, and commercial dealings between the Roman Empire and the pre-Old English Germanic tribes, were carried over from the continent into Old English: e.g. *camp*, *mile*, *street*, *cheese*, *wine*, *gem*, *linen*, *wall*. These words must have been part of the core vocabulary of the first bands of Germanic warriors crossing the English Channel in the middle of the fifth century.

Christianity and monastic culture. The most significant early influence of Latin on English comes through the adoption of Christianity by the Anglo-Saxons. This important cultural and political event took place in England between the end of the sixth and the middle of the seventh centuries, and its impact was felt on the language for several centuries thereafter. A large number of the Latin words borrowed in that period were words related to the Christian religion and religious practices; most of these words go back to Greek prototypes:

---

[14] A full list of these loans can be found in Andrew Breeze, "Seven types of Celtic loanword" in Filppula, Klemola, and Pitkänen (eds.), *The Celtic Roots of English*, pp. 175–83. Most of the OE loanwords from Celtic cited by Breeze (pp. 175–76) have been lost, suggesting regional and dialectal limits on their circulation.

OE *abbod* 'abbot,' Lat. abbatem < Gk.   OE *diacon* 'deacon,' Lat. diaconus < Gk.

OE *cleric* 'clerk,' Lat. clericus < Gk.   OE *idol* 'idol,' Lat. idolum < Gk.

OE OE *creda* 'creed,' Lat. credo 'I believe' OE *paradis* 'paradise,' Lat. paradisus < Gk.

Latin borrowings attested in Old English are also *candle, congregation, devil, disciple, eternal, martyr, mass, pope, noon, offer, testament*. The monasteries were not only centers of religion, they were centers of scholarship and writing. Through increased literacy and enhanced interest in translating the religious and philosophical treatises popular in Europe at the time, a great many learned words entered the language. Scholarly words adopted through translations of Latin learned and literary texts and having to do with reading and writing are:

OE *(e)pistol* 'letter,' Lat. epistula < Gk.   OE *paper* 'paper,' Lat. papyrus < Gk.

OE *brefian* 'to state briefly,' Lat. breviare   OE *scol* 'school,' Lat. schola < Gk.

OE *notere* 'notary,' Lat. notarius   OE *studian* 'to take care of,' Lat. studere

In this group are also *alphabet, describe, discuss, history, mental*, and the word *translate* itself. Other Latin borrowings from that period have become common everyday words: *fever, giant, port, mount, pear, plant, polite, radish*. Like the continental borrowings, the Latin words adopted during Anglo-Saxon times through religion and learning have blended completely with the native vocabulary; it is only the number of syllables in the longer words that betrays their origin to a speaker of Modern English. In the centuries following the adoption of Christianity and the subsequent rise in literacy, new words, especially for "elevated" usage, continued to be borrowed from classical and medieval Latin, from its Romance descendants French, Italian, and Spanish, and later, during the Renaissance, from New Latin. We return to the contribution of these languages to the English vocabulary in Chapter 3.

2.1.2   The Scandinavian element

One of the major influences on the early vocabulary and grammar of English comes from its North Germanic neighbors. From the eighth century until the eleventh century, the Anglo-Saxons were subjected to a series of attacks and invasions by Scandinavian seafarers. One can think of these invasions as the second Germanic onslaught on Britain, only this time the invaders and the invaded were close relatives, linguistically speaking. The Scandinavians (also known as *Vikings*) spoke a version of Old Norse, the precursor of Danish and Norwegian in the North Germanic subgroup. The earliest written texts in Old Norse do not appear until the eleventh century (but inscriptions using the pre-Christian Runic alphabet exist from the third century AD). Judging from the written records, there was probably a considerable degree of mutual intelligibility between English and the language of the Vikings. During the Anglo-Saxon period, a very significant part of the northeast Midlands of England had to be surrendered to the Viking invaders. In 878 the English King Alfred (871–99) signed a treaty establishing the *Danelaw*, or Danish area, an independently administered Danish territory to the northeast of a boundary stretching approximately from London to Chester. Although the territory changed hands again in the next century, the Viking raids continued unabated and culminated in the complete usurpation of the English throne by Danish kings between 1014 and 1042.

Reconstructions of Viking customs and way of travel suggest that many of the seafarers arrived in England without womenfolk. Intermarriages must have been common as more and more of the invaders became settlers and inhabitants of what they came to see as their own country. These social and historical circumstances would have been very favorable for the transfer of vocabulary from Scandinavian to Old English. The first linguistic link between Vikings and Anglo-Saxons is found in the large number of Scandinavian place names in the northern and eastern parts of England, as many as 1,400. These are place names containing or ending in *-beck* 'stream' (*Beckbury, Beckford, Blackbeck*), *-by* 'settlement, dwelling' (*Carnaby, Ellerby, Rugby, Thirtleby*), *-thorpe* 'hamlet' (*Barleythorpe, Grimsthorpe, Hamthorpe, Hilderthorpe, Low Claythorpe, Fridaythorpe*), *toft* 'farmstead' (*Toft, Thurdistoft*), *-thwaite* 'clearing' (*Applethwaite, Hampsthwaite, Hunderthwaite, Husthwaite, Thwaite*). The loanword *by* 'dwelling, town' survives only in the now obscure compound *by-law*, originally 'town-law.' *Thwait(e)* and *thorp(e)* are now rare and obsolete as separate words.

Demographically, it is hard to reconstruct reliably the extent to which the Scandinavian invasions, victories, and settlements swelled the ranks of the Anglo-Saxon population. However, there are more than 750 Scandinavian name-forms in records concerning medieval Yorkshire and Lincolnshire alone, the best known of which is the ending *-son*, as in *Henryson, Jackson, Robertson*. Judging by the density of Scandinavian place names and the considerable rate of survival of *-son* names, we can assume that the newcomers represented a large and vigorous minority. There were probably as many Scandinavian speakers as English speakers living in the Danelaw. As the lexicon is the language layer most responsive to socio-political and cultural changes in the history of a nation, it is easy to see why English borrowed almost 1,000 words from Scandinavian between the eighth and the eleventh centuries.

Unlike the adoption of Latin vocabulary, which was initiated and promoted primarily by a small subsection of the population, the learned priests, monks, and scribes, the adoption of Scandinavian words did not involve special education or writing skills. It occurred naturally in the mixed households, in the fields, and in the marketplace, among people at comparable levels of cultural development. In addition to the propitious social conditions, the borrowing of words was facilitated by the linguistic closeness of Scandinavian and Old English. It is not surprising that loanwords that came into English during this period are not easily recognizable as foreign, nor are they marked as belonging to a special more literate or more elevated level of usage. Scandinavian borrowings in Old and Middle English are common words such as:

ceallian 'to call'	*feolaga* 'fellow'
cnif 'knife'	*legg* 'leg'
hæfen 'haven'	*utlaga* 'outlaw'
husbonda 'householder, husband'	*wrang* 'wrong'

The list includes also *bag, cast, crawl, crave, die, hit, root, skin, sky, sprint, ill, until,* the prepositions *till* and *fro* (as in *to and fro*), and the pronouns *they, them, their*. There is probably Scandinavian influence on the pronoun *she*, the verb form *are*, and the quantifiers *both* and *same*. In some regional varieties of English today Scandinavian words exist side by side with the more familiar word from the standard language: *garth* vs. *yard, kirk* vs. *church, nay* vs. *no, trigg* vs. *true*. Since the Vikings spoke a Germanic language, sharing words with Old English, but pronouncing them differently, we find that one and the same word with two pronunciations, Scandinavian and Old English, has evolved into a pair of historically related words which are now two separate lexical items. Such pairs in Present-Day English are *dike* vs. *ditch, scrub* vs. *shrub, skirt* vs. *shirt*.

2.2   English becomes a hybrid

The Norman Conquest. The next important historical event which has left a lasting mark on the composition of the English lexicon is the Norman Conquest of Britain in **1066**. In that year, William, Duke of Normandy, attacked and defeated the English army at Hastings on the south coast of England. He was then crowned king of England, replacing the Saxon line which had begun with Alfred the Great's grandson Ecgberht in 802. By the end of the eleventh century the positions of influence, prestige, and learning in England were occupied by Norman nobility, churchmen, and clerics. The exact number of new settlers following the Conquest is unknown, though some scholarly estimates have been offered. Here is how one well-known source describes the social and demographic consequences of the Conquest:

> One may sum up the change in England by saying that some 20,000 foreigners replaced some 20,000 Englishmen; and that these newcomers got the throne, the earldoms, the bishoprics, the abbacies, and far the greater portion of the big estates … and many of the burgess holdings in the chief towns.[15]

The key to understanding the enormous effect of the Norman Conquest on the vocabulary of English is in the political and social standing of the conquerors. William of Normandy lived on as king of England for twenty years after his conquest. During that time members of the Saxon aristocracy were executed or driven away from their castles and their lands. Their property was now in the possession of Norman barons and retainers who had come with William or had followed him soon thereafter. This led to a new correlation between social

---

[15] Cited in Baugh and Cable's *A History of the English Language*, p. 111, from a statement by F. York Powell in H. D. Traill (eds.), *Social England*, vol. 1, p. 346.

standing and language: the peasants working in the fields or doing the manual jobs around the noblemen's estates were speakers of English, and the overlords spoke French. In terms of sheer numbers, the speakers of English were unquestionably the dominant group: they constituted between 90–98 percent (or even more) of a total population of approximately 1,500,000.[16]

The social boundaries within which French was used were quite narrow, however. As Nicholas Ostler puts it:

> … the spread of Norman French would have been limited by the very rigidity in the social hierarchy over which the Normans presided. Within the feudal system, the status of every English man and woman was largely determined by birth, with the church providing the only paths for advancement through merit, and that was severely limited through the constraints of celibacy. As a result the French-speaking nobility remained almost a closed society … and there was little or no scope for people to better their prospects through aping their masters. In feudal England, people knew their place …[17]

For upwards of two centuries, therefore, the country's "important" affairs were conducted in Anglo-Norman or Latin, and that's what determines the dominant role of these languages as sources of enrichment during that period. In the only form of language we have from the period, *written* language, the vocabulary of the post-Conquest period is marked by rapid absorption of words from all spheres of interaction characteristic of the higher social status of the French-speaking nobility: literature, religion, government, law, warfare, architecture, art, science, medicine. The new rulers brought with them legal, administrative, military, political, and ethical terms which often paralleled existing English words:

Old English	Anglo-Norman French loan
burh 'town, borough'	*city* (1225)
(ge)mot 'court, council,' PDE *moot*	*council* (1125), *assembly* (1330)
deman 'to judge,' PDE *deem*	*judge* (1225)
deor 'any animal,' PDE *deer*	*beast* (1220), *animal* (1398)
freodom 'freedom'	*liberty* (1374)
wundor 'wonder'	*miracle* (1230), *marvel* (1300)
rum 'room'	*chamber* (1225)

The numerical and social discrepancies between speakers of French and speakers of English worked against the development of widespread bilingualism. Nevertheless, the linguistic barriers between the two groups were not impenetrable. Given their dependence on local labor, the conquerors had to communicate with the conquered. The French-speaking upper clergy had to talk to the lower clergy and listen to the preachers whose sermons had to be in English. Instructions

---

[16] The demographic estimates are from Roger Lass, *The Shape of English: Structure and History* (London: J. M. Dent and Sons, 1987), p. 56.

[17] Nicholas Ostler, *Empires of the Word: a Language History of the World* (New York: HarperCollins, 2005), p. 461.

had to be given and understood in every walk of life. The majority of the population spoke English natively, but many people must have learned enough French to fulfill requests and obey orders from their French overlords. A smattering of French would have been sufficient for some French words to gain access to English; that was enough of an opening to allow the initial trickle to become a flood.

The Norman French masters, on their part, gradually got out of touch with their French origins. At the beginning of the thirteenth century King John who, like William, had started out as King of England and Duke of Normandy, lost his Norman title and territory. This forced many of the French-speaking nobility in England to abandon their continental ties, either because their lands in Normandy had been confiscated, or because they themselves divided their possessions between their offspring, discontinuing the practice of having lands both in England and in Normandy. As new generations came along and constant travel between the two countries was made unnecessary, the Normans in England assimilated linguistically to the (Middle) English-speaking majority. Although the interaction between the two languages following the Conquest resulted in quite dramatic vocabulary changes, the language of England remained *English*.

The linguistic influence of the Norman Conquest is marked by an interesting historical fact: though French-speaking, the Normans were just a couple of generations removed from their North Germanic Viking ancestry themselves. The word *Norman* is a reduced form of "North-man," the name of the Scandinavian tribes that had raided the north of France since the middle of the ninth century and had established the dukedom of Normandy in 911. The variety of French that the Normans brought to England was different from the variety of French spoken around Paris and in southern France. During the immediate post-Conquest period in England, Norman French was the main donor of Romance vocabulary. Norman French (also known as Anglo-French or Anglo-Norman) was one of the provincial dialects of French. As the political scene in England changed after the end of the twelfth century, the linguistic connections between English and French shifted to central and southern France. Middle English was receptive to new Romance vocabulary from both sources. Originally driven by demographic and economic necessity, the influence of French grew during the thirteenth century and after through English–French political contacts and through the cultural prestige of French in Europe. The massive influx of French words in post-Conquest England changed the proportion of Germanic vs. non-Germanic words in the language. Old English had a relatively *homogeneous* lexicon, while Middle English became lexically *heterogeneous*.

2.2.1   French loanwords in Middle English

The unprecedented enrichment of the lexicon through borrowing altered the etymological composition of English after the Conquest. Data on the exact number of words borrowed from French is difficult to obtain, but according to one estimate the number of French words adopted during the Middle English period was slightly over 10,000. Of these, about 75 percent have survived and are still used in Present-Day English.[18] The large volume of new words changed the etymological balance from approximately 3 percent of foreign (Latin) words in Old English, to 25 percent of borrowed words in Middle English. At no other time in the history of English had such a dramatic change in the composition of the vocabulary occurred. Moreover, this was only the beginning. The trend of borrowing from other languages that was started with the post-Conquest English–French mixture was to continue steadily throughout the history of English and it is still with us today.

Interestingly, at these early stages of massive diversification of the vocabulary of English, there seem to be no negative attitudes to borrowed words. Literacy in medieval times was very much an accomplishment related to social standing. It is likely therefore that the large majority of the people who could read and write were either members of the Norman aristocracy, or people trained to serve the Normans in some capacity: clerks, scribes, chroniclers, religious and court writers, scholars, poets. This situation might conceal both potential negative attitudes and the rate at which new words were actually adopted by speakers of English. Thus, an early record of a French word is no guarantee that that word was familiar and current throughout the linguistic community. Conversely, we can imagine that many words, especially words which would not make their way easily into religious, legal, or didactic writing, might have been used in the spoken language for decades before they actually went on record.

More manifestly, the class-based distinction between the literate and the illiterate is reflected in the type of words that Middle English borrowed from French. The two chronological layers of borrowings discussed below show how the new political and social realities shaped the English lexicon.

Early post-Conquest borrowings. For approximately the first two centuries after the Conquest the source of new words was mainly Norman French. Though the Normans were Scandinavian in origin, they had adopted the language and culture of medieval France. William and his men spoke French when they first came to England, but the linguistic assimilation that had happened to the Northmen in Normandy was replicated in England. From about the middle of the thirteenth century, English was gradually replacing French (and Latin) as the language of government, administration, and learning. By the middle of the fourteenth century French was taught as a foreign language, even in ethnically Norman households. For reasons which perhaps have much to do with the keeping and survival of records, the overall number of documented borrowings before 1250 is relatively modest: about 900.[19] Among the words which entered English at that early stage are such common words as *air, beast, beauty, color, dangerous, diet, feast, flower, jealous, journey, judge, liquor, oil, part, peace, soil, story,*

---

[18] See Baugh and Cable, *A History of the English Language*, p. 174.
[19] The estimate is from Baugh and Cable, *A History of the English Language*, p. 164.

tender. Many of the early borrowings also reflect social class relations: *baron, noble, servant, throne.*

Central French. In 1204 King Philip of France took Normandy from England, severing the immediate administrative and political ties between the dukedom and the Anglo-Norman rulers of England. England's military, economic, and cultural interests shifted to central France. From the thirteenth century on, therefore, the French spoken in and around Paris became the source of new loans in English. More and more members of the upper classes adapted to the linguistic environment by learning English. This paves the way for yet another strand of linguistic influence, namely from Central Old French, creating rivalry between the Anglo-Norman and the French forms of the same word. Some surviving pairs are:

Anglo-Norman	Central Old French
catch	*chase*
Karl	*Charles*
cattle	*chattel*
warranty	*guarantee*
warden	*guard(ian)*

Thus, in effect, and according to legal histories, Anglo-Norman survived as a true vernacular language only for a couple of generations after the Conquest. Thereafter, any form of French was a learnèd tongue, like Latin.

Again, throughout Middle English the word-stock continued to be enriched with words reflecting the leading position of the new aristocracy in the legal, military, administrative, political, religious, and cultural spheres. Many Old English words in these areas were either duplicated or replaced by Romance borrowings: *army, assembly, council, defense, empire, mayor, navy, parliament, record, soldier, state, statute, tax.* Predictably, words from the fields of literature, art, science, medicine came into the language in large numbers, including the words *literature, art, science, medicine,* and *number* themselves: *figure, grammar, image, logic, music, pain, physician, poet, remedy, romance, study, surgeon, tragedy.* Many of these loanwords can be traced back to Classical Greek and Latin.

After the fourteenth century English became once again the dominant language of administration, commerce, art, and learning. From that point onwards, the rate at which common words were adopted from *any* foreign source into the language slowed down. The rapid and far-reaching vocabulary growth of Middle English permanently changed our lexicon, making it etymologically non-homogeneous. Already contemporaries of Chaucer (d. 1400) would not have considered words borrowed from French such as *very, river, city, mountain, close, glue, haste, ease,* and so on as "foreign"; such words had become an inseparable part of English. The rapid growth of the vocabulary through absorption of foreign elements has an interesting effect on the creation of new words through derivation and compounding. In Old English newly derived words (root plus affix, e.g. PDE *kingdom, winsome, weakling*) and compounds (e.g. PDE *Englishman, quicksilver, underlie*) used native building-blocks, so that the resulting word was etymologically homogeneous. In Middle English, however, **hybrid** word-formation becomes quite common. Here are some examples of hybrid compounds:

English + French

town-clerk (1386)
breastplate (1386)
freemason (1376)
bedchamber (1362)

French + English

safe-keeping (1432)
gravel-stone (1440)
riverside (1366)
dinner-time (1371)

Similarly, in some newly derived words the native roots combined with borrowed affixes and borrowed roots with native affixes:

English + French

talka*tive* (1432)
unknow*able* (1374)
wiz*ard* (1440)
love*able* (1340)

French + English

color*less* (1380)
joy*ful* (1290)
manner*ly* (1375)
*fore*taste (1435)

One further etymological comment: as noted in Section 1.1, Old French, the forerunner of French and its Anglo-Norman variety spoken in England, is ultimately a development of a vernacular form of Latin, known as Vulgar Latin. Vulgar (popular) Latin, as distinct from the stylized and frozen Classical Latin, was spoken in the provinces of the Roman Empire, roughly between the second and the eighth centuries AD, by which time it started to evolve into the various early forms of the Romance languages, including Old French. Therefore, in many cases the new Anglo-Norman words would be indistinguishable from their ultimately Latin proto-types, which makes it difficult to state with precision what the source of the borrowing is. The practice of recording the etymological source varies. In *A Chronological English Dictionary*,[20] the entries are assigned etymologies according to the *immediate* source of borrowing. Thus, for example, in the 1150–1450 time-bracket we find: *excuse*, n., v. (OF), but *excusable* (Lat.); *exemplar* (OF), but *exemplary* (Lat.); *lineage* (OF), but *lineation* (Lat.); *violence* (AN), but *violent* (OF), *visage* (AN), but *vision* (OF). Convenient cover-terms for all of these are "Latinate" or "Romance" loanwords.

The next chapter will look at the sources of borrowing after the Middle English period and their effect on the etymological composition of Present-Day English.

---

[20] Thomas Finkenstaedt, Ernst Leisi, and Dieter Wolff, *A Chronological English Dictionary* (Heidelberg: Carl Winter Universitätsverlag, 1970).

3 Composition of the Early Modern and Modern English vocabulary

1 The Early Modern English cultural scene

The linguistic period identified as *Early* Modern English began some time during the second half of the fifteenth century. There is no single historical event comparable to the Norman invasion of 1066 for Middle English which can be taken conveniently as the boundary between Middle and Early Modern English. The language changes which characterize the transition of Middle to Early Modern English coincide chronologically with several major cultural and social changes. The most notable among these is the introduction of the printing press, by Sir William Caxton, in **1476**. This year is commonly taken as the cut-off date because it marks a turning point in the production and accessibility of books. It is also easy to remember. Another historical event which coincides roughly with the beginning of Early Modern English is the discovery of the New World in **1492**. While its effect on our word-stock was not as immediate as the availability of printed books, the discovery of the Americas has had extraordinary consequences for the composition of the English lexicon.

The end-point of Early Modern English coincides with two important events which occurred in the second half of the eighteenth century. We have already mentioned the appearance in **1755** of the first really influential dictionary of English, the *Dictionary of the English Language* (in two volumes) by Samuel Johnson. That dictionary boosted enormously the prestige of English lexicographical research. It was the first dictionary to use quotations, and it contributed more than any other eighteenth-century work to the establishment of spelling standards. Another demarcation point of immense cultural and social significance is the American Revolution of **1776**, when along with their political independence Americans began to develop more linguistic autonomy relative to British English. Enclosed within these four dates, 1476/1492 at one end and 1755/1776 at the other, are the three centuries that comprise Early Modern English.

The Early Modern linguistic period, roughly 1476–1776, does not overlap completely with the usual chronological boundaries of the English *Renaissance*. Most histories identify the Renaissance with the time prior to the revolutionary events of the middle of the seventeenth century: the English Civil War of the 1640s, Oliver Cromwell's Protectorate, and the Restoration of Charles II in 1660. The broader time-span for Early Modern English is justified for two reasons. First, the cultural aftermath of the Renaissance continued beyond the political events in the seventeenth century. The revival of classical learning had a powerful and permanent effect on the intellectual life of the following century. Second, even at that highly literate stage in the history of the language, recorded "first" entries of new words in the language can be off by one or two generations. Since the focus in this book is on "words," we will ignore the time differences and will use Renaissance and Early Modern English as loosely synonymous terms.

The main cultural difference between Middle and Early Modern English, stated in most general terms, is in the number of people who had access to books and could read. Heightened *literacy* means wider exposure to new texts and new words; the more people read, the smoother the channels for the adoption of new words. Living in highly literate societies, we may find it shocking that reading was not common before the end of the fifteenth century. Medieval peasants were almost all illiterate, and most of the nobility were able to read only with considerable effort, if at all. Although literacy was highly respected and could ensure one a privileged place in society, reading and writing were skills expected only from the clergy and specially trained copyists known as scriveners. After 1476 the reading scene began to change dramatically. More than 20,000 titles, several million individual copies of books or pamphlets, were printed in the fifty-to-sixty years after Caxton set up the first printing press in London.[1] Books became part of everyday middle-class life. Easy access to printed materials brought about reforms of the educational system, and within three generations the inhabitants of England, the lower classes as well as the nobility, went from 2 percent literacy to as high as 50 or even 60 percent. Virtually all middle- and upper-class males learned to read. Women of the aristocracy were generally literate also, but it was a skill not taught to most females until the Industrial Revolution about 200 years later.

The rise of literacy in Early Modern English was accompanied by a parallel rapid expansion of the lexicon. According to one estimate based on counting entries in the *OED*,[2] as many as 4,500 new words were recorded in English during each decade between 1500 and 1700. Two-thirds of these words were creations based on already existing roots and affixes,[3] but an impressive one-third were straight borrowings. Eliminating new words of unknown origin, and words not

---

[1] These numbers are cited in Baugh and Cable, *A History of the English Language*, p. 195. The first dated book printed in English, *Dictes and Sayenges of the Phylosophers*, appeared in November 1477. By the time of his death (1491) Caxton had published over 100 items, including *The Canterbury Tales* and other poems by Chaucer, John Gower's *Confessio Amantis*, Sir Thomas Malory's *Morte Darthur*, and much of John Lydgate; see "Caxton, William," in *Encyclopædia Britannica*, retr. January 17, 2008, from *Encyclopædia Britannica Online*: www.search.eb.com/eb/article-9021929.

[2] Charles Barber, *Early Modern English* (Edinburgh University Press, 1997), p. 220. Our figures are a recalculation of Barber's original counts which cover 2 percent of the entries in the first edition of the *OED*, i.e. Barber's 2 percent count amounts to about 95 words per decade.

[3] The terms will be explained fully in Chapter 4. For the moment, *affixes* can be taken as meaning roughly 'word-endings,' in the case of those that typically occur at the ends of words, or 'word-beginnings,' in the case of those that typically occur at the beginnings of words. In this book the position of an affix relative to the word can be read off by the placement of the hyphen: the affix is at the left edge when the hyphen follows, as in *re-*, and at the right edge when the hyphen precedes, as in *-ness*.

recorded after 1700 (one-third of the entries), English adopted for permanent use over 20,000 borrowings in two centuries. In Middle English the corresponding estimate for double that time is about 7,500 surviving borrowings; the different numbers are due to the availability of books and the popularization of literacy and education in Early Modern English. New intellectual activities, the rediscovery and reappraisal of the ancient philosophical, religious, and literary masterpieces went hand in hand with the realization that like Greek and Latin, English should be capable of expressing the full range of abstract ideas and subtle emotions conveyed in the classical writings. Vocabulary enrichment was one of the consequences of the unparalleled interest in the classical heritage; the *Renaissance* was not only a time of re-birth, but also a time of invention, growth, and expansion.

The word *Renaissance* itself expresses the idea of looking back and looking forward at the same time. Its first element, *re-* means 'again,' or 'backwards from a certain point,' and *nais-* 'be born' is a form that developed in French from the Latin root *nasc-* still found in words like *nascent, native, nation*. What may come as a surprise is that *Renaissance* is not a word that speakers of Early Modern English would have recognized. The word was borrowed from French in the eighteenth century in the strictly religious sense of 're-birth,' and it was only later, since about the 1840s, that *Renaissance* developed its present-day cultural and historical associations.

2   Vocabulary enrichment during the Renaissance

The great intellectual movement of reinvention and reinterpretation of the classical models began in Italy during the early Middle Ages, spread in Europe, and reached England during the fifteenth century. From that time on, the importance of French loans decreased, while English turned increasingly towards Latin and Greek for new learned words. Scholarly and everyday words continued to be borrowed from French in the sixteenth century: *fragrant* (1500), *elegance* (1510), *baton* (1520), *accent, adverb* (1530), *amplitude* (1540), *cassock* (1550), *chamois* (1560), *demolish* (1570), *pounce* (1580), *admire* (1590), *avenue* (1600), yet the *Chronological English Dictionary* from which these dates are cited, shows that as the century advances, the share of words identified as French goes down at the expense of words from Latin and Greek.[4]

During the Renaissance proficiency in Latin and Greek became equivalent to being educated. Much of the scholarly work and academic writing was conducted in a form of Latin known as Neo-Latin, or Renaissance Latin. To a well-educated Renaissance person Latin was like a second language, it was taught, read, and used for learned discourse. Much energy and enthusiasm went into translating the classics into English. The translators often found it easier to introduce a new word for an unfamiliar notion than to worry about coining an English equivalent

---

[4] See Finkenstaedt, Leisi, and Wolff, *Chronological English Dictionary.*

and risk being misunderstood. An interesting example of how widespread this practice was comes from a count of the Latin innovations in a c. 1485 translation by John Skelton, a prominent poet and writer. In turning *The History of the World* by Diodorus Siculus into English, Skelton introduced more than 800 Latin words new for the language, many of which are recorded by the *OED* as later borrowings.[5]

Learned words make up the largest portion of the new Latin vocabulary. From the fields of classical civilization, philosophy, religion, and education, Early Modern English added words such as: *alumnus, arena, contend, curriculum, elect, exclusive, imitate, insidious, investigate, relate, sporadic, transcendental.* Among the loanwords from the fields of mathematics and geometry, botany, biology, geography, medicine are: *abdomen, antenna, calculus, cerebellum, codex, commensurable, compute, evaporate, lacuna, larva, radius, recipe, species.* Along with these, a substantial number of everyday words were also adopted; they probably started out as specialized words, but quickly became part of the common vocabulary: *frequency, parental, plus, invitation, susceptible, offensive, virus.* An important aspect of the process of borrowing during these two centuries was the naturalization of a great many affixes from Latin: *-ence, -ancy, -ency* < Latin *-entia, -antia*; Latin *-ius, -ia, -ium, -ous*, and Latin *-us, -ate* were borrowed unchanged. Borrowed prefixes such as *ante-, post-, sub-, super-* became part of the productive morphology of English.[6]

Classical Greek was another source of learned words during the Early Modern English period, though the path of entry of Greek words into English is very often indirect, as noted in Chapter 2, Section 1. The Romans knew and admired the Hellenic heritage; the vocabulary of Latin included many learned Greek words. Similarly, French had adopted many Greek words, either through Latin, or directly. The Greek words we use today are therefore as likely to have come into English through Latin and French, as they are through direct borrowing. Greek words which came through Latin or through French are words such as *atheism, atmosphere, chaos, dogma, economy, ecstasy, drama, irony, pneumonia, scheme, syllable.* Learned borrowings from Greek through higher education – i.e. the study and translation of Greek documents – are *asterisk, catastrophe, crypt, criterion, dialysis, lexicon, polyglot, rhythm, syllabus.* In some cases such as *amoral, homosexual*, the Greek first elements of the words: *a-* 'non-, not,' *homo-* 'same,' combine with the Latin elements *moral, sexual* < Latin *moralis, sexualis.* Other examples of hybridization are the words *epicenter* < Gk. *epi* 'on, upon' + *center* < Latin/Old French, and *chronic* 'long lasting, inveterate' < Gk. *chronos* 'time' + *-ic* < Old French *-ique*, Latin *-icus.*

Another interesting aspect of the new Renaissance vocabulary was that words that had already been borrowed into English from French could be re-borrowed

---

[5] The example is cited in Baugh and Cable, *A History of the English Language*, p. 210, fn. 1.
[6] "Productive" means that they are still used to make up new words: *postwar* (1908), *subset* (1902), *superstar* (1925). Other affixes in the language are no longer productive, like the fossilized *th* in *growth, warmth, health, wealth*, or *with-* in *withstand, withdraw, without.*

from Latin; the different pronunciation of the pairs shown below is due to the changes that had occurred to the Latin words in French.

ME loanword	EModE loanword	Source
count (1325)	*compute* (1634)	Lat. *computare*, OFr. *cunter*
cross, v. (1391)	*cruise* (1651)	Lat. *cruc-em*, OFr. *croiz*
debt (1225)	*debit* (1682)	Lat. *debitum*, OFr. *dete, dette*
frail (1382)	*fragile* (1513)	Lat. *fragilis*, OFr. *fraile, frele*
ray (13–)	*radius* (1597)	Lat. *radius*, OFr. *rai, ray*

The adoption and assimilation of the hundreds of new words from the classical languages is not easy to trace. The ultimate sources can be obscured by intermediate borrowings and changes: Latin borrowed freely from Greek, and it is often hard to distinguish between words borrowed into English directly from Latin, and words borrowed from Latin through French. Nevertheless, it is beyond doubt that during Early Middle English three or four times more words were borrowed from an immediate classical source through reading and translating classical texts than words coming directly from French. We will return to the identification of the source or sources of borrowed words in Section 3.

Other European Languages. The New World. The Renaissance spirit of intellectual renewal and discovery manifested itself in adventurous travel and heightened political, economic, and cultural interest in other countries and peoples. The conditions for the adoption of words from languages other than French and the classical tongues were good. For the first time in the history of the language, many speakers of English were exposed to the customs and achievements of other Europeans. More and more members of the rising English merchant class maintained active ties with their European partners in travel and navigation, manufacture and commerce. Compared to classical borrowings, the volume of Early Modern English borrowings from other European or non-European languages is not overwhelming, but they set a trend that has been steady and increasing to this day: the trend to welcome words not just from the highly prestigious languages of the past, but from any other contemporary language.

Along with French, Italian was the source of many borrowed words. During the first two centuries of the period the words borrowed from Italian were distributed evenly between words having to do with everyday life, military activities, architecture, and the arts. From that period we have inherited *artichoke* (1531), *bazaar* (1599), *gondola* (1549), *vermicelli* (1669), *squadron*, (1562), *balcony* (1619), *fresco* (1598), *opera* (1644), *rotunda* (1687), *stanza* (1588). At the beginning of the eighteenth century, Italian music and especially Italian opera became very fashionable in England, and with that came a new wave of Italian loanwords. Indeed, there was a real explosion of new musical words in English. Here is a small selection of some of these words with their dates of entry:[7]

---

[7] All dates are from the *Chronological English Dictionary.* Some of the dates of the pre-1700 loans are cited in Barber, *Early Modern English*, pp. 229–31.

adagio (1746)	impresario (1746)
allegretto (1740)	lento (1724)
andante (1742)	libretto (1742)
aria (1742)	maestro (1724)
bravo (1761)	mezzo-soprano (1753)
cantata (1724)	moderato (1724)
coda (1753)	operetta (1770)
coloratura (1753)	oratorio (1727)
concerto (1730)	pianissimo (1724)
contralto (1730)	pianoforte (1767)
crescendo (1776)	soprano (1730)
divertimento (1759)	sotto voce (1737)
duet (1740)	tempo (1724)
falsetto (1774)	trombone (1724)
forte (1724)	violoncello (1724)

The addition of the Italian musical terms to English illustrates well the importance of innovation, leadership, and prestige to the composition of the vocabulary. During the eighteenth century it became impossible, as it still is, to speak about western music in English without using an Italian word. At the beginning of the twenty-first century it is probably impossible to speak about computers in any language without using some English words.

During the Renaissance and after, there were strong commercial and cultural ties between Britain and the Low Countries. Early loans from Dutch into English are words like *drill*, v. (1622), *foist*, v. (1545) *knapsack* (1603), *pickle*, v. (1552) *smuggle*, v. (1687), *rant*, v. (1598), *trigger* (1621), *yacht* (1557). These are not learned or specialized words; the same tendency for borrowing popular words from Dutch continued in the eighteenth century:

bully, v. (1710)	ogle, v. (1700)
cookie, n. (1730)	roster, n. (1727)
crap, n. (1721)	scoop, n. (1742)
gin, n. (1714)	scuffle, v. (1766)
kid, n. (1769)	snuffle, n. (1764)
kit, v. (1725)	track, v. (1727)

There is an interesting difference between Dutch and the Italian borrowings. The Italian words, in addition to being more specialized, are all nouns, while the words borrowed from a related Germanic language, Dutch, are a fair blend of verbs and nouns. Clearly, Dutch words were adopted through direct contacts between people speaking English and Dutch, while the Italian terms must have been transmitted mostly on paper. The structural closeness between Dutch and English probably allowed English speakers to produce sentences mixing the two languages, where the foreign item could either point to new objects (nouns), or also describe new types of action (verbs).

Spanish and Portuguese borrowings also reflect the cultural traditions and accomplishments and the naval and military exploits of the countries of origin. Spain and Portugal led Europe in the colonization of the New World, and some of the words borrowed from Spanish had been borrowed into Spanish from American Indian languages. Early borrowings from Spanish include *buoy* (1596), *cargo* (1602), *guava* (1555), *hammock* (1555), *masquerade* (1654), *mestizo* (1588), *negro* (1555), *potato* (1565), *siesta* (1655). Some eighteenth-century loans from these languages are:

adobe (1748)

albino (Portuguese) (1777)

banjo (1764)

cocoa (1707)

demarcation (1727)

fandango (1700)

flotilla (1711)

hacienda (1760)

jerk (1707)

lasso (1768)

mantilla (1717)

mesa (1775)

palaver (Portuguese) (1733)

poncho (1748)

quadroon (1707)

torero (1728)

Compiling statistics about the exact sources of the new words in Early Modern English is hard because of uncertainties surrounding their etymologies. Nevertheless, an approximate picture of how the vocabulary changed is useful. A count of the new loanwords between 1500 and 1700 in a sample of 1848 words of "reasonably certain etymology" in the *OED* shows that the sources break up as follows:[8]

Latin (62.9%) (*393*)

French (19.3%) (*121*)

French or Latin (3.2%) (*20*)

Greek (5.5%) (*35*)

Italian (2.5%) (*16*)

Spanish/Portuguese (2.5%) (*16*)

German/Dutch (1.5%) (*9*)

Other languages (2.4%) (*15*)

Loanwords total: 625

You can visualize the distribution of the loanwords classified by their origin in the following chart:

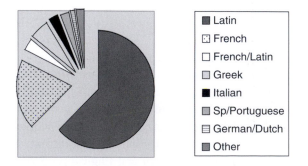

- ■ Latin
- ⊡ French
- □ French/Latin
- ▨ Greek
- ■ Italian
- ▨ Sp/Portuguese
- ▤ German/Dutch
- ■ Other

---

[8] Our percentages are based on Barber's numbers (Early Modern English, p. 221), here in italics. Barber's chart is based on the same 2 percent sample of the *Oxford English Dictionary* used to estimate the overall number of borrowings during the period 1500–1700.

Latin at nearly 63 percent was by far the most important donor of new words during the first two centuries of Early Modern English. French comes in as a distant second. Closer to the end of the eighteenth century, however, the balance shifted in favor of the living languages of travel and commerce. The trends in borrowing in the final quarters of the last three centuries, based on the *OED* records, are illustrated in the following chart:

The ten most frequent sources of loanwords in each period:[9]

1775–1799 (*305*)	1875–1899 (*816*)	1975–1999 (*84*)
French (33%)	Latin (40.5%)	Latin (20%)
Latin (30%)	German (18%)	French (16.5%)
German (5%)	French (15.5%)	Japanese (8.5%)
Sanskrit (5%)	Italian (4%)	Spanish (8.5%)
Italian (3%)	Japanese (3%)	German (7%)
Malay (2.5%)	Spanish (3%)	Russian (3.5%)
Urdu (2.5%)	Greek (2%)	Hindi (3.5%)
Hindi (2%)	Yiddish (1.5%)	Italian (3.5%)
SAfr. Dutch (1.5%)	Hawaiian (1%)	Zulu (3.5%)
Spanish (1.5%)	Swedish (1%)	Greek (2.5%)

The growing share of non-classical loanwords in English is clear in the data for the late eighteenth and the late twentieth centuries. The relatively high percentage of Latin loans for the corresponding decades in the nineteenth century is due to a very substantial number, 184, of words based on "Scientific Latin," which Durkin defines as "Latin in taxonomic and medical use" (p. 30). These are words such as *magnolia*, n., *macadamia*, n., and their derivatives. Modern English continues to coin new terms using classical roots. Nineteenth-century loans from German are also comparatively numerous; these are mostly scientific words based on classical roots, but attested first in German, from where English has borrowed them. Some examples of such nineneteenth-century loans are *merispore, meroistic, metabiosis*. Looking at the end of the twentieth century, we are not surprised by the large portion of Japanese words in English, clearly reflecting the tighter links between Japan and the English-speaking world. The trend which started with the Renaissance, and which was so prominent during the eighteenth century, continues to this day. In the twenty-first century we can talk of the globalization of our vocabulary: for genuinely new words covering previously unfamiliar geographical areas, customs, and civilizations, English keeps turning to the living modern languages.

A special chapter dedicated to the most recent borrowed vocabulary of English is included in the online Workbook.

[9] The chart is based on table 3 in Philip Durkin's highly informative article "Lexical borrowing in Present-Day English" (*Oxford University Working Papers in Linguistics, Philology & Phonetics*, ed. Daniel Kölligan and Ranjan Sen, vol. 11, 2006), p. 29. We have added the total numbers of loans for each period in italics. Durkin provides fascinating information about the areas in which these words were borrowed, their social status, regional usage, and much more.

3   Transmission, etymology, source identification

The biological metaphor of language families is convenient for describing the evolution of languages from a common source, but it says nothing about the way our vocabulary reacts to outside influences. Like biological families, languages can grow and move away from their original genetic pool by borrowing and absorbing new (grammatical) features and (lexical) items. Unlike people, however, languages never grow old or become dysfunctional with time. When they do die out, i.e. cease to be spoken, it is almost always because of non-linguistic changes in the society where they are spoken. Focusing only on the vocabulary, languages constantly renew themselves by discarding unnecessary words, changing the meaning of existing words, by creating or borrowing new lexical items. The vocabulary turnover in English has been quite remarkable; etymologically, the English we speak now does not look like the offspring of Old English at all. More than 80 percent of the vocabulary used a thousand years ago has been replaced with words created or borrowed since the Norman Conquest.

The *transmission* of borrowed vocabulary into English has been both direct (oral transmission), and indirect, mediated by writing, education, and literacy. Face-to-face communication is the easiest and most obvious mode of linguistic transmission. When the Roman troops battled or traded with the pagan Germanic tribes in the early centuries of the Christian Era, it must have been the immediate exchanges between them that led to the adoption into Germanic of words such as *chalk, cheese, street, wall, wine*. It must have been through direct conversation with the Scandinavian settlers that the words *bag, call, fellow, skin* came to be part of the vocabulary of English after the tenth century. Some words borrowed from the Anglo-Normans after 1066 must also have been heard and learned in conversation: *air, beast, mountain, river, story, very*. Oral transmission continues to be part of our everyday experience: words like *bagel, cockroach, gumbo, macho, moccasin, pajamas, sherbet, sushi* are words which were probably heard, understood, repeated in everyday conversations long before they were written down in documents and recorded in dictionaries.

The situation is quite different with learned words, which of course comprise a very large portion of our borrowed vocabulary. They do not come directly from the battlefield, the marketplace, or in a bilingual family setting, and their meanings tend to be more abstract. The transmission of "bookish" words is more likely to change their meaning in some way, sometimes quite radically. Often one and the same Indo-European root with several meanings emerges with different meanings in Old English, French, Latin, Greek, etc. Words which start out from the same root, but which merit separate dictionary entries, are called *cognates*. We will return to a more specific description of cognates in the following chapter; here we only illustrate the way cognates enter the language and the vast variation of form and meaning that occurs during the process of transmission.

Let us start with a simple example. Old English and other Germanic languages borrowed from Latin the word *discus* 'a flat round plate.' In Old English this word was used to refer to the flat plates on which food was served, and it also came to mean platter, or bowl, and, by extension, the food itself. The form of the word was changed from *discus* to *disc*, pronounced the same way as our word *dish*. It is most likely that the word, first used in ecclesiastical writings and sermons, continued to be transmitted directly from speaker to speaker. Then, in the seventeenth century, the French word *disque*, or its source, Latin *discus*, was borrowed again, this time strictly with the meaning of 'flat surface,' especially the surface of the sun, the moon, etc. The word was pronounced [disk], spelled either *disc* or *disk*, and was first recorded in 1664. It must have come into the language through the medium of education or reading. This second borrowing quickly spread to medical, zoological, and botanical uses; later it evolved into a technical term, as *disc brake*. The musical meaning of *disc* 'phonograph record' was first recorded in 1888. After the Second World War the word *discothèque* was coined in French, borrowed into English in 1951, where it produced *disco* by shortening in 1964. The word was modified yet again and given a specialized new meaning more recently with the introduction of the *disk camera* (1973) and *compact disc* (1979). The invention and popularization of computers gave it new life and new meanings too: *floppy disk*, *hard disk*, *disk drive*, and the diminutive *diskette*. But that's not all: during the seventeenth century the word *discus* was borrowed, directly from the Greek word *diskos*, with its specialized athletic meaning that we associate with the Olympic discipline of discus throwing. Adding to the richness of this cognate group is the Old French version of the Latin *discus* which turns up in English as *dais* 'raised platform.'

Another intriguing example of the vagaries of transmission is provided by the Indo-European root **bha-* 'speak,' whose word-family shows how repeated contacts, the reading and production of literary or administrative documents, can change meaning. The Latin forms of the same root are *fa-*, *fe-*, and the Greek forms are *pha-*, *phe-*. The word *fame*, 'being spoken about,' was borrowed in Middle English from Latin or French and it meant just having a reputation, good or bad. It probably came into the language orally. Its cognate *infamy*, a fifteenth-century loan, entered the language through Latin legalistic texts, in which the word *infamia* had no English counterpart; the transmission was mediated. Another cognate, the rhetorical term *euphemism* 'the avoidance of offensive terms,' 'speaking well' (where *eu-* means 'well, good'), was a purely literary seventeenth-century borrowing from Greek. The word *infant* (first recorded in 1382) may have been borrowed either orally or through literacy, but *infanta* 'the daughter of a king of Spain or Portugal' (1601), was strictly a learned word borrowed through political discourse. Both words have the negative prefix *in-* 'not': *infant* originally meant 'one who does not speak,' or simply 'not speaking,' while *infanta* assigns a very special and restricted meaning to the 'one who does not speak.' Since the word can be used only in reference to a royal female offspring in Spain and Portugal, speakers of English were not likely to encounter this word in their everyday life.

Cognates such as *dish, diskette, discus, fame, infamy, infant* show traces of their origin, no matter what the manner of historical transmission is. The semantic relationships are quite intricate, however. *Fame* and *infant* preserve the idea of speaking, but the legal term *infamy* meaning 'loss of rights as a consequence of earning a bad reputation' is less transparently linked to the original *fa-*. Then there are surprising cognates, such as *infantry* or *bandit*, where the semantic traces are fully obscured. *Bandit* was borrowed into English from an Italian form *bandetto* (1593), which itself was borrowed from earlier Germanic through Late Latin. This explains why the word is *bandit* rather than **fandit*, since in Germanic the Indo-European *bh-* had changed to *b-*, but in Latin, the ancestor of Italian, it changed to *f-*. In Italian, the form had come to mean not just 'to speak,' but specifically 'to summon, to muster, to band together'; the meaning of *bandit* is derived from the activities of outlawed gangs.[10] *Infantry* is an Italian word, *infanteria*, army units made up of young soldiers who did everything on foot, hence the meaning 'foot-soldiers.' The word was borrowed from Italian into French, and from French into English (1579). Thus, whether or not cognates share the same form, their meanings can be far removed from each other and from the original. Figure 3.1 summarizes some of the changes of Indo-European **bha-* 'speak' in its various daughter languages:

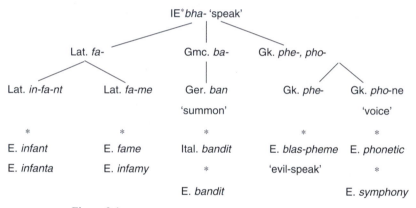

Figure 3.1

Etymology. Etymology is the historical study and recovery of formal and semantic links among words. Literally, etymology means 'the study of *true* meanings,' coming from the roots *etym* 'true' and *o-log-y* 'the study of' or 'the theory of.' An important point to understand in learning about etymology is that many semantic associations exist independently of historical cognate developments, and at the same time many cognate relationships exist (like *bandit, fame, infantry, euphemism*) in which the semantic connections are extremely remote and obscure. The historical (diachronic) relation between *dish* and *diskette*, or *infant, fame*, and *bandit*, would be lost to us without the additional insight provided by these words' etymology. They have a common origin, yet, from a *synchronic* point of view, they are separate

---

[10] It. *bandito* 'proclaimed, proscribed,' in pl. *banditi* n. 'outlaws,' past participle of *bandire* = Med.L. *bannīre* 'to proclaim, proscribe': see BAN *n.* and *v.*, and cf. BANISH in the *OED*.

modern English words. The following chapters describe various ways in which the etymology of English words can become more transparent. Before we go on to the principles and methods of parsing and semantic change, here are some facts about the etymological composition of our present-day vocabulary.

The historical survey in Chapter 2 and this chapter makes it clear why and how our language developed its rich and varied vocabulary, both in terms of numbers of items, and in terms of sources. The vocabulary of Old English was *homogeneous* (*homo* 'same' + *gen* 'origin'); as many as 97 percent of the words used by the Anglo-Saxons were Germanic words. The cultural changes following the Norman Conquest created conditions for the development of a *heterogeneous* (*hetero* 'other, diverse') vocabulary. A modern speaker's awareness of the genetic diversity of the word-stock depends on education, interests, familiarity with other languages, and many other highly individual factors. One perception we all share, however, is that when we speak, read, or write, we encounter words whose 'foreignness' is beyond doubt. We may use confidently, or we may stumble at words like *blasé, glasnost, niño, mbongo, gyoza, pas de deux,* or *echt*; in either case we *know* that these words are somehow different from our garden variety English words. If one thinks of the vocabulary as being distributed over a scale of *native < — > foreign*, obviously borrowed words such as *blasé, glasnost, niño, mbongo, gyoza,* are clearly at the "foreign" end of the scale. Many learned words with which we are comfortable are probably stored mentally as non-native: *convalesce, deduce, exorcism, hermaphrodite, hibernation, paradigm, polygamy.* For most people words such as *hesitate, machine, neuter, pantry, supply,* would not carry any "foreign" associations, though all of them are post-Conquest loanwords. Finally, words like *arrive, dinner, dollar, face, mountain, really, river, sky, very* will seem "native"; time and frequent use have allowed these early borrowings to blend with the genuinely native words, but for the etymologist, they remain "outsiders." We can represent the recognition of "native" and "foreign" words as a continuum:

Native	Early borrowings	Recent borrowings	*Foreign*
< -- >			
mother	animal	prospectus	kolkhoz
green	crimson	gelatinous	ecru
sleep	spouse	supplement	mbongo

The composition of the modern English vocabulary reflects the historical circumstances of its growth. Table 1 shows the percentages of Old English and post-Conquest etymologies in the 10,000 most frequent words in English.[11]

Table 1

Old English	French	Latin	Other Gmc.	Other languages
31.8	45	16.7	4.2	2.3

[11] The percentages are from A. H. Roberts, *A Statistical Linguistic Analysis of American English* (The Hague: Mouton, 1965), p. 36.

These numbers allow us to see how significant the turnover of vocabulary from Anglo-Saxon times to this day has been. Only one-third of the first 10,000 words we learn and use are *native*, i.e. Germanic words which have been in continuous use since Old English times. The imbalance between native and non-native sources becomes quite striking if we take French and Latin together; the ratio then approaches two to one in favor of Romance borrowings.

The figures in Table 1 should be treated with caution. They reflect only the *immediate sources*, the languages from which a word was directly borrowed into English. The *ultimate source*, the language where the word first originated, is not recorded in these data. Thus *telegraph* which contains two Greek roots: *tele* 'distant' and *graph* 'write,' is counted as French; a predecessor of the telegraph, a contraption with movable arms sending signals at a distance, was invented in France in 1792, and that's the immediate source of the word in English. Similarly, a word like *agony* from the Greek *agōniā* 'struggle to win an athletic contest' counts as French in this classification. The route of transmission is from Greek to Latin to French. The Romans borrowed the word in its more general sense of 'any mental or physical struggle,' and it was modified in Old French to *agonie*, 'mental anguish,' which is the meaning first recorded in English after 1382. *Draco* was an Athenian lawgiver in 621 BC, known for having established the first rigorous code of laws in ancient Greece, 200 years before the classical period, but the word *draconic*, first recorded in English in 1680, comes to us via Latin. These are examples where the distinction between ultimate and immediate source is clear. Often, however, the boundaries between the sources can be very fuzzy: we can't tell whether *destructive, cooperation, position, solid*, come to English from Latin or from French.

Etymological classification is also hampered by mixed-language word-formation. As pointed out in Chapter 2, Section 2.2.1, hybridization of the vocabulary in Middle English led to the formation of new items whose etymology is mixed. Native affixes modify the borrowed roots in *un-important, prince-ly, over-estimate, respect-ful*, while native roots combine with borrowed affixes in *woman-ize, re-fill, foresee-able. Clergyman, nobleman, superman* count as native, because of the key element *-man*, but *man-hour, manservant*, and *manpower* do not qualify as native. The vocabulary of English is truly heterogeneous only in terms of its immediate sources. Ultimately, well above 95 percent of the words in our language are of Indo-European origin; the remaining portion is made up of words found only in the Germanic branch of Indo-European (see Chapter 2, Section 2.2.1), and in the non-Indo-European donor languages such as Arabic, Malay, Japanese, Hawaiian, Zulu, Hopi, Chinese. This is unsurprising in view of the geographical and cultural distance between English and non-Indo-European languages for most of the language's long history.

The percentages in Table 1 are somewhat problematic also because a blanket count of all 10,000 words obscures the important correlation between etymology, the frequency of a word, and the context and style in which it is used. More specialized contexts and more elevated styles rely heavily on borrowed or

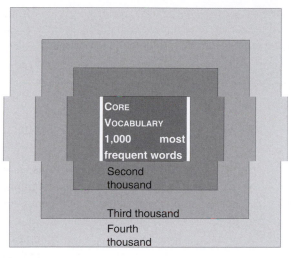

Figure 3.2

uncommon words. The most frequent words form the core of the vocabulary, shared by all adult speakers, but outward from that core lie layers of words of decreasing familiarity. Here is how the editors of the *OED* describe the situation:

> … the vast aggregate of words and phrases which constitutes the vocabulary of English-speaking people presents … the aspect of one of those nebulous masses familiar to the astronomer, in which a clear and unmistakable nucleus shades off on all sides, through zones of decreasing brightness. The English vocabulary contains a nucleus or central mass of many thousand words whose "Anglicity" is unquestioned; … but they are linked on every side with other words which are less and less entitled to this appellation and which pertain ever more and more distinctly to the domain of local dialect, of slang, … of the peculiar technicalities of trades and processes, of the scientific terminology common to all civilized nations, and of the actual languages of other lands and peoples.[12]

Figure 3.2 is a graphic representation of the core–periphery distribution for the first four deciles; more layers can be added around the ones shown here.

The dividing lines between the layers are only approximate. Word-frequency counts depend on the nature of the texts from which the data have been drawn. Nevertheless, large-scale vocabulary studies are quite informative about the etymological composition of English in relation to the relative frequency of words. Table 2 shows the results of one such study, based on more than 15 million running words, over half of which were recorded in business and personal correspondence reflecting ordinary everyday activities:[13]

---

[12] *OED*, 2nd edn., p. xxiv.
[13] The original results of the investigation were published in Roberts, *A Statistical Linguistic Analysis of American English*, pp. 35–38. The tabulation of the results used here is from Joseph M. Williams, *Origins of the English Language: A Social and Linguistic History* (New York: The Free Press, 1975), p. 67.

Table 2

Sources of the most frequent 10,000 words of English				
Decile	English	French	Latin	Norse	Other
1	83%	11%	2%	2%	2%
2	34	46	11	2	7
3	29	46	14	1	10
4	27	45	17	1	10
5	27	47	17	1	8
6	27	42	19	2	10
7	23	45	17	2	13
8	26	41	18	2	13
9	25	41	17	2	15
10	25	42	18	1	14

Possible individual variation aside, the figures in Table 2 prompt some interesting observations. The percentages in the first row bear out the assertion that the core vocabulary of English, the words which are indispensable in our daily life, such as *water* and *food*, *go*, *sleep*, *wake*, *sister* and *brother*, *green* and *yellow*, are most likely to be of native origin. The more complicated and abstract our notions become, e.g. *cognition*, *psychoanalysis*, *reverberate*, *telethon*, the more likely English is to turn to loanwords. The higher deciles include words from the realm of ideas, art, science and technology, specialized discourse; there the proportion of borrowed words increases. Going from higher to lower frequency of usage, we notice a very significant drop: only 34 percent of the second layer of words are words that have survived directly from the time of King Alfred, about 1,000 years ago. In that same frequency range, the 1,000 to 2,000 decile, the proportion of combined French and Latin words jumps from 13 percent in the first decile to an impressive 57 percent. After that, the proportion of native words goes down more slowly, and remains approximately steady at 25 percent in the last four deciles. The share of French and Latin remains remarkably steady in the outer layers. Starting with the second decile, the percentages of "other" sources are on the rise. Since the study on which these figures are based does not separate Greek sources from any other sources, including words of uncertain and unknown etymologies, the increase in this column is largely due to the presence of Greek borrowings.

The correlation observed in English between frequency of usage and etymology is not necessarily true of every language. Some languages – German is a case in point, within Germanic – have traditionally turned to their own resources for enriching the vocabulary with words for more sophisticated notions or new products. For example, *Übersetzung* is equivalent to our word 'translation,' but it literally means 'setting over.' *Fernsehen* is equivalent to 'television' but it literally means 'far-seeing.' *Lautlehre* is equivalent to 'phonology,' but

it literally means 'sound study.' That is, in German, native roots are combined
to form new compounds having the same meaning as the classical-based compounds. This method of vocabulary enrichment is familiar also in English:
doorbell, horseshoe, lighthouse, shorthand, stronghold are all compounds containing native elements only. However, compared to German, English has been
less inventive in producing new words from its own roots; instead, it has added
and creatively recycled roots from other languages. Chapters 5, 6, and 7 in this
book address the mechanisms of borrowing roots and affixes from the classical
languages in detail.

4   Summary of early British history and loanwords in English

The vertical center-line below is a time line, from earlier to later. Many
of the dates have to be taken as approximate:

500 BC or earlier	Celts in Britain
from c. 200 BC	Roman contacts with Germans
56 BC, final conquest after AD 43	Romans in Britain
by c. 430	Romans out of Britain
449 Germanic settlement of Britain	**Beginning of Anglo-Saxon period**
	Old English
450–600	Pre-Christian England
597	Christianity to England
from c. 700	First Old English texts
850–1066	The Danelaw
1066 Norman Conquest	**End of Old English**
1066 Norman Conquest	**Middle English**
1086	Doomsday Survey, 1.5 million population
1204–5	King John loses Norman estates
from c. 1150	Literature in English revives
until c. 1450	Laws written in Latin and French
1363	Parliament opens in English
1383	First will written in English
1400	Death of Chaucer[14]
1476	William Caxton introduces the printing press
1489	French no longer used in statutes of Parliament
	End of Middle English
1476–1650	20,000 titles printed

---

[14] About 12 percent of the words used by Chaucer are borrowed from French.

1500–1600	Translations of classical books[15]
1564	Shakespeare born
from c. 1550	Literacy borrowings (dated below)

Latin 1500–1600: *cadaver, arbiter, integer, genius, torpedo, pollen, cornea, fungus, vertigo, acumen, folio, alias, peninsula, regalia, abdomen, animal, appendix, miser, circus, aborigines, axis, vacuum, genus, medium, species, terminus, caesura, caveat, multiplex, corona, hiatus, innuendo, cerebellum, decorum, compendium, radius, sinus, albumen, delirium, stratum.*

Latin 1600–1700: *premium, torpor, equilibrium, specimen, spectrum, series, census, cerebrum, plus, vertebra, squalor, affidavit, arena, apparatus, agendum, veto, fiat, curriculum, query, imprimatur, onus, impetus, alumnus, data, insignia, copula, stamen, album, complex, desideratum, vortex, honorarium, pendulum, nebula, rabies, tedium, lacuna, minimum, dictum, residuum, serum, fulcrum, calculus, stimulus, lumbago, status, antenna, momentum.*

Latin 1700: *nucleus, inertia, propaganda, alibi, auditorium, ultimatum, maximum, insomnia, bonus, extra, prospectus, deficit, addendum, habitat, humus, referendum, moratorium.*

Greek through French before 1500: *academy, atom, bible, center, character, climate, diet, diphthong, dynasty, ecstasy, emblem, fancy, fantasy, frenzy, galaxy, harmony, horizon, idiot, ink, logic, magic, magnet, melon, mystery, nymph, pause, plane, pomp, rhetoric, rheum, scandal, schism, spasm, sphere, stratagem, surgeon, theater, tragedy, turpentine.*

Greek through Latin before 1500: *abyss, agony, allegory, artery, asphalt, centaur, chaos, chimera, comedy, crypt, cycle, demon, echo, halcyon, hero, history, hyena, mania, mechanic, meteor, paper, piracy, plague, siren, theme, thesis, thorax.*

Greek after 1500: *irony, trophy, elegy, drama, tome, dilemma, phrase, idea, trope, enigma, scene, rhapsody, crisis, tragic, cynic, machine, scheme, cube, caustic, isthmus, rhythm, chorus, chemist, despot, topic, nausea, chord, cylinder, prism, basis, skeptic, larynx, skeleton, pathos, amnesty, climax, diatribe, comma, acrostic, nomad, critic, ode, epic, trochee, disaster, python, chasm, cynosure, stigma, theory, energy, enthusiasm, strophe, orchestra, acoustic, clinic.*

---

[15] Thucydides, Xenophon, Herodotus, Plutarch, Caesar, Livy, Tacitus, Aristotle, Cicero, Seneca, Ovid, Horace, Homer, Boethius.

4 Smaller than words: morphemes and types of morphemes

1 The smallest meaningful units

We think of words as being the most basic, the most fundamental, units through which meaning is represented in language. There is a sense in which this is true. Words are the smallest free-standing forms that represent meaning. Any word can be cited as an isolated item. It can serve as the headword in a dictionary list. It can be quoted. It can be combined with other words to form phrases and sentences. In general the word is the smallest unit that one thinks of as being basic to saying anything. It is the smallest unit of sentence composition and the smallest unit that we are aware of when we consciously try to create sentences.

But actually there are even smaller units that carry the fundamental meanings of a language. Words are made up of these units. Consider just the unit *gen* in Figure 4.1. It is clearly not a free-standing word, but rather some kind of smaller unit which goes into the make-up, the composition, of words:

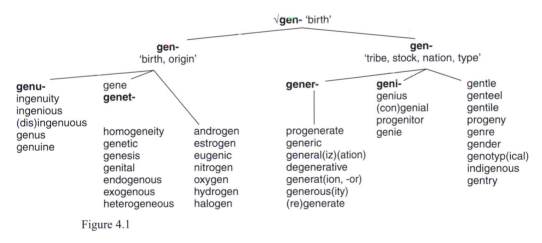

Figure 4.1

These smaller units are called **morphemes**. *Gen* is a morpheme. It has a basic single meaning 'birth' which has split into two distinct, yet related and overlapping meanings, 'birth, origin' and 'tribe, stock, nation, type.' Looking at the words that appear under each of these meanings, one can readily see the difference. The meaning 'origin' is most easily seen on the middle branch below it, in words like *genetic* or *genital*. The meaning 'type' is easily seen in words like *general*. The meaning 'gentle' is derived from the notion 'belonging to a good tribe/family, coming of good stock.' There is also some overlap: words like *generate* could just as reasonably be attached to the left branch ('create, give birth'), while *genus* straddles 'origin' and 'type.' *Gentile* originally, in the Vulgate translation of the Bible from Hebrew into Latin, simply meant 'nations/tribes other than the Jews.' A later, seventeenth-century re-borrowing of the same word, *gentil*, from French, originally also meaning 'of good stock,' resulted in our word *genteel*, which has changed its erstwhile positive meaning of 'having proper breeding,' 'elegant, stylish,' to its rather ironic and disparaging current meaning. The meaning of *gentry* as 'rank by birth' has been extended to 'any middle class' in *gentrification*. *Genius* comes about through Roman mythology. It meant 'The tutelary god or attendant spirit allotted to every person at his birth, to govern his fortunes and determine his character, and finally to conduct him out of the world' (*OED*). It is a short step from 'attendant spirit' to 'having a genius for music' to 'being a musical genius.' *Genre* is used by literary scholars to mean 'a literary type.' *Gender* refers to types, or categories, of nouns, in the usage of grammarians. In general usage it has become the accepted term for types of humans differentiated by virtue of their sex.

1.1   What is a morpheme?

Since morphemes are the smallest carriers of meaning, each word must contain at least one morpheme: *out, just, grace, person, ozone, London*. One word may have more than one morpheme: *outing, justly, ungracious, personalize, ozonation, Londoner*. The word *morpheme* itself is made up of two morphemes: *morph* 'form, shape' and *-eme* 'linguistically distinctive unit.' So a *morpheme* is a form associated with some distinctive meaning. The essential point about morphemes is that they cannot be dissected further into smaller meaningful units: they are themselves the smallest ones. But one might challenge this claim by pointing out that *morph* itself consists of four sounds represented by <m> plus <o> plus <r> plus the <ph> (=<f>). Why are these not smaller units? The answer is that they are not units of **meaning**. They are units of **sound** (or spelling); the string of these sounds or letters together represents the morpheme. The relationships between sounds, morphemes, and meanings is like this, taking √*gen* and √*graph* as our example:

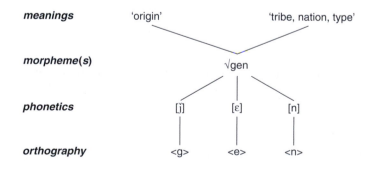

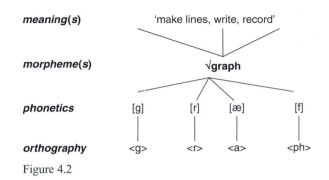

Figure 4.2

In Figure 4.2 we find some technical symbols. The checkmark in front of the morphemes √*gen* and √*graph* simply means 'This is a morpheme,' in analogy to the common mathematical meaning of the symbol 'root.' As noted in Chapter 3, note 3, and in the Workbook (Chapter 2), we mark affixes with hyphens to the left or to the right, depending on where they are attached, so *prefixes* such as *be-*, *for-*, *re-* go to the left of roots, and *suffixes* such as *-ly*, *-ness*, *-ity* go to the right of the root. The square brackets on the level below √*gen* and √*graph* indicate pronunciation. They are used for phonetic writing, also known as phonetic transcription. Don't worry if you don't recognize all the phonetic symbols: we will explain them later. Finally, in the orthography/spelling row, the angle brackets mean 'This is a letter of the alphabet traditionally used to spell this sound in this word.'

Morphemes are the subject of study by the branch of linguistics known as *morphology*. As we turn to morphology in this and the following three chapters, we remind the reader that more broadly, the study of words (Gk. √*leg-*, √*log-* 'word, speak') is the target of more than one field of humanistic endeavor. Here, from the *OED*, are the definitions of these fields and the earliest attestations in English of the words covering them:

- **Lexicography** (1680): the writing or compilation of a lexicon or dictionary; 'the art or practice of writing dictionaries.' Webster in his *American Dictionary of the English Language* (1828) used the word *lexigraphy* to mean 'the art or practice of defining words.'
- **Lexicology** (1828–32): the branch of knowledge which treats of words, their form, history, and **meaning**.
- **Morphology** (1870): the study of the structure, form, or variation in form (including word-formation, change, and inflection) of a word or words in a language.

Topics from English lexicology and lexicography are discussed elsewhere in this book; here we concentrate on morphemes and their properties.

1.2   The properties of morphemes

We summarize below the properties of morphemes in an effort to show how they differ from other linguistic units like syllables, words, and individual sounds. The properties which uniquely differentiate morphemes from other linguistic units are these:

(1) *A morpheme is the smallest unit associated with a meaning.* As an example, consider the following words:

car	**car**e	**car**pet	**car**digan
carpal	**car**ess	**car**ve	**car**amel
carrot	**car**bon	**car**ibou	s**car**let
bac**car**at	mas**car**a	myo**car**dial	Os**car**
vi**car**	s**car**e	dis**car**d	pla**car**d

Each of these words contains the spelling <car>. How can we determine whether this fact is significant or not? Answer: Ask whether there is some constant meaning in each word that can be attributed to a morpheme having the form <car>. It is obvious that *care* has nothing to do with *car* – the meaning of *car* is completely independent of the meaning of *care*. Take *caress*: although superficially *caress* resembles *car* the way *princess* resembles *prince*, there is clearly no shared meaning in the first pair. *Carpet*, on the other hand, looks as though somehow (imaginably) there might be a connection: perhaps *carpet* could be a little *carp* (as *tablet* is a little *table*), but of course it is not, nor is *carpal*, an adjective, 'relating to the wrist,' a ride-sharing friend. *Carpet* is a single morpheme, and can be written √carpet. We can also write √care, √carve, √caribou, √baccarat, √Oscar, √cardigan, √carrot, √caress, √caramel, √scare, and √vicar, following the same logic in each instance. They merely "accidentally" contain <car>, but they do not contain the morpheme √car. (Why can we not do this also with *discard*, *myocardial*, and *placard*?)

(2) *Morphemes are recyclable units.* One of the most important properties of the morpheme is that it can be used again and again to form many words. The morpheme √care can be used to form *uncaring, careful, careless, caregiver*, and we saw in Figure 4.1 that √gen is used in forming dozens of words. If you did not know the meaning of the words *cardigan* and *caramel*, and if you thought that they might contain the morpheme √car, one way to test your conjecture would be to see whether the remaining material can be used in other words, i.e. whether it is another morpheme. Obviously, *-digan*, and *-amel* do not meet our first definition of a morpheme, they are not contributors of independent meanings, nor are they recyclable in the way in which the morphemes √care+-*ful*, or *un*-+√care+ -*ing*, or √care+√give+-*er* are. One should be careful, however: recyclability can be deceptive, as it was in the case of *carrot, carpet, caress, carpal*. Though all morphemes can be used over and over in different combinations, non-morphemic parts of words may accidentally look like familiar morphemes.

The test defined in (1) above, namely that what makes a sequence of sounds a morpheme is its ability to convey independent meaning, or add to the meaning of the word, should always be applied first. However, there are some interesting cases for which the decision on whether some part of a word is a morpheme or not requires a combination of tests (1) and (2). If we try to parse the word *happy*, we can easily isolate *-y* as a morpheme: it adds to the grammatical meaning of the word by turning it into an adjective, as in *show-y, trend-y, summer-y*. But what about *happ-*? Taken in isolation, it does not mean anything to a speaker whose knowledge of etymology does not extend to Old Norse. In Old Norse there was a noun *happ*, meaning 'luck, chance.' The word was borrowed into English in the twelfth century. That morpheme is no longer likely to appear by itself; the last attestation of the noun *hap* is dated 1888 in the *OED*, but the morpheme has kept its ability to turn up in various words and to form the core of their meaning: *mishap, happen, happenstance, happily, hapless, happiless, happify, perhaps, slap-happy, unhappiness*, and even the (converted) verbal form *to perhaps*. In other words, the recyclability of √*hap(p)-* in the language today confirms its status as a morpheme, even without the etymological information. As you will see, many of the classical morphemes we will be dealing with in this book are of the √*hap(p)-* type.

(3) *Morphemes must not be confused with syllables.* A morpheme may be represented by any number of syllables, including none, though typically only one or two, sometimes three or four. Syllables have nothing to do with meaning. Syllables are units of pronunciation. In most dictionaries, hyphens are used to indicate where one may split the word at the end of a line. Hyphens are also used to separate the word into syllables. A syllable is the smallest independently **pronounceable** unit into which a word can be divided. The number of morphemes in a word is very likely to differ from the number of syllables. √*Car* and √*care* are one syllable each; √*carpet*, √*caress*, √*carrot*, and √*carat* are two syllables each; and √*baccarat*, √*cardigan*, and √*caramel* have three syllables. But each of these words is a single morpheme.

Morphemes may be **less** than a syllable in length, too. Consider *car* vs. *cars. Cars* is one syllable, but two morphemes, namely √*car+-s*, where *-s* is the morpheme that means 'plural,' i.e. more than one. Other examples of morphemes which are not syllables include the *-ed* of *cared, caressed, rubbed*, and the *-th* of *growth, warmth*. Generally, however, morphemes are independently pronounceable and are at least one syllable in length, like √*gen*, √*morph*, √*hap(p)-*, and *-y*. In some (few) instances, a morpheme may be present only by inference. If we say *The sheep are grazing*, we have to infer that *sheep* is plural, even though its form is the same as the form of the singular. If we say *I cut some flowers yesterday*, we understand *cut* to be in the past tense because of *yesterday*, not because of any morpheme attached to *cut*. The longest single morphemes tend to be names of places or rivers or Indian nations, like *Mississippi, Massachusetts, Potawatomi*, or *Saskatchewan*.[1] In the indigenous languages of America from which these names were borrowed, the words were polymorphemic, but that information is completely lost to us, as English speakers.

(4) *One and the same morpheme may take phonetically different shapes*. Different forms of the same morpheme are called 'allomorphs' (which means 'other forms' – √*allo* 'other'+√*morph* 'form'). This general property of allomorphic variation is called **allomorphy**. Recognizing different allomorphs of the same morpheme is one of the surest ways to extend one's vocabulary and to identify relationships between words. Any speaker of English will identify the nouns *cares, caps*, and *classes*, as sharing the plural morpheme *-s*, though both the spelling and the pronunciation of the morpheme vary in the three words. That is, the morpheme has three allomorphs. But although the allomorphy of the plural *-s* is part of everyone's core knowledge of English, there are many morphemes where this knowledge is not at all automatic. Consider the morpheme meaning 'take' or 'contain' whose most familiar allomorph is √*cap*, as in words like:

> **cap**able   **cap**sule   **cap**tive   **cap**acity

It also has the allomorph √*cep* in words like

> ac**cep**t   de**cep**tion   inter**cep**t   per**cep**tible   re**cep**tacle

It has a third allomorph √*cip* in words like

> anti**cip**ate   eman**cip**ate   in**cip**ient   parti**cip**ate   prin**cip**al   re**cip**e   re**cip**ient

The fourth allomorph is √*cup* in a few words like *occupy, recuperate*, and the legal term *nuncupative*, 'of a will or testament: declared orally' (*OED*). In Chapter 9 we will discuss the fact that the meaning of the morpheme *cap* is **transparent** in some of these words – e.g. *captive* is 'one who has been taken,' *capable* is 'able to take,' *participate* is 'to take part.' But it is **opaque** in others. For example, it is not obvious what *perceptible* has to do with the basic meanings 'take' or 'contain.' Perhaps the association is something rather vague like 'able to take in [through one of the senses].' It is even more opaque in *recuperate* – perhaps something like 'to take back [one's health],' and *anticipate* 'take beforehand.' Finally, the connection between *recipe* and √*cap* is recoverable only with the help of an etymological dictionary: it is the imperative form of the verb 'take' in Latin. That's how the word *recipe* acquired its first meaning of a 'formula for a medical prescription.' Later, it was extended further into cooking and, of course,

---

[1] An unconfirmed Answers.com search shows the 49-letter name of a lake in Massachusetts, Chargoggagoggmanchauggauggagoggchaubunagungamaugg, as the longest place name in North America. It is also called Lake Webster.

today, into general transferred use as a 'list of ingredients and a set of actions' in phrases such as 'a recipe for success, a recipe for disaster' – a far cry from the basic meaning of √*cap*. The interplay of formal variation and semantic variation is very complex; we will be returning to these issues in the following chapters.

These, then, are the four essential properties of all morphemes: (1) they are packaged with a meaning; (2) they can be recycled; (3) they may be represented by any number of syllables; and (4) morphemes 'morph,' i.e. they may have phonetically different shapes.

2   Types of morphemes

While all morphemes share the properties discussed in the previous section, there are important functional and structural differences between them; not all morphemes are equally central to the formation of a word. The first major split in the overall inventory of morphemes we find in English is between **roots** and **affixes**. First, we turn our attention to roots.

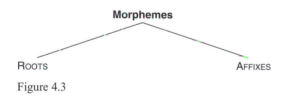

Figure 4.3

2.1   Roots

Any sound or sound sequence identified as a word by a speaker has at least one root. Roots are at the center of word-derivational processes. They carry the basic meaning from which the rest of the sense of the word can be derived. Morphemes such as *Chaplin, host, fair, red, travel, schmooze*, are roots; their meanings carry over into *Chaplinesque, hostess, unfair, redden, travelable, schmoozaholic*. Roots like *host, fair, travel* also happen to be free forms, i.e. independent syntactic entities with identifiable word-class properties. But quite often, and especially in the borrowed vocabulary, roots are like √*seg* in *segment*, √*gen* in *genetics*, √*card* in *cardiac*, √*sequ* in *sequence*, √*brev* in *brevity*, √*pter* in *pterodactyl*. These cannot stand alone as words. They are called **bound root morphemes**, as distinct from **free root morphemes** (the ones that are also independent words); this is shown in Figure 4.4.

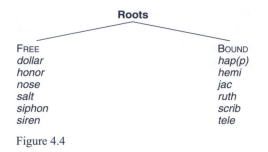

Figure 4.4

Most bound roots found in the language today are of classical origin – i.e. they were borrowed into English from Latin or Greek or other European languages during the Renaissance and after. Moreover, we usually borrowed words from these languages wholesale, i.e. the classical roots came into the language nested inside derived forms such as *segment, genetics, cardiac*, etc. Sometimes, though not very frequently, borrowed roots do make their way into the inventory of free forms too: *contra* in the meaning of 'counterrevolutionary' (1981), *graph* (1878), *phone* (1866), *retro* with reference to fashion and style (1974), are some examples. As you can see from the dates of their first recorded appearance in English, such roots which are also independent words are fairly recent and formed by shortening of the classical words or phrases that contain them, i.e. their transition from bound to free roots has occurred on English soil. So, it would be fair to say that roots borrowed from classical sources are nearly always bound roots.

The 'boundedness' of borrowed roots does not reflect their status in the donor language. The basic numerals in the classical languages, which were free forms in Greek and Latin just as the corresponding numerals are in English, have provided the bound roots out of which many English compounds are formed: e.g. *un(i)-* 'one' in *unanimity, unilateral, penta-* in *pentagon* 'having five angles,' *sept-* in *septet* 'a group of seven,' *oct-* in *octagonal* 'having eight angles.'

On the other hand, the number of bound roots of Germanic origin like *hap(p)* 'luck, fortune,' as in *hapless, happy*, is comparatively small. Of Germanic origin are the bound roots of *feckless, reckless, ruthless, listless, uncouth, unkempt*. What has happened in all these cases is a straightforward historical change: a root, which used to be also a word at earlier times, became obsolete or disappeared completely as a free-standing word, leaving behind only a derivative. Thus *feckless* is derived from a sixteenth-century Scots word *feck*, a shortened form of *effect*. Later *effect* was reintroduced into Scots, replacing the form *feck*, yet its derivative *feckless* 'ineffective' is still around. We consider *ruth* in *ruthless* as a bound morpheme today, but it used to be a common word in English meaning 'pity, sorrow' well into the eighteenth century. Though it appears as an entry in many dictionaries, the word is obsolete in Present-Day English, but note its connection with the verb 'to rue,' from which the noun was obviously derived originally. In any case, the historical processes we are illustrating here are not recoverable without the aid of specialized dictionaries. For the ordinary speaker of English *feck-*, *hap(p)-*, *ruth-*, etc. are bound roots.

To be completed, bound root morphemes require that another morpheme be attached to them. This additional morpheme may be either another root or an affix. If it is another root, the result is a **compound**. Some issues related to compounds and compounding were discussed in Chapter 1: you will remember that words like *airship, birdcage, bookmark, flagship, hemisphere, hydrogen, phonograph, polymath, telephone*, etc. are compounds. They all contain two roots. If a bound root is not attached to another root, as in **brevity, capable, cardiac, gentile**, etc., it must be accompanied by an **affix**.

2.2   Affixes

All morphemes which are not roots are affixes. Affixes carry little of the core meaning of a word. Mainly affixes have the effect of slightly modifying the meaning of the **base** – a base is either a root or a root plus an affix, or more than one root with or without affixes – to which more affixes can be attached.[2] Affixes change either the lexical meaning and/or part of speech of the base, or its grammatical properties; we address the latter in Section 2.3 below. Here we start with the difference between derivational affixes and roots. The most common modification introduced by derivational affixes is to change the word-class, the part of speech, to which the word belongs. Thus *child* (a noun) becomes an adjective in *childish*. That adjective can in turn be changed to an adverb: *childishly*, or to a different kind of noun – an "abstract" noun – by adding another affix to the base *childish*, as in *childishness*. This process, known as derivation by *affixation*, is one of the two most fundamental processes in word-formation (the other is compounding, discussed in Chapter 1 and below). Words formed by affixation are called *derivatives*, or *derived* words. Let us examine more closely the properties of derivational affixes in comparison to roots.

Affixes differ from roots in three ways.

(1)   Affixes do not form words by themselves – they have to be added on to a **base**.

(2)   Affixal meaning, in many instances, is not as clear and specific as is the meaning of roots, and many of them are so opaque as to be almost completely meaningless.

---

[2] The term *stem* is also used to refer to the part of the word to which further affixes can be added; however, *stem* is most frequently used in the context of inflection rather than derivation; *stem* is the part of the word that remains after inflectional affixes are removed.

(3)   Compared with the total number of roots, which is very large (tens of thousands in any language), the number of affixes is relatively small (a few hundred at most).

In English, all the productive affixes ("productive" in the sense that they do a lot of work) are either attached at the end of the base – **suffixes** – or at the front of the base – **prefixes**. Here are examples of common prefixes where the meaning is clear:

co+occur 'occur together'	**peri**+meter 'measure around'
mid+night 'middle of the night'	**re**+turn 'turn back'
mis+treat 'treat badly'	**un**+filled 'not filled'

And here are examples of common suffixes where the meaning is also clear:

act+**ion** 'state of acting'	child+**ish** 'like a child'
act+**or** 'person who acts'	child+**hood** 'state of being a child'
act+**ive** 'pertaining to being in action'	child+**less** 'without a child'

Many of the affixes are, unfortunately, less clearly associated with a meaning than these. We will provide more detailed information on them later, matching them to some of the possible meanings they may have.

All affixes, by definition, are bound morphemes. Historically it is possible for free morphemes to lose their independence and become affixes, and therefore become bound. One transparent example is the suffix *-less*: its origin in the adjective *less* 'devoid of' and its connection with the word *less* do not require specialized knowledge. The suffixes *-dom*, *-hood*, and *-ship* once had independent meaning as nouns. *Dom* meant 'doom, judgment, statute' and is the ancestor of the modern word *doom* as well as the suffix *-dom*. The suffix *-hood* meant 'condition' or 'state of affairs'; it has no modern independent counterpart, however, and is unrelated to our word *hood* 'covering for the head,' though the more recent word *hood* (1969) is a clipping of the derived word *neighborhood*.

The opposite development, whereby a bound morpheme escapes into the list of free morphemes, is unusual. This is more true of affixes than it is of roots. There has been a recent trend in the language to detach affixes and bound roots and elevate them to the status of free roots. Here belong the noun *ex* 'a former spouse' (1827), the verb *ex* 'to delete' (1935), the verb *dis*, v. 'to disrespect' (1980). Yet another affix that has been detached to become an independent word itself is the form *pro* from the word *professional*, which originally meant 'one who declares (*fess*) forth (*pro-*).'[3] We no longer think of *pro* in a phrase like *pro golfer* as having

---

[3] The process is reminiscent of *clipping*, see Chapter 1, Section 3.3, though clipping typically ignores morphemic boundaries.

anything to do with the prefix *pro-* that occurs in *process, provide, profess. The Lady is a Trans*, meaning 'a transgendered person,' was a 1996 musical hit.[4] Another typical example is *anti*, used both as an adjective and as a noun. We can say things like, "It doesn't matter what the principle is, he is so stubborn that he's bound to be anti." Some of these examples are still considered "humorous" or "non-standard." We already mentioned some "escapees" from the bound roots group such as *contra* (1981) and *retro* (1974). Other examples of this kind, more or less acceptable, include *hyper* (1942), *sub* (<submarine sandwich, 1955), *mini* (1966), *maxi* (1967), *semi* (1912), *stereo* (<stereophonic, 1954). The status of affixes vs. roots and bound roots vs. free roots is therefore in flux. Still, the occasional encroachment of affixes into the realm of free roots does not change the basic norm that affixes are bound forms which must be attached to bases.

2.3 Functions of affixes

The types of affixes according to their function are summarized in Figure 4.5:

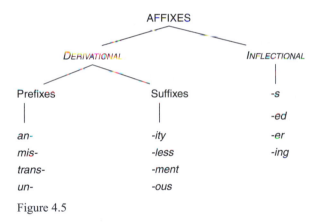

Figure 4.5

Affixes have two quite different functions. The first is to participate in the formation of new words. The affixes which do this are called **derivational** affixes; they are an important topic in this book. The other type of affix, which does not participate in word-formation at all, is called **inflectional**. Inflectional affixes, of which English has only a very small number compared with Latin or Greek or Old English, are really part of syntax, though some inflectional affixes are the indicators of very broad semantic categories like tense (*play-s, play-ed*) or number (singular–plural, as in *girl-Ø, girl-s*). The most typical inflectional affixes for nouns, in most Indo-European languages, serve to indicate which

---

[4] Cited in the *Barnhart Dictionary Companion: A Quarterly of New Words*, vol. 10, no. 1, Summer 1997, p. 69 (Springfield, MA: Merriam-Webster, Inc.).

word is the subject of the sentence or which word is the object of the verb. Thus Latin:

Ama-t   puer   puella-m
'love-s   boy–NOM   girl–ACCUS'

NOM means 'nominative,' the case for marking the subject of the sentence. ACCUS means 'accusative,' the case for marking the object of the verb. The three words can be arranged in any order without changing the meaning – they all just mean 'The boy loves the girl':

Puer puellam amat
Puellam puer amat
Puellam amat puer
Puer amat puellam

Since inflectional affixes are nothing more than markers of sentence structure and organization, they occur outside the derivation of new words and are therefore of little interest in the present context. They are always added at the rightmost edge of the stem (they are always *suffixal*) and they are subject to fewer restrictions: e.g. with some well-defined exceptions, *all* English nouns take the plural inflection *-(e)s*. It should be acknowledged, however, that this is a simplified picture: there are cases where the addition of an inflectional affix can result in the development of a new meaning, detached from the original semantic category represented by the affix, as in *customs*, *news*, *spectacles*. Similarly, the present and past participle affixes, *-ing* and *-ed*, lead a dual life: they can be purely inflectional as in "They were *building* the new dorm," "They *painted* the wall," or they can behave like derivational affixes and produce new parts of speech: "The *building* on the corner, the *painted* walls."

    If we think of the root as the **nucleus** of the derivation, the affixes are like satellites; furthermore, they have to circle the nucleus at different distances, vaguely like the solar system. As an example, consider the word *uninhabitableness*. The base is *habit*. Now, can we add *un-* to *habit*? Of course not: *unhabit* is not a word. So in this derivation, *in-* must be added first. Again we ask: can *un-* be added to *inhabit*? Same answer.[5] And so on: we keep adding morphemes on the right-hand side until we get to *inhabitable*. Now we can put *un-* in front of the formation. Why is this? Because after we added *-able*, we had finally created an adjective. It is one of the properties of *un-* that in Present-Day English it normally attaches to adjectives, adverbs, participles used as adjectives. There are a few funny counterexamples where the negative *un-* attaches to underived nouns like

---

[5] Note that the *un-* which we are examining here has the meaning of 'not, negation, contradiction,' and it can only be attached to adjectives and participles which function as adjectives. The *un-* meaning 'reversal,' which can be placed in front of verb roots such as *unbutton, undo, unfasten*, is a different prefix which requires a verb with a special 'reversible' meaning. The verb *unhabit* in our example is clearly not of that type, though the potential for this formation exists – the *OED* records a single attestation of *unhabit*, v. 'to free from a habit' in 1650.

unbook, uncola, undeath (and there are also some unsurprising common forms such as *unrest, unconcern*), but precisely the reason why a novelty-word like *uncola* in the 7-Up commercial in the US is effective is that it violates the majority pattern of word-formation with the prefix *un-* in English. And of course we can't attach *un-* to just any adjective whatever: with few exceptions such as *unable, unkind, unwise*, simple adjectives can't take *un-*: **unbad*, **unsmall*, **unglad*, **ungood*, **unstrong*, **unwarm* are not possible. Derived adjectives and adverbs, on the other hand, take the negative prefix freely: *uninteresting, unreliable, unimportant, unsympathetically, unpremeditatedly*, etc. We can represent this hierarchical property of word-formation by affixation onto the original root *habit* in the tree diagram in Figure 4.6.

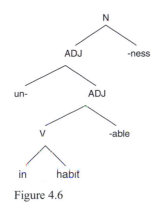

Figure 4.6

Note that the root *habit* can have the prefix *in-* attached first, followed by the suffix *-able*, because both *inhabit* and *inhabitable* are words. By the same logic, *-ness* can only be added after the word has become an adjective, or an adjectival participle. Thus the affix *-ness* is constrained in its use: it cannot be attached to roots with a clear verbal meaning, therefore *habitness*, or *inhabitness* are as impossible as **eatness*, **jumpness*, **sleepness*. The isolated example of *forgiveness* is not really an exception because it is probably a simplification of the adjectival past participle *forgiven+-ness*, which would be a regular formation. Thus, with *-ness* too, in order to get to the proper form of the noun we have to attach the adjective suffix first. Another type of restriction governs the use of the suffix *-able*: it can be added to verbs that take objects, such as *enjoy, pay, know, notice, biodegrade, read, interpret*, but not to verbs like *snow, rain, fall, rise, arrive*.

Throughout this book we have indicated the position at which an affix attaches to a base by placing a hyphen either before or after it, depending on which side the affix is added to: thus *trans-, un-*, but *-ment, -ous, -ly, -ness*. Affixes have a fixed position: they are either prefixes or suffixes, and speakers are not at liberty to switch around their place in order to create a different meaning. There is very strict ordering of the morphemes in terms of types, i.e. what affix can attach to what kind of base, and the strictness is applicable to their linear ordering too. A simple example: *un+happ+y+ness* is the only option we have for combining the morphemes in this word; any other combination is linguistic garbage: **y+happ*, **un+ness+y+happ*, **happ+ness+un+y*, **un+ness+happ+y*. The linear order of the derivational suffixes determines the part of speech: *self -> selfish*, adj. -> *selfishness*, n.

The affixes which have the function of deriving new words, then, are often restricted with respect to their position and with respect to the base that they can attach to. They often change the part of speech. They can go before or after the base, and they can be nested inside the final form, like *in-* in *un-in-habit-able*. Note again that when we string affixes on either side of the base, it is the last *derivational suffix* that determines the part of speech.

Figure 4.7 summarizes all the types of morphemes discussed above.

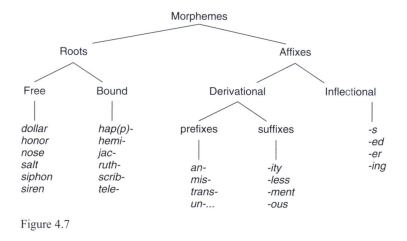

Figure 4.7

We already introduced the process of compounding in Chapter 1, Section 2.3. Here we will add some more information on the structure of compounds. A compound is a word which contains two or more roots. It may also contain affixes, because a compound is a base, just like a simple non-compound root. The roots in a compound may be either free or bound, but there must be at least two of them. Thus *orthodontist* is a compound consisting of two *bound* roots and a suffix:

√orth 'right'+√odont 'tooth'+√ist 'one who'

Pterodactyl is a compound consisting of one *bound* root and one *free* root:

√ptero 'wing'+√dactyl 'finger'

Dactyl is a free root only in one special sense, having to do with poetic meter. The *OED* gives no current citations in any other sense, and the only sense listed in the

Merriam-Webster Tenth Collegiate Dictionary is this one. So in the sense 'finger,' *dactyl* should be viewed as a bound root. Less controversial examples would be *stratosphere*, *hemisphere*, and *biosphere*, in all of which the second root is *sphere*, which is clearly a *free* root:

$$\left.\begin{array}{l} \sqrt{}\text{strato 'spread out'} \\ \sqrt{}\text{hemi 'half'} \\ \sqrt{}\text{bio 'life, living'} \end{array}\right\} + \sqrt{}\text{sphere 'ball'}$$

Airport, *backpack*, *getaway*, *leftmost*, and *killjoy* are familiar compounds in which both members are *free* morphemes. This is an enormously productive pattern: *downsize*, *laptop*, *shareware*, *trackball*, are all late twentieth-century compounds – speakers continue to create them on a daily basis. Once a compound is formed, it acts like any other base – it can take affixes in accord with the properties of the base: so *blockhead* → *blockheadish* → *blockheadishness;* *downsize* → *re-downsize* → *re-downsizeable* → *unre-downsizeable* → *unre-downsizeability*. The roots of a compound do not have to be immediately adjacent. They may be separated by an affix: in *overreact*, *underperform*, *photoreduction* the first root is added to the prefixed words *react*, *perform*, *reduction*.

4 Hyphens

The principle of fixed linear ordering is valid for all affixes, so our first point here is that you should note the position of the hyphen when you encounter an unfamiliar affix.

If a morpheme is not marked with a hyphen, it may still be a bound morpheme that can occur only in compounds or as the root of a base. Even when root morphemes are free forms, however, it is not possible to predict whether in compounding other forms will occur necessarily before, or necessarily after, them. This is true of all roots, native and borrowed, free and bound; compare *baby-sit* to *crybaby*, *crowbar* to *scarecrow*, *horsepower* to *racehorse*. Similarly, with borrowed and bound roots, √*tele* generally occurs as the first root in a compound, but √*phon*, √*dict,* √ *graph*, and √*card* may occur in either position: compare for example *telephone* with *phonology*, *dictaphone* with *verdict*, *graphotype* with *ideograph*, *cardiogram* with *myocardium*.

One further comment on compositionality and hyphenation: the insertion of hyphens in compounds is largely unregulated. Under the rubric "Combinations," the *OED* recognizes the difficulty of deciding which compound is fully unified and should not be hyphenated.[6] There are some clear-cut cases such as *postman*,

---

[6] "The formal union and the actual by no means coincide: not only is the use of the hyphen a matter of indifference in an immense number of cases, but in many where it is habitually used, the combination implies no unity of signification; while others, in which there is a distinct unity or specialization of meaning, are not hyphenated" (www.oed.com/archive/oed2-preface/gen-combinations.html).

headline, wallpaper; these are written as one word. Another type is represented by compounds where hyphenation signals a special relationship between the two bases, as in *fine-tuned*, *head-to-head*, *open-minded*. Then there are many compounds, usually descriptive names, which are not hyphenated: *Black Jack*, *Santa Monica*, *Old English*. These are just the *typical* cases. There are many compounds for which the practice in different dictionaries will differ or for which all three spellings are acceptable. Following this unsettled state of affairs, the *OED* "Find Word" search function ignores hyphens and does not distinguish hyphens and spaces, so a search for *database* will find *database*, *data-base*, and *data base*.

<table>
<tr><td>5</td><td>Cognates</td></tr>
</table>

In Chapter 3 we defined cognates as words which start out from the same ancestral root, but which develop into separate dictionary entries. Both roots and affixes can have cognate relations: historically *hyper* is cognate with *super*, *hemi-* is cognate with *semi-* in the same way that *bha-* is cognate with *fa-* and *phe-*. The word *cognate* actually contains a form of the root with which this chapter started, namely √*gen*. The word breaks down like this:

co- 'together'+√*gn* (=√*gen*) 'birth'+*-ate* 'being, adj.'

or, roughly, 'being born together.' All root morphemes that can be traced back to a common origin, or having the same *etymon*, are said to be cognate. Being cognate does not at all entail that such roots would today be viewed as examples of allomorphy. Being cognate is a *historical* relationship. Allomorphy is a synchronic relationship usually recognized by the speakers of the language as it is today. The two sometimes merge rather closely into each other, as we will see. In principle, all allomorphs are also cognates, but cognates do not have to exhibit allomorphy. As we will see in Chapters 5–8, allomorphy varies from being transparent synchronically to being discoverable only with reference to a good etymological dictionary. Therefore, what may be considered two separate morphemes or two allomorphs of the same morpheme in Present-Day English will vary from speaker to speaker.

There are many fairly extreme examples of obscured common origin where the divergence is so radical that the relationship of allomorphy cannot be invoked without reference to sophisticated historical knowledge. This is the story of the IE **bha* root which, as we saw before, surfaces in a number of common words: *bandit, fame, infant, phonetic,* and *symphony* all contain this root (in the forms √*ban*, √*fa*, and √*phon*). These roots are cognates. But would we invoke the relationship of allomorphy between them? Not automatically, and probably not at all for the ordinary speaker of the language, though it is always interesting to know what the etymological relationship is. Let us reproduce here the family tree of the root *bha from Figure 3.1. in Chapter 3.

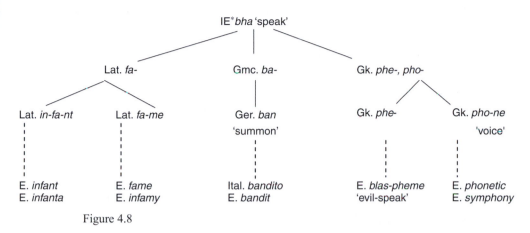

Figure 4.8

Looking at the "family tree" of the morpheme *bha in Figure 4.8 may give you the impression that there is a continuous line of inheritance from the older to the modern languages. But this is not always true, especially for words which have come into English more recently, say within the last four or five centuries. The Germanic form of *bha, ban 'to summon, to proclaim, to band together' did not produce the word *bandit* directly. What happened was that first (Late) Latin borrowed the Germanic allomorph *ban*, in addition to its own allomorph *fa-*, then Italian used the new allomorph to create the word *bandito*, and finally English imported the word from Italian at the end of the sixteenth century. Thus, at a certain point, the line of transmission can break, a fact which we represent here with a dotted vertical line. What this means is that the link between the IE form and the form we use in English today is not a natural inheritance, but rather a borrowing. When borrowing takes place, it may easily happen, as here, that the borrowed form no longer resembles the cognate forms in the borrowing language. It is therefore no longer recognizable as related through allomorphy. It is just a different root altogether, from the point of view of the borrowing language. The "natural" root here is √ban. It does not look at all like √fam or √phon, and when the latter two are borrowed they are not associated with √ban in the minds of the speakers of English who borrowed them in the first place or learned them later.

For English speakers the most accessible and fairly rich account of cognate relationships among English roots is to be found in the Appendix of the *American Heritage Dictionary* (4th edition, 2000), under "Indo-European Roots" (www. bartleby.com/61/IEroots.html). It is also available as a separate publication, but that version is more difficult to use because one needs the cross-references to the Appendix that are found in the regular dictionary entries. The *AHD* online adds a separate category "etymology," where there is reference to the IE root of the word, if the connection has been established. Here, for example, is the etymology entry for the noun *retrospect*:

> ETYMOLOGY: From Latin *retrōspectus*, past participle of *retrōspicere*, to look back at : *retrō-*, retro- + *specere*, to look at; see **spek-** in the Appendix.[7]

By way of comparison, the *OED* entry for the noun *retrospect* reads: "L. type *retrōspect-us*, f. *retrōspect-*, vbl. stem of *retrōspicere* to look back: cf. *prospect*." Therefore, if one is interested in the deepest roots of a word, the best source would be the *AHD*, but if we want to know where the word used in *English* was coined and borrowed from, we should consult the OED.

5.1   Shared structure

If several words share the same root, they are cognates, but what if words share a common structural element: that is, they are based on different roots but they share a common derivational affix or set of affixes? It is rather like saying, "All the members of this group have red hair, though they may differ in every other way." Consider the sets *childless, humorless, painless, timeless*, or *apologize, dramatize, digitize, terrorize*. These words are cognates only in a very trivial way: they resemble each other because they contain a recognizable recurring part of the word, the affixes *-less*, and *-ize*. When a set of words shares an affix or even several affixes, they are said to have a shared structure. Thus *biped, expedite*, and *impede* are derived from the same root √*ped* "foot," they are cognates, but they don't share structure.

Sometimes classifying a set of words as cognates or as words with shared structure can be tricky. Suppose we make a list of some of the words, or parts of words, that end in *-ology*. (There are hundreds of them including many "sportive nonce-words," as the *OED* describes them, such *as hatology, nothingology, commonsensology, keyboardology, undergroundology*. Colloquially, the "clipped" noun *ology* has been in use in English since the early nineteenth century.) Our list might look like this:

bio-	-ology	phil-	-ology
cosm-	-ology	phon-	-ology
herpet-	-ology	physi-	-ology
immun-	-ology	rheumat-	-ology
music-	-ology	robot-	-ology
neonat-	-ology	ur-	-ology
ornith-	-ology	vir-	-ology

---

[7] From www.bartleby.com/61/96/R0199600.html. The form **spek** is linked to the IE Root List. The *OED* does not have a reconstructed IE entry, though the relevant cognates are listed under "etymology."

It is clearly not the case that all of these words are full cognates: they simply share a "combining" form, namely *-ology*, which is actually the base *-o-log-y*, that is, three morphemes together. All of the morphemes to the right are the same and therefore obviously cognate with each other (being identical is sort of an empty sense of being cognate). But the initial roots and bases are not cognate; the unrelatedness of the first roots will be sufficient to disqualify the words from being classified as full cognates. *Infant* and *fame* are cognate in this sense: they share a root. But *biology* and *virology* are not full cognates, even though they share the form *-(o)logy*, because √*bio* and √*vir* are not descended from a common ancestral root. By way of compromise, we can call sets in which only some parts are recognizably and meaningfully cognate *partial cognates*.

5.2   Shared form and meaning

If two words contain a shared form with a constant meaning, there will necessarily be a semantic relation between them – the meanings will be similar in some clear way. In the list above, *-(o)logy* means 'the study of.' These words mean, therefore, 'the study of life,' '... the cosmos,' '... snakes,' '... immune systems,' etc. It is one of the curiosities of natural languages that a pair of words may actually be true cognates, and even have completely shared base forms, yet still be, at least on the surface, quite different in meaning. Such pairs are *outcome* vs. *income*, *graceful* vs. *disgraceful*, *pertinent* and *impertinent*. Knowing pairs like *output* vs. *input*, *organized* vs. *disorganized*, *plausible* vs. *implausible*, where it is obvious that the entire difference in meaning depends on the opposition between *out* and *in*, or the negative polarizing sense of *dis-*, *in/im*, we should be able to infer that *outcome* is the opposite of *income*, or *disgraceful* is somehow the opposite of *graceful*. Even more dramatic is the difference between the cognates *ease* and *disease*; indeed, for most people the connection between these two words comes as a surprise. But such mismatched pairs are not typical: usually we can infer the meaning of the whole from the meanings of the parts.

6   Finding roots in a dictionary

Before we end the discussion of morphemes and the types of morphemes that make up the words of English, we should find out how roots and affixes are identified in dictionaries. Many dictionaries mark words into syllables; the *OED* is a notable exception. The division into syllables is done mainly to enable the reader to decide where to hyphenate at the end of a line. Most dictionaries also indicate pronunciation, including especially marking where the accent falls in polysyllabic words. And of course they provide meanings and usage notes and all sorts of encyclopedic information. But curiously, most dictionaries do not divide up words into morphemes, and even if they do, they do not label roots and affixes as such. Rather, they give some etymological information from which the user is supposed to figure out what the root morphemes and other morphemes are. There is no dictionary, anywhere, in which the editors have neatly marked up the words of English into their constituent morphemes, though there are dictionaries of roots and dictionaries of affixes. Here is the relevant part of a dictionary entry (from the *Concise Oxford*) for *municipal*:

> **municipal** †pert. to the internal affairs of a state; pert. to local self-government, esp. of a town. xvi. -L *municipalis*, f. *municipium* Roman city of which the inhabitants had Roman citizenship, f. *municeps*, *-cip*, f. *munia* civic offices+ *capere* take.

From this information how do we find the root(s)? We have to know what the abbreviations mean, first. They're all listed in the front of the dictionary. In this entry, the symbols and abbreviations we need to know are the dagger, "†" for 'obsolete' (i.e. the first meaning is obsolete, not the word), the Roman numeral xvi, which tells us that the word appears in English for the first time in the sixteenth century, L for 'Latin,' f. for 'formed on,' and most important the hyphen which precedes the 'Lat.' The hyphen marks the beginning of the etymological information. This means 'adoption of' – that is, the word was borrowed from the Latin form *municipalis*, with just a small change, namely we dropped the final *-is*. Now we look at the etymology itself – the material that follows the hyphen. This is where we find the roots, but only indirectly. We must look at the ultimate source of the word – the very last entries in the etymology, where in this case it says "f. *munia* civic offices+*capere* take." This tells us, first, that this word is formed on two roots: the word is a compound, combining the root that means 'civic offices' and the root that means 'take.' Now comes the hard part: we have to be able to subtract from the forms that are given here any part of these forms that are not themselves roots. In the case of *munia*, for example, we have to know that *-a* is a suffix. We don't have to know very much Latin to know this, but we do have to know this much. It doesn't matter what suffix it is, or what it means: it only matters that it is a suffix, and can be subtracted to find the root. In this case, then, the first root is *muni*. The second root is given as *capere* 'to take.' Once again we have to know a little Latin: we have to know that *-ere* is some kind of suffix. It happens to be the suffix that marked the infinitive in a certain class of verbs. One thing we can count on, in looking at etymologies that contain Latin sources, is that whenever we find *-are*, *-ere*, or *-ire* at the end of a word, and the word is translated as a verb, then it is an infinitive, and the *-are*, *-ere*, *-ire* can be subtracted to get the base. That base will also be the root if the whole word has been maximally broken down, as in this case.

5   Allomorphy, phonetics, and affixation

1   Morphological rules

It is common knowledge that over time words may change both their form and their meaning. Knowing the etymology of a word requires familiarity with the ways in which its phonetic shape has evolved, and familiarity with the evolution of its semantic content. Recognizing the variants of the word components enables us to link words together in more interesting and revealing ways. This and the following two chapters will deal with some regular changes in the phonological form of roots, affixes, and whole words. We will refer to these regularities as **morphological rules**.

1.1   Types of allomorphy

Many of the alternations that we find in roots and affixes can be attributed to the interaction of phonological properties, in which case we talk of *regular allomorphy*. Regular allomorphs are said to be transparent because one can easily recognize that the two forms are variants of a single form. The changes that the morphemes undergo may affect only the pronunciation of a morpheme, or both its spelling and pronunciation. In either case the variation can be described in terms of regular changes; in that sense, the allomorphs are predictable.

The first type of regularity is illustrated by the pair *invent–convene*, both derived from the root √*ven* 'come, bring.' More examples of this type of allomorphy are *locus–allocate* from √*loc* 'place,' *dysphagia–necrophagous* from √*phag* 'eat,' *psychiatry–pediatric* from √*iatr* 'treat,' *bibliophile–philosophy* from √phil 'love,' *sole–solitude* from √*sol* 'alone, single.' While the spelling of the recurring morphemes in these sets remains unchanged, their pronunciation varies according to regularities in the phonology of English to which we return in Section 2.6. below.

Regular variation may change both the spelling and the pronunciation of the allomorphs of the same morpheme. Here we can illustrate this type by examining the allomorphs of the morpheme *syn-* 'with, together' in these words:

symmetry	[-m]	*symphony*	[-m]
syllable	[-l]	*syngamy*	[-ŋ-][1]

---

[1] The symbol [-ŋ-] 'eng' represents a variant of the pronunciation of the sound [n] before [g], see below, Figure 5.2 and the discussion there.

Note that the *syn-* has changed its final sound in accordance with the initial sounds of the roots to which it is attached. In the great majority of instances, a morpheme will have only two allomorphs, occasionally three. Later in this chapter and in Chapters 6 and 7 we summarize some rules that help us recognize morphemes which exhibit regular allomorphy.

Not all variant forms of the same morpheme with the same meaning can be explained by reference to "rules," however. The second type of allomorphy we find is *irregular allomorphy*. Because of the historical depth and the indirect entryways of the words into our lexicon, we can recognize two levels of unpredictability among the morphemes with irregularity. First, there are morphemes which are now irregular because some sound change took place years ago in one of them but not the other. Irregular allomorphy arises also when the conditions for some process are no longer in place, making the surviving allomorphs synchronically **opaque**. Such is the relationship between √*gen–gon–gn* 'birth, origin' in **gen**esis–**gon**ad–**cognate**, or between √*opus–oper* 'work' in **opus–operate**, or between √*fa–pha–ba–*'speak' in **infant–aphasia–ban**. In these instances, along with recoverable alternations that have a good historical explanation and can be linked to a valid regularity in the distant past, we will find a very large number of "exceptions." Irregularities in this group come under headings such as vowel gradation, rhotacism, Grimm's Law, and some Latin–Greek correspondences – we will see how these work in Chapter 8.

The other subgroup of morphemes with irregular changing forms includes totally unpredictable sets. Even if such morphemes were, at some ancient stage in the history of the source language(s), subject to some regularities that linked them, these patterns have become completely obscured and for our purposes it would be pointless to try to recover them. They do not represent the shards of broken allomorphy, but rather they are just cognates. More examples of unpredictable sets of forms are not hard to come by: √*ab-* = *abs-* 'from, away,' √*bene* = *bon* 'good, well,' √*can* = *cyn* 'dog,' √*ced* = *ceed* 'go, let go,' √*erg* = *urg* = *org* 'work,' and many more. The only bond between the different forms in these examples is their common etymological origin – again, they are simply cognates.

Figure 5.1 summarizes the different types of allomorphy we have identified:

Types of Allomorphy	Scope	Examples
Regular	Pronunciation only	*sole–solitude, venue–convene*
	Orthography and pronunciation	*syncope–symmetry–syllable*
Irregular	Restricted application; fossilized	*opus–operate, genetic–cognate*

Figure 5.1

A note on the use of the designation *cognate* vs. *allomorph*. You will recall (Chapter 4, Section 5) that, in principle, all allomorphs are cognates. A question which arises in this connection is whether allomorphic variation can produce forms which are so far apart in both sound and sense that they are no longer recognizable allomorphs. There comes a point, admittedly not easily defined, when some members of a word-family become unrecognizable as variants of a single morpheme. For the modern speakers, even for many highly sophisticated and well-educated speakers, such allomorphy is completely dead, or at least fossilized. In the same way that fossils tell us the story of earlier geological times, fossilized variants of a single morpheme take us back to earlier layers of linguistic history. If we go into considerable time-depth, we can find cognate relationships which are not recognizable any longer: that is, forms which are no longer seen as being *allomorphs* at all: √*graph* and √*gram* 'write' in *mono**graph*** and *mono**gram***, √*glot* and √*glos* 'tongue, speech' in ***glot**tis* and ***glos**sary*, √*vac*, √*van*, √*voi* 'empty' in ***vac**ant*, ***van**ish* and ***voi**d*, in which the etymological roots have appeared in alternate shapes for ages, but the reasons for the alternation are not recoverable. As noted above, such completely fossilized variants are simply cognates, not allomorphs. Put differently, while all allomorphs are cognates, not all cognates are allomorphs in the narrower, synchronic understanding of *allomorphy*. So, in spite of the fact that sets such as √*ced*=*ceed* 'go, let go,' √*erg* = *urg* = *org* 'work' may have been allomorphic at some stage in history, for us they are unpredictably variable cognates.

In a discussion of allomorphy, we should also note that a large number of morphemes appear to preserve both their spelling and their pronunciation in all forms. Here are some examples of morphemes which remain mostly unchanged in all of their derivatives:

√chron 'time'	√dys 'bad, badly'	√morph 'form'
chronic	dyslexia	morpheme
anachronism	dysentery	amorphous
chronometer	dyspeptic	allomorph
diachrony	dystrophy	geomorphology
synchronize	dyslogistic	isomorph(ic)

We say "mostly" because even in these forms which appear at first glance to be very stable, there are differences of pronunciation that follow from the position of the stress in the derived word: the vowel of √*chron* has one pronunciation in **chron**ic, where it is stressed, and a "reduced" pronunciation in ***chron**ology* and *syn**chron**ize*. Reduction of vowels in unstressed syllables is perhaps the variation closest to being automatic. We will assume that this type of variation is sufficiently transparent to require little discussion.

1.2   Origins of allomorphy and variability of cognates

Language change is inexorable. It occurs at every level of structure, in every community, and unless a language is dead, like Latin, or artificial, like Esperanto, its features are subject to constant change. As we saw in the *syn*- example above, the shape of morphemes may change because of their phonetic environments. If a particular phonetic change spreads part way through a derivationally related set of words but not all the way, we will perceive allomorphy, because the change will have occurred in some words but not in others. Consider the words *compel* and *compulsion*. √pel is the root that means 'push.' If the [l] at the end of √*pel* comes to be followed by a suffix beginning with a consonant, as in *pulse* or *compulsion*, then the <e> changes to <u>. As in the change of *syn*- to *sym*- in *symmetry*, the change of √*pel* to √*pul* in certain phonetic environments is a regular process which has the effect of creating a new allomorph of the morpheme whose base form is √*pel*.

Another major source of historical variability of the base form is borrowing cognate words from two different languages or from the same language at different times. The connection between such forms coexisting in English will no longer be transparent or predictable from the phonetic environment. From Greek we borrowed √*onym* 'name,' as in *pseudonym, anonymous, heteronym*, and from Latin we borrowed √*nom*, which also means 'name,' as in *nominal, nominate, nomenclature*, etc. As a result of this double borrowing we have a pair of roots √*onym* and √*nom*, meaning the same thing. Similarly, the Latin root √*via* 'way' is preserved in borrowings such as *via* 'by way of,' *viaduct, trivia*, but in borrowings from French the same root shows a change to √*vey*, √*voy*, as in *convey, envoy*. Such historical connections can be made only by specialists familiar with the early phonological history of Greek, Latin, or French; for us the link between the alternate forms √*onym* and √*nom*, √*via* and √*voy* is solely etymological.

1.3   Some triggers of phonetic change

Allomorphy emerges as a result of phonetic changes. The operation of these phonetic changes and therefore the applicability of the rules of allomorphy may depend on a number of structural, historical, or social factors. Before we look into the details of individual rules, let us examine briefly five general principles which may trigger or influence the way in which a particular phonological rule is likely to create allomorphy. These are:

(1)   Ease: some phonetic sequences are preferable to others because they are easier to pronounce.

(2)   Transparency: some phonetic sequences are more transparent to the ear than others, even though they are harder to articulate. Ease of perception may be in conflict with or even override ease of articulation.

(3)   Frequency: more frequent forms are more likely to be reduced by erosion than uncommon forms.

(4)   Origin: native words often behave differently from borrowed words, because different languages favor different processes of phonetic change.

(5)   Age: phonetic sequences are slowly modified by time. Metaphorically, erosion due to years of usage may show the age of an item.

Let us examine these five principles in more detail:

Ease of pronunciation. When morphemes are strung together to form a word, the sounds at the point of contact between the adjacent morphemes may not be compatible, or may require extra effort from the speaker. For example, consonantal sequences such as [n+p] are commonly changed to the "easier" sequence [m+p], e.g. *in+possible* becomes *im+possible*. In many languages sequences of two syllabic vowels tend to be avoided. Thus √*meta* 'transcending, changed'+√*onym* 'name' becomes *metonym*, not *meta-onym*. In other words, we can expect that there will be changes which simplify or eliminate uncomfortable phonetic combinations whenever they arise in the course of deriving a more complex word.

The principles which govern, for any given language, what sequences are judged to be comfortable to pronounce, and what sequences are uncomfortable or difficult or even impossible, are called **phonotactic constraints** (√*phono*- 'sound'+√*tact*- 'arrange'). These constraints vary from one language to another: the consonant clusters [mn-] or [ps-] can appear word-initially in Greek or Russian, but they are avoided and simplified in English. Even within one single language the phonotactic preferences and constraints can change historically. In Old English the first two consonants in words like *know, knee, knight* were actually pronounced as [kn-]. Similarly, the words corresponding to *write, wrist, wrong* started with [w-], and there were words beginning with [hn-], [hl-], [hr-], which we now consider impossible word-initial consonant clusters. So, phonotactic constraints are not absolute, except for some very general principles which will block combinations that are hard to pronounce or completely unpronounceable, say, four consonants or four vowels in a row, but these are not of interest to us here: we are concerned with strings of sounds that *can* be pronounced, but are fully or partially avoided, usually for a discernible phonetic reason. Even then, the constraints are sometimes violated when we borrow from other languages. Thus we can force ourselves to pronounce successfully (though this is frequently accompanied by a substantial distortion of the original sound sequence), but still find strange, combinations such as ***Brno**, **Bedřich**, **chihuahua**, **Dniepr**, **Dvořak**, **Dzershinsk**, **gnocchi**, **Nkruma**, **Mbabane**, **Lhotse**, **Tsangpo**, **schwa**, **Zweig***, and many others.

Transparency. Transparency is the opposite of **ease**. When we change pronunciation to make it easier, we often make the word harder to process. Consider the difference between *unfurl* and *imbibe*. The first would be easier to pronounce if it were **umfurl* because [m] is more similar to [f]. But this would make the identity of the prefix *un-* less transparent. The second would be easier to understand if it were **inbibe* because the prefix *in-* would be immediately recognizable. But this would make it somewhat harder to articulate. Pronouncing the last three consonants of *length* is not easy at all, but any shortcut which changes the cluster to say, *lent*, would also damage the transparent relationships of this word with *long* and with a number of other nouns ending in *-th*: *depth, warmth, wealth*. It is not predictable whether ease will win – as in *imbibe*, or whether the need to maintain transparency will block the effect of ease as in **unfurl**, **unfulfilled**, **midtown**, **midsummer**, **subclass**, **subsection**, where the prefixes may resist phonetic change in spelling and in careful pronunciation and would thus favor maintaining transparency.

Frequency of use. The correlation between frequency of use and the degree of change is not a straightforward matter, but for purely phonetically induced changes we can say that the more frequent a word is, the more likely it is to change. Speaking metaphorically again, as with any mechanism, excessive wear can be a factor in determining how well the mechanism survives. On the other hand, the most frequent lexical items are firmly entrenched in our lexicons since child-hood and sheer repetition of the same form may prevent them from changing.[2] In addition to these contradictory effects of frequency, the importance of this factor for the shape of the loanwords in English is hard to assess because the frequency of an item in the donor language may differ considerably from its frequency in English. By definition, borrowed words will not be very frequent upon entry into a new language, so initially their shape will be guided primarily by phonetic ease and transparency of structure. In many cases where transparency is paramount, frequency may not play a role in the implementation of otherwise predictable changes.

Origin. The etymological source of a morpheme is also important. Often the applicability and generality of the phonetic rules depend on the entire system. In the case of English, it matters whether the word is of Germanic descent, or whether it is to be traced to a non-Germanic, non-Old-English source. Some rules are shared by native and borrowed morphemes. Thus we find [n] preserved before a vowel in both the native *an* (indefinite article, originating in the Old English numeral *an*, 'one'), and in the common negative prefix *an-* 'not' borrowed from Greek via Latin, so **an** *opportunity*, but **a** *perspective*, *an+arch+y* >*anarchy*, but *an+political* >*apolitical*. Other rules apply only to morphemes of classical origin. Thus a rule which changes [n] to [m] (or [l] or [r]) under certain conditions, as in the morphemes *syn-*, *in-*, affects only non-native morphemes ending in *-n*: *sym-pathy, syllable, imbibe, illogical, irresponsible*. The morpheme *un-*, which is the Germanic prefix corresponding to Latin negative *in-*, retains its [n] in the same environments: **unbiased**, **unlawful**, **unready**. The decision to label some mor-phemes native and some foreign will depend on how far back in history we want to go. The accepted practice is to classify morphemes common to most Germanic languages as **native**; morphemes which have come into the English language from Latin or Greek, sometimes via French, Spanish, Italian, are lumped together as

---

[2] In the findings of Betty Phillips (*Word Frequency and Lexical Diffusion*, New York: Palgrave Macmillan, 2006) both the most frequent and the least frequent words in the language can be at the forefront of a change, depending on how much analysis of the innovative form is required by the speaker.

Romance borrowings (where "Romance" includes "classical," especially since many of the Latin borrowings are quite late, after 1500, from the European *lingua franca* of science and higher education, known as New Latin).

Age or time of entry of the word into English. Roots and words which were borrowed or coined at a relatively early stage in the history of English or the donor language are more likely to have undergone a number of phonetically driven changes. More recent borrowings or new coinages, on the other hand, are likely to preserve the original form of the morphemes. The words *Antarctic* and *antagonist* are both early (fourteenth and sixteenth centuries) borrowings – they are ultimately Greek, but passed through Latin and French before entering English. They show a change in the original language whereby the morpheme *anti* lost its second vowel when attached to a vowel-initial root. In more recent formations, however, the second vowel of *anti-* is retained: ***anti**-American* (1773), ***anti**-attrition* (1833), ***anti**-imperialism* (1846), ***anti**-abortion* (1936). The *OED* records two forms for some words in which the same vowel might be subject to loss: *anti-acid* and *antacid*, *anti-emetic* and *antemetic* and even *antodontalgic* (1880).[3]

2   The sounds of English

Before we go on to the discussion of specific rules of allomorphy, we need to survey briefly the inventory of sounds in English. Knowledge of the basic facts will help you understand and remember many of the rules governing allomorphy in English.

2.1   Phonetic notation systems

The sounds of all languages can be written reliably in phonetic notation systems, of which the International Phonetic Alphabet (IPA) is the most famous. However, there is not just one single phonetic notation system. Different dictionaries use different systems, and to discover the details of their systems you must check the introduction, and the bottom of the pages in the main part of the dictionary, where you will find a pronunciation key in most dictionaries. American phoneticians and lexicographers in general use a slightly different set of symbols from those used by European phoneticians. The important thing to understand is that phonetic symbols are arbitrary, codified, representations of language sounds. Any well-defined system is, in principle, as good as any other. However, because the IPA is used in the *OED* and its various derivative dictionaries, although it is not used in *Chambers* nor in any of the general purpose American dictionaries, we have used (a simplified version of) it here. We believe it is becoming more widely known in general education anyway, as it certainly should. Later in this

---

[3] As in the previous chapters, references to the age of borrowing are from *OED* online.

chapter we provide a comparison between the symbols of the IPA, of *Chambers*, of the *American Heritage Dictionary*, and of a very broad respelling system of the type that is commonly used in newspapers to indicate the pronunciation of unfamiliar words, so that you can see what the differences and similarities are.

2.2   Phonetic symbols in square brackets

When symbols of the alphabet are intended specifically to represent language sounds, they are enclosed in square brackets: [p, t, k] means the sounds at the beginnings of the words *pill, till, kill*. Once a symbol is enclosed in square brackets like this, it no longer refers to the spelling, only to the sound. Thus the first letter of the word *philosophy* is *p*, but the first sound is [f]. The first letter of *pneumonia* is *p*, but the first sound is [n]. It is common in our highly literate western world to confuse the **sounds** of words with the **spelling**. We must keep these two separate from each other, because many etymological statements can be quite confusing if misunderstood as statements only about about spellings or only about sounds.

Most of the phonetic symbols of the IPA will be familiar to you from the standard spelling of English words. A few new symbols will have to be introduced, however, to avoid ambiguity, since the basic idea of phonetic writing is to use a single symbol for a single sound, and always to use the same symbol for the same sound. For example, we will use the symbol [θ] to represent the initial consonant sound in words like *thigh* and *think* (this symbol, the Greek "theta," is the standard IPA symbol), because the actual sound is a single sound (i.e. it is not *t* plus *h*).[4] The IPA symbol [ð], known as "eth" or "edh," will be used to represent the initial consonant sound in words like *them* and *though*. If you are uncertain about the difference between these sounds, compare *ether* (like *thigh* and *think*) with *either* (like *them* and *though*) and you should hear it easily. To represent the initial sound in words like *shout* and *she*, we will use [š] "s wedge" instead of the IPA symbol [ʃ] "esh," simply because it is typographically easier. There is a similar, but not identical sound in the middle of the word *measure* and at the end of the word *triage*. We will represent this sound with [ž] "z wedge," although the IPA symbol is [ʒ] "yogh." Four other deviations from standard IPA are not in principle damaging to the general utility or purposes of IPA phonetic writing. The first, [č] "c wedge," represents the initial and the final sound in the word *church*. A similar sound occurs as the initial and final consonant in the word *judge*. We will represent this sound as [ǰ] "j wedge." We can write [ng] instead of IPA [ŋ] "eng" in words like *sing* and *singer*. Finally, we write [y] instead of [j] for the first sound of words like *year*, *yes*, because writing [j] is an unnecessary source of confusion for English speakers. The [y] notation for this sound is also the practice of the *American Heritage Dictionary*, 4th edition (2000).

---

[4] The names of the IPA symbols can be found in the very useful *Phonetic Symbol Guide*, 2nd edn, by Geoffrey Pullum and William Ladusaw (Chicago: University of Chicago Press, 1996).

2.3   Consonantal parameters

When describing the articulation of the consonants of English (or any language), it is necessary to consider three parameters:

(1)   **Place of articulation**: precisely where does the tongue or lower lip – the two moveable "articulators" – make closure or near-closure with some point along the roof of the mouth? The possibilities are (a) the upper lip, (b) the upper teeth, (c) the area directly behind the upper teeth called the alveolar ridge, (d) the hard palate, and (e) the soft palate, also called the velum. One can feel all five of these with a single sweep of the tip of the tongue from the upper lip to the furthest point back along the roof of the mouth that the tip can reach.

(2)   **Manner of articulation**: what is the degree of the closure or near-closure (i.e. some kind of hindrance of the airflow through the mouth) that is made between the articulator and the place of articulation?

(3)   **Voicing**: are the vocal cords vibrating or not during the production of a particular sound?

These three parameters are spelled out in more detail below.

2.3.1   Place of articulation

This parameter in the description of consonants refers to the regions of the vocal tract involved in the production of a given sound. For instance, the sounds [p, b, m, w], as in *pill*, *bill*, *mill*, *will*, involve both lips. We refer to these sounds as bilabial. The sounds [f, v], as in *fairy*, *very*, are articulated with the lower lip and the upper teeth, and are therefore referred to as labiodental sounds. There are six major places of articulation relevant for English consonants:

Bilabial [p, b, m, w]: articulated with both lips.
Labiodental [f, v]: articulated with the lower lip and upper teeth.
Dental [θ, ð]: as in *thistle*, *this*, articulated with the tongue touching the back of the teeth.
Alveolar [t, d, s, z, r, l, n]: as in *too*, *do*, *sue*, *zoo*, *rue*, *loo*, *new*, articulated with the tongue contacting or approaching the bony (alveolar) ridge behind the upper teeth.
Palatal [š, ž, č, ǰ, y]: as in *shoe*, *genre*, *chew*, *jew*, *you*, articulated with the tongue contacting or approaching the hard palate behind the alveolar ridge.
Velar [k, g, ng]:[5] as in *kill*, *guilt*, and the last sound in *sing*, articulated with the back part of the tongue raised toward the soft palate.

2.3.2   Manner of articulation

"Manner" of articulation is a reference to what happens to the air as it escapes from the lungs through the mouth and/or nose as the sound is produced.

---

[5] The sound [w] also involves a velar articulation, and is often classified as both bilabial and velar.

For example, during the production of the consonants [p, b, t, d, k, g], there is a brief period when the air is completely **stopped**, and so these consonants are called **stops**.[6] During the production of the consonants [f, v, θ, ð s, z, š, ž], the air is allowed to flow out of the mouth, but there is some friction which results in a hissing sound, so these are called **fricative continuants**. In the production of the consonants [č, ǰ], the air is stopped for a brief period, and then is released with a certain degree of friction, and the consonants are called **affricates** (half stop and half fricative). Stops, fricatives, and affricates as a group are called obstruents. In the production of [m, n, ng] the airflow is stopped in the oral tract but allowed to continue through the nose, so they are called **nasal sonorants** (sonorants are sounds which can be hummed). The other sonorants deflect the airstream in various ways: [l] is called a **lateral sonorant** because it deflects the airflow around the side of the tongue; [r] is called a **retroflex sonorant** because the airflow is redirected up over the curled-back tip of the tongue. There are thus five major manners of articulation relevant for English consonants:

Stops [p, b, t, d, k, g]: the air is completely stopped for a brief period – you should be able to feel this stoppage at the beginning of *town*, *down*, or in the middle of words like *upper*, *rubber*, *sucker*, *mugger*.

Affricates [č, ǰ]: the air is stopped, then released with a degree of friction – *pitcher*, *ledger*.

Fricatives [f, v, θ, ð, s, z, š, ž]: the air passes uninterrupted, with a degree of friction[7] – *fan*, *van*, *through*, *this*, *sip*, *zip*, *sure*, *azure*.

Nasals [m, n, ng/ŋ]: the air is released through the nose, rather than the mouth – *mom*, *nun*, *hung*.

Approximants [r, l, y, w]: the air is allowed to flow more freely than for the other types of consonants, but with coloring introduced by tongue shape. Examples: *rear*, *lull*, *yell*, *wow*. Within that larger set, [r, l] are called **liquids**; [r] is variable in the different varieties of English, and we use the symbol [r] as a convention to cover all types. [l] is a **lateral** – the tongue touches the roof of the mouth, but there is no contact at the sides, where the air escapes freely. [y, w] are also called **glides** or, sometimes, **semi-vowels**.

2.3.3   Voicing

The final parameter relevant to the phonetics of consonants is voicing. In English, all consonants except the sonorants are either **voiced** or **voiceless**. When the vocal cords are vibrating during the articulation of a sound, we say that the sound is voiced. When the vocal cords do not vibrate during the articulation of a sound, we say that the sound is voiceless. You can feel your vocal folds vibrating by placing your fingertips on your larynx (Adam's apple) as you say the sound zzzzzzzzzzz. You should be able to feel a vibration beneath the skin. Then try the

---

[6] Another name for the stops is *plosives*.
[7] Another commonly used term for the fricative consonants is *spirants*.

same experiment, but instead say *sssssssssss*. You should feel no vibration beneath the skin this time. This is because the fricative [z] is voiced, whereas the fricative [s] is voiceless. Now try saying *s-z-s-z-s-z*. You should be able to feel the voicing turning on and off. The voiceless consonants of English are [f, θ, s, š, p, t, k, č]. The voiced consonants are [v, ð, z, ž, b, d, g, ǰ, m, n, ŋ, r, l].

2.3.4   English consonants: summary

All this information about consonants is displayed in Figure 5.2.

	MANNER PLACE	LABIAL	LABIODENTAL	DENTAL	ALVEOLAR	PALATAL	VELAR
Obstruent	STOPS	p b			t d		k g
	AFFRICATES					č/tʃ ǰ/dʒ	
	FRICATIVES		f v	θ ð	s z	š/ʃ ž/ʒ	
Sonorant	NASALS	m			n		ŋ
	LATERALS				l		
	APPROXIMANTS	(w)			r	y	(w)

Figure 5.2 *English consonants*

In each box of Figure 5.2 where there are two symbols, the one on the left is voiceless, the one on the right is voiced. Jointly, the consonants in the lower three rows [m, n, ŋ, r, l, w, y] are called **sonorants** – they are always voiced in English, unlike the stops, fricatives, and affricates which can be voiced or voiceless. Further, sonorants can be *oral* [r, l, w, y] or *nasal* [m, n, ŋ] depending on whether the airstream can exit through the mouth or not. As noted above, the sound [w] also involves a velar articulation; we indicate this by placing (w) in parentheses in both cells.

The only English consonant which is not listed in Figure 5.2 or discussed above is [h]. This is because the place of articulation of [h] depends on the adjacent vowel. It is really a type of vowel: it is in fact a voiceless vowel. That is why in most of the phonetic rules which concern vowels, the rules work in the same way whether the vowel is preceded by [h] or not. A source of confusion for some readers may be the common assumption that there really is an [h] in the sounds represented by the spellings <th, ch, sh, ph>. The fact is that the orthographic symbols <th, ch, sh, ph> do not contain or represent an [h] at all, phonetically. The [h] in these instances is simply a diacritic mark used in conjunction with the symbol to which it is adjacent to indicate an altogether different sound, namely [θ, ð, č, š, f].

2.4   English vowels

Except for the diacritic spellings with <h> discussed above, English orthography represents the consonant sounds with a high degree of consistency and reliability: not perfectly, but still straightforwardly. There are jokes about it, like the question attributed to George Bernard Shaw, "What does *ghoti* spell?" – the answer, of course, is *fish*.[8] On the other hand, the main source of dismay on the part of foreigners learning English, and of English-speaking children learning to spell, is the extreme variability of English orthography in the representation of vowels. They are more difficult than consonants to characterize phonetically, partly because we don't have the same easy articulatory reference points as we do with the consonants, and partly because the manner in which our orthography represents them is erratic. When the spelling system of English is criticized, the basis of the criticism is usually this very fact, the inconsistency of the vowel system. The sound represented by the letters *ee* as in *beet* is also spelled *ie* in *niece*, *ea* in *neat*, *i* in *machine*, *e* in *complete*, and so on.

Vowel sounds are maximally sonorant – there is no consonantal-type obstruction at all. All that happens is that the size and shape of the resonating cavities of the vocal tract, namely the upper throat and the mouth, are varied in such a way as to produce different vowel qualities. How may we represent those variations in a consistent manner? On the whole, vowels play a less important role in what might be called "visual" allomorphy – i.e. the differences which turn up visually in the writing system (the ones we are mainly concerned about in looking at classical allomorphy). On the other hand, they are central to variation that does not necessarily affect the spelling – we will return to these patterns below. First, however, we lay out the main parameters of vowel production but without the refinements needed to develop serious skills of vowel discrimination. Nonetheless, it is necessary to understand the rudiments of vowel articulation in order to interpret the phonetic indications of preferred pronunciation found in dictionaries, and in order to understand certain etymological processes described below.

2.4.1   Vowel variation

The precise details of how vowels are articulated vary strikingly across the English-speaking world, and any description of the vowel system will be correct only within some selected geographic area. In Britain, one of the widely accepted norms is usually referred to as "Received Pronunciation," based on the pronunciation of educated speakers in southern England. Sometimes (especially in America) it is called "BBC English."[9] It is this pronunciation which is recorded in the *Oxford English Dictionary* and in the many editions of Daniel Jones' *English Pronouncing Dictionary*.[10] The one we shall use in this book is referred

---

[8] For those who are not familiar with the joke <gh> spells [f] as in *tough*, <o> spells [I] as in *women*, and <ti> spells [š] as in *revolution*.

[9] The *American Heritage Dictionary* defines BBC English as "A pronunciation of British English based on the speech of the upper class of southeastern England, formerly used as a broadcast standard in British media."

[10] Jones' first pronouncing dictionary was published in 1907. Its latest, 17th, version, appeared in 2006. It was renamed *Cambridge Pronouncing Dictionary* by Daniel Jones (Author), Peter Roach (Editor), James Hartman (Editor), Jane Setter (Editor). It includes British and North American pronunciation.

to as "General American," which means – by and large, though we shall simplify it somewhat – the pronunciation recorded in *A Pronouncing Dictionary of American English*.[11] What is recorded there is basically the variety of American English spoken west of the Appalachians and north of the Ohio River on a line extending westward at approximately the 40th parallel until the Rockies, and then the area spreads north and south like a great fan and there comes to be minimal variation throughout the whole area.

2.4.2   Vowel parameters

To understand the way vowels are produced and differentiated, you must become aware of some fairly subtle differences in the way your tongue is positioned in your mouth. Begin with the doctor's instruction: say AH. Why does the doctor ask anyone to say AH? Because if you say AH, you have to open your mouth wide, and your tongue will be lying along the very bottom of the jaw (on the inside). Only then can the doctor see your throat, since otherwise your tongue is in the way. The sound you make with your mouth wide open is called an "open" or "low" vowel. That particular vowel is the most open of all vowels. On Figure 5.3, you will find this vowel represented as [ɑ] in the box that shows the intersection between LOW on the vertical axis and CENTRAL on the horizontal axis.

Figure 5.3 presents an overview of the vowels of English. Some typically southern standard British variants are marked as (BrE). The colon symbol (:) is a commonly used convention to indicate that the vowel is long; more on that below. The representations [ey/ei] and [ow/ou] for [o] indicate that the vowels of PATE, BOAT are diphthongal – they start and end with the tongue in a different position from where it started. In American English, the diphthongization is much more noticeable in the Midlands and on the East Coast than around the Great Lakes.

Figure 5.3 is a schematic representation of the relative height and frontness of the tongue in producing these vowels. Think of the left side of the diagram as the front of the mouth, just behind the teeth, and the right side is the back of the mouth, where it turns down into the throat. You should be able to feel what is happening to your tongue if you say, in fairly rapid alternation, EE – AH – EE – AH. You should feel your jaw (and tongue) dropping in going from EE to AH and then closing as the tongue moves up high again for EE. Now try moving your tongue from the most open position, the doctor's AH position, very slowly up to the EE position. You should hear the vowel quality gradually change, going through the inter-mediate front vowels along the way.

Taking the doctor's AH (i.e. phonetic [ɑ]) in Figure 5.3 as the maximally open reference point in the system, we can establish two other such reference points, namely the vowels at the other extreme, maximally close.

---

[11] John S. Kenyon and Thomas A. Knott (Springfield, MA: Merriam, 1953). See also *Longman Pronunciation Dictionary*, 3rd edn by J.C. Wells (Harlow [England]: Pearson Education Ltd., 2008).

	FRONT	CENTRAL	BACK
HIGH	iy/(i:) (PEAT)		(BOOT) uw/(u:)
(lower) HIGH	ɪ (PIT)		(PUT) ʊ
MID	e(y) (PATE)	ɜ: (BrE)[12]	(BOAT) o(w)
(lower) MID	ɛ (PET)	ə (CUT)	(CUT) ʌ (BrE)
(higher) LOW	æ (PAT)		(PAW) ɔ(:) (POT) ɒ (BrE)
LOW		ɑ (POT, FATHER)[13]	

Figure 5.3 *English vowels*

(1) The maximally close **front** reference point is the vowel represented by [iy/i(:)] (the intersection of HIGH and FRONT in Figure 5.3). This is commonly spelled with "double *e*" in English orthography, as in words like *geese, meet, beet, feet, keep*, but also *ea* as in *beat, bean, grease, flea*, or *ie* as in *field, pierce, bier*. The only English words which use the letter *i* to represent this vowel sound are relatively recent borrowings from French, like *machine, mystique, fatigue, regime*. The use of *i* to represent this sound phonetically is no doubt due to the fact that in most European languages the letter *i* is the regular representation of the sound we are discussing: consider French *oui*, Spanish *si*, Italian *si*. English is the odd language in this respect.

(2) The maximally close **back** reference point is the vowel represented by [uw/u(:)] (the intersection of HIGH and BACK in Figure 5.3). This is commonly spelled with "double *o*" in our orthography, as in words like *goose, moot, boot, loop*.

You can feel these three reference points by saying *me–ma–moo* – i.e. phonetically [mi – mɑ – mu]. You'll find that the third vowel, [u], not only requires that you move your tongue to the high back position, but you must also pucker your lips, or as phoneticians say, you must "round your lips." This lip rounding is an additional parameter, but it is automatic in English and requires no special discussion.

Figure 5.3 also contains information about another difference between the vowels of English: the cells for HIGH, MID, and LOW are further divided into lower HIGH, lower MID, and higher LOW. These additional specifications are needed because the set of **tense**, or **long**, vowels of English, [iy, ey, uw, ow] are higher and more peripheral than the corresponding **lax**, or **short**, vowels in the

---

[12] This symbol represents the southern British English development of the [r] that Americans have in such words as *bird, word, rehearse, first, sir*. The IPA representation of this vowel is [ɝ] ("right-hook schwa") for the r-colored schwa. For the American [r] as in the *-er -ur-* of *father, further*, we write [-ər], both stressed and unstressed.

[13] For many American speakers the vowels of POT, FATHER, and PAW are identical.

same cell. We will return to the history of these vowels in Section 2.6. Here we just note that while in pre-Chaucerian English and in the the classical languages the "short" and the "long" vowels differed primarily in duration, in PDE the "long" vowels are very different from their "short" counterparts, though both may continue to be written with the same letter: compare the values of the letter <i> in *hide* and *hid*, the letter <e> in *pet* and *Pete*, the letter <a> in *grade* and *gradual*, the letter <o> in *sole* and *solitude*.

Up to this point, we have discussed mainly the **monophthongs** of English. That is, they are relatively "pure" vowels (though see our earlier comment on the vowels of PATE and BOAT in Figure 5.3 above). We must also have a notation for certain combinations of two vowels, called **diphthongs**, which behave like single long vowel units but are in fact carriers of the height and frontness properties of two vowels. Diphthongal vowels are produced by starting with the first vowel and gliding quickly toward the second vowel position, which may or may not be fully articulated. The four common diphthongs in English are shown below; the slashes separate alternative ways of representing them phonetically:

[ɑi]/[ɑy]   as in BITE, LIE, HIDE, MIGHT, DINE
[ɑu]/[ɑw]   as in BOUT, BOW, BOWED, DOWN, NOUN
[oi]/[oy]   as in BOY, AVOID, GROIN, COY
[iu]/[yu]   as in BEAUTY, CUTE, FUME, DISPUTE

For many speakers [**iu**] appears also in *duty, dues, news, sue, tune*, but in America more often these words have the vowel [**uw/u:**] instead of [**iu**] whenever the vowel follows a consonant in the dento-alveolar series ([t, d, s, z]) as in these words.

All of the points in the vowel space can be calculated from the three extreme positions [**i u ɑ**]. Working from the key words given in Figure 5.3, you can determine precisely what sounds are represented by which phonetic symbols. In Figure 5.4 we display these sounds in four notation systems:

(1)   Simplified IPA, with alternatives discussed above (our system)
(2)   *American Heritage Dictionary* (4th edition 2000)
(3)   *The Chambers Dictionary* (1998)
(4)   Newspaper "respelling"

Examples	IPA	*AHD*	*Chambers*	Respelling
bead, see, niece	[i]/[i:]	ē	ē	ee
bid, his, sin	[ɪ]	ĭ	i	i
paid, may, came	[e]/[ei]	ā	ā	ay
bed, said, bread	[ɛ]	ĕ	e	e
bad, pack, jazz	[æ]	ă	a	a

pod, lot, father	[ɑ]	ŏ[14]	o	o
pawed, caught	[ɔ][15]	ô	ö	aw
bud, was, rough	[ʌ] ([ə])	ŭ	u	u
hoed, coat, note	[o]/[ou]	ō	ō	oa
good, would	[ʊ]	oo	oo	oo
boot, food, noon	[u]/[u:]	o͞o	o͞o	oo
beauty, review	[iu]	ȳ	ū	yoo
eye, mine, pie	[ɑi]/[ɑy]	ī	ī	igh
how, bout, loud	[ɑu]/[ɑw]	ou	ow	ow
boy, loin, point	[oi]/[oy]	oi	oi	oy
bird, hurt, fur	[ər], [ɚ]	ûr	û(r)	ur
uh, a(bout)	[ə]	ə	ə	uh

Figure 5.4

2.5   Reduction of vowels ▬▬▬▬▬▬▬▬▬▬▬▬▬

The distinction between full and reduced vowels depends on the presence or absence of prominence, marked with boldface type in the example below. Compare the different allomorphs of the morphemes *tele* and *graph*:

> **te**le-graph –[ˈtɛlə-græf] or [ˈtɛlɪ-græf]

vs.

> te**le**-graph-y – [tə ˈlɛ -grəfi]

Notice that the first syllable of *tele-* when accented almost rhymes with *belly*; when unaccented, its first syllable has the same vowel as the word *but*. This change in the quality of the vowel is called **vowel reduction**, and it is directly associated with loss of prominence. Vowel reduction replaces whatever the stressed vowel is by the most neutral and under-articulated vowel in the system, namely the one called *schwa*, represented by the upside-down e, namely [ə]. In Figure 5.4 the only symbol that is agreed upon by IPA, *AHD*, and *Chambers* is schwa. It is also used by *Merriam-Webster's*, starting with their great unabridged

---

[14] The *AHD* has a separate symbol for the stressed vowel in father, [ä].
[15] Not distinguished from the vowel of *pod*, etc. in some dialects. The representation of the vowel in r-dropping BrE *pore, sore* would require a length mark: [-ɔ:]. In American English it requires an off-gliding *schwa*; see immediately below.

dictionary of 1961. Vowel reduction is pervasive in both the native and the Latinate vocabulary of English. Even when the borrowed morpheme remains orthographically stable, the shifting of stress away from a vowel is bound to trigger reduction – this is what we had in mind in Section 1.1. above when we said that otherwise stable morphemes such as √*chron*, *dys-*, √*morph* show allomorphy due to vowel reduction. Here some more examples of vowel reduction:

Unreduced	*Reduced*
val**i**d [væ-]	val**i**dity [və-],
Canada [kæ-]	**Ca**nadian [kə-]
co**me**dian [-mi:-]	co**me**dy [-mə-]
idi**o**tic [ɪdɪ-ɑ-]	idi**o**t [-ət]
expl**a**natory [plæ-]	expl**a**nation [-ə-n-]

2.6   **Long-vowel shifting**

Returning to the discussion of allomorphy in the first part of this chapter, we can now be more specific about some of the alternations we find in morphemes such as √*mani* 'intense desire' in *mania* and *maniacal*, √*mim* 'copy, imitate' in *mime* and *mimic*, √*riv* 'shore, river' in *arrive* and *river*, √*pro-* 'before, in space or time,' as in *profess* and *proactive*, to mention but a few. Such pairs show how orthographic zero allomorphy can be associated with different pronunciations. This section surveys the history and the mechanism of these alternations.

For a start, consider the **phonetic** differences between the vowels of the root syllables of words in columns A–B in Figure 5.5:

A		B		Spelling
sane	[ey]	*sanity*	[æ]	<a>
serene	[iy]	*serenity*	[ɛ]	<e>
final	[ɑy]	*finish*	[ɪ]	<i>
reduce	[iu]	*reduction*	[ʌ/ə]	<u>
abound	[ɑw]	*abundant*	[ʌ/ə]	<u, ou>
melodious	[ow]	*melodic*	[ɑ]	<o>
school	[u:]	*scholar*	[ɑ]	<o>

Figure 5.5 *Vowel alternations in borrowed words with shared roots*

Superficially, there appears to be little in common between the vowels of column A and the vowels of column B. But the spelling identity between the boldfaced vowels and their letter representation in the rightmost column suggests that there is something basic that they share.

Suppose we temporarily give up on phonetic notations such as those in columns A and B above. Such notations, often necessary and factually correct, actually obscure the relationships. We can replace the first of each pair of phonetic notations with the "name vowel" for them: [A-E-I-YU-OU-O-OO] = [ey-iy-ɑy-iu-ɑw-ow-uw]. The concept "name vowel" is not quite perfect – it only works for [A-E-I-O]. For [U] we have to supply a different onset, perhaps [YU] as in *beauty*; and for *bound* we use its most common spelling [OU]; and finally for the *food* vowel again we resort to its most common spelling, namely [OO]. That gives us seven vowels with non-phonetic names which, just by their grade-school names, bring the relevant sounds into play.

The above paragraph would not have much point if it were only a memory trick, a sort of esoteric naming game. The point is this: these seven vowels were the most important members of the full set of **long vowels** in late Middle English and Early Modern English times – roughly the 200 years between Chaucer's death (1400) and Queen Elizabeth's death (1603). At the beginning of this period each long vowel – the "name" vowels, recall – sounded like a longer version of the corresponding **short vowel** – namely [æ: – e: – i: – o: – u:], such that these are read "long ash," "long e," "long i," "long o," "long u," and referred to as "the long vowels of late Middle English." Without the colon they would be read as "short ash," "short e," "short i," "short o," "short u," and referred to as "the short vowels of late Middle English." The two sets would have sounded alike except for length – this is shown in Figure 5.6, in a vowel chart configration; some correspondences are simplified to make the principle clear.

$$\begin{array}{ll} \text{i: – i} & \text{u – u:} \\ \text{e: – e} & \text{o – o:} \\ \text{æ: – æ} & \text{ɔ – ɔ:} \\ \quad\quad \text{ɑ: – ɑ} & \end{array}$$

Figure 5.6 *The Middle English long–short vowel correspondences*

You will note that Figure 5.6 does not show the same pairs of long–short matching vowels as Figure 5.5. In Figure 5.7 we show PDE words that sound approximately like the vowels in Figure 5.6 do today:

$$\begin{array}{ll} \text{beet – bit} & \text{pull – fool} \\ \text{bait – bet} & \text{cot – coat} \\ \text{---- – bat} & \text{---- – caught} \\ \quad \text{calm–bomb} & \end{array}$$

Figure 5.7 *Approximate values of the vowels in Figure 5.6*

It is clear that the pairings in Figure 5.7 do not strike English speakers as natural. The point is, the pairing of long and short vowels was, in Chaucer's time, phonetically transparent, whereas something has happened to make such pairs opaque. A pair like [sæ:n] – [sænɪti] with the pairing based on length used to form such a natural "matched set," maintaining the transparency of the allomorphy.

What happened after the fourteenth century was that the "long vowels" – the "name vowels" in Figure 5.6 – changed their pronunciation and moved away from their earlier mates, creating unseemly long–short vowel pairings in words that had previously been natural and obvious sets, both native and borrowed: ***heal–health***, ***wide–width***, ***knee–knelt***, ***nation–national***, *revise–revision*, *seduce–seductive*, ***sole–solitude***. The direction of the long-vowel change was upwards to the next higher position on the vowel chart, unless they were at the top; if they were already at the top, they became diphthongs of a special type, namely out-gliding diphthongs

(diphthongs ending in [-y] or [-w]) that we now recognize as the name vowels A, E, I, O, U. With this proviso it becomes clear that the examples mentioned above and in *anglo**phile*** and ***phil**osophy*, *gre**garious*** and *e**gregious***, ***river*** and *ar**rive***, ***mime*** and ***mim**eograph*, etc. the boldfaced roots are still one and the same morpheme. They look the same in the spelling, they used to be pronounced the same (except for length), as in Figure 5.6, and now each set of these long–short pairs is a matched pair in our identity space even though they are phonetically quite different from each other. How did this come about?

Basically, the short vowels stayed at home, unchanged, and did not undergo any kind of phonetic drifting. (Our simplified account assumes identity of the short vowels in Figure 5.6 with the lax vowels of PDE in Figure 5.3, [ɪ, ɛ, æ, ʊ, ʌ, ɔ].) At the same time, the long vowels went wandering in a highly systematic way. To describe their phonetic behavior (which still goes on), remember "Rising on the periphery, sliding down the center, and fill vacated space."

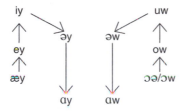

Figure 5.8 *Directionality of the long-vowel shift*

The changes shown in Figure 5.8 are commonly referred to as *The Great Vowel Shift*, though we prefer to avoid that label.[16] The most important aspect of the long-vowel changes in the context of this course is that they create a new pattern of allomorphy in the language which applies to borrowed words, as in Figure 5.5, and is indeed part of the *historical* allomorphy of English itself, as in *heal–health*, *wide–width*, *knee–knelt*, *five–fifth*, but they are not normally reflected in the orthography. From a linguistic perspective such pairs, as well as pairs like *photograph–photography*, *serene–serenity*, *resign–resignation*, *deprive–deprivation*, etc. present interesting analytical challenges and are much studied.

3   The affixes of English[17]

While by far the largest number of English morphemes are roots, the most frequently occurring morphemes are the affixes. Almost every word that has

---

[16] For an alternative interpretation of the shifting, see Robert Stockwell, "How much shifting actually occurred in the historical English vowel shift?" in D. Minkova and R. Stockwell (eds.), *Studies in the History of the English Language: A Millennial Perspective* (Berlin: Mouton de Gruyter, 2002), pp. 267–82.

[17] The main source of detailed information about English affixes, on which we have drawn freely, is Hans Marchand, *The Categories and Types of Present-Day English Word-Formation* (Munich: Beck, 1969).

come down to us from the classical languages Greek and Latin, or that has been newly created from Greek or Latin roots (as is done these days as well as earlier in history in nearly all fields of learning), has one or more affixes. The same affixes occur over and over again; because of their frequency, they are not hard to recognize and memorize.

Roots vs. derivational affixes: how they differ. Recall from Chapter 4, Section 2.2, that roots have a clear meaning, in and of themselves. While some affixes are like that (e.g. *un-* means "not"), affixes do not usually have such clear meanings. They are also extremely subject to a process of "bleaching," in which their original meaning is bleached out completely and what is left behind is almost impossible to specify; this is the case with the English suffixes *-dom, -hood, -ly*. In addition to the differences between roots and derivational affixes discussed already, you should be aware that not all affixes are equally distinct from roots. While suffixes are, in general, easy to identify as non-roots, prefixes tend to be more root-like. Historically roots frequently become prefixes (or "combining forms," to use the *OED* label), as in *ambi, mono, tele,* or conversely, by clipping off the root, they become roots themselves: *anti, dis, ex, pro*.

In the lists below, meanings are given that reflect the basic sense of each affix, but one cannot count on that meaning as being the only sense that one will ever encounter.

3.1   Prefixes

Counting-prefixes: those which in some way quantify the root

a- or *an-* 'lacking' as in *asymmetric, amoral, atonal*
ambi- 'both, around' as in *ambidextrous, ambiguous, amphibious, amphitheater*
arch- 'chief, principal, high' as in *archbishop, archduke*
bi- 'twice, double' as in *bifocal, biennial, bipolar, bisulfate*
di- 'two' as in *dioxide, ditransitive, dichloride*
mono- 'one' as in *monograph, monosyllabic, monomorphemic*
multi- 'many' as in *multifaceted, multivalent, multiform*
oligo- 'few' as in *oligarchy, oligotrophic*
omni- 'all' as in *omnipotent, omniscient, omnidirectional*
pan- 'all, comprising or affecting all' as in *panorama, pandemic*
poly- 'many' as in *polychromatic, polyangular, polygamy*
tri- 'three'[18] as in *triangle, tridimensional*
uni- 'one' as in *unisex, unidirectional, univocal*

---

[18] One might also list the prefixes for 4, 5, 6, 7, 8, 9, and 10, namely √*quadri* (*quadrilateral*) or √*tetra* (*tetrahedron*), √*penta* (*pentagon*), √*hex* (*hexagonal*), √*sept* (*septuagenarian*), √*octo* (*octogenarian*), √*nov* (*November*), √*dec* (*December, decasyllabic*).

Involvement prefixes: those which say something about the kind of involvement of the participants in the action of the root

anti- 'opposed, instead' as in *antidote, antisemitic, antacid, antonym*
auto- 'self' as in *automaton, autobiography, automobile*
co-, con- 'together, jointly' as in *coexistence, cooperate, concur*
contra- 'against, opposite' as in *contradiction, contrary*
vice- 'in place of, instead' as in *vice-consul, vice-president*

Judgment prefixes: those which make a judgment about the root

dis- used as an intensifier as in *disturb, disgruntle, disannul*
dys- 'bad, badly' as in *dyslogistic, dyspeptic*
eu- 'good, well' as in *eugenics, evangelical, euphoria*
extra- 'outside the scope of' as in *extraordinary, extramarital*
mal- 'ill, evil, wrong' as in *malfeasance, malodorant, malpractice*
meta- 'transcending, changed' as in *metaphysics, metamorphosis*
mis- 'badly, wrongly' as in *misspent, miscalculate, mislead*
pro- 'on behalf of' as in *pro-British, pro-education*
proto- 'first, chief' as in *protoorganism, protoplasm, prototype*
pseudo- 'false, deceptive resemblance' as in *pseudonym, pseudo-prophet, pseudo-archaic*

Locative prefixes: those which say something about place or direction

ab- or *a-* or *abs-* 'from, away' as in *abnormal, abstinence, abjure*
ad- or *a-* 'toward' as in *admit, advance, admonish, ascribe, avenue, avenge*
ana- 'up, back' as in *anatomy, anachronism, anaphora, analogy*
apo- 'away, from' as in *apocryphal, apostasy, apology*
cata- 'down, away, back, opposite' as in *catapult, catastrophe*
circum- 'around' as in *circumnavigate, circumspect, circumcise*
counter- 'against, opposite' as in *counterfeit, counterbalance*
de- or *di-* or *dis-* 'away from, down' as in *debase, depend, digest, direct, dismiss*
dia- 'across, through' as in *diameter, diachronic*
ecto-, exo- 'external' as in *ectoplasm, ectoderm, ectophyte, exocentric, exocardial*
en- 'in, into' (a form of *in-*) as in *encapsulate, enclose*
endo- 'internal' as in *endodontic, endogenous, endocardial, endocrinology*
epi- 'on, over' as in *epiglottis, epidermis, epicycle*
ex-, ec- 'out from, away' *ex consul, ex-wife; eccentric;* in reduced form *educate, eradicate, emit*
in- 'in, into, within' as in *inaugurate, inchoate*
infra- 'below, beneath, within' as in *infrastructure, infrared, infraterritorial*
inter- 'between, among' as in *interchange, interpose, intersect*
intra-, intro- 'inside' as in *intracity, intramural, intracellular, introvert*
ob- 'toward, against' as in *obdurate, obfuscate, occasion, obsequious*

para- 'beside, along with' as in *paramedic, parallel*
per- 'through, thoroughly' as in *perspire, pernicious, pervade*
peri- 'around, nearby' as in *perimeter, peristomatic*
pro- 'in front of' as in *proposition, proscenium, propel*
pros- 'concerning, towards' as in *prosody, proselyte*
retro- 'backwards, back' as in *retrogression, retrospection*
sub- 'under, below' as in *subdivision, subtraction, subtitle*
super- 'over, above' as in *supernatural, supererogatory, superman*
sur- 'over, above, beyond' as in *surtax, surrealistic*
syn- 'with, together' as in *synthetic, synchronic*
trans-, tres-, tra- 'across, surpassing' as in *transalpine, transoceanic, transhu-man, trespass, trajectory, traduce, tradition*

Measurement prefixes

crypto- 'secret, hidden' as in *cryptography, cryptanalytic*
hemi- 'half' as in *hemisphere, hemicircle, hemistich*
holo- 'whole, entire' as in *holocaust, hologram, holarthritic*
hyper- 'over, to excess' as in *hyperactive, hypersensitive*
hypo- 'under, slightly' as in *hypotactic, hypoglossal, hypotoxic*
is-, iso- 'equal' as in *isochrony, isosceles, isotope*
macro- 'large, broad scale' as in *macroeconomics, macroclimatology*
mero- 'part, partial' as in *meroblastic, merocracy, meronym*
micro- 'tiny, small scale' as in *microorganism, microscope*
mid- 'middle' as in *midwinter, midlands, midnight*
semi- 'half, partly' as in *semicolon, semifinal, semi-annual*
ultra- 'beyond, extreme' as in *ultraliberal, ultramodest, ultraviolet*

Negative prefixes

dis- 'apart, reversal, lacking' as in *displease, disallow, distaste*
in- 'negative' as in *indiscreet, ineffectual, incredible, illegible*
non- 'not' as in *nonsense, non-resident, non-intervention*
ob- 'inverse, in the opposite direction' as in *object, obverse*
se-, sed- 'apart' as in *separate, select* 'chosen apart,' *sedition, seduce*
un- 'not' as in *unclean, uneven, unmindful, unbearable, uncouth*
un- 'opposite, reverse' as in *untie, unlock, uncoil*

Temporal prefixes: those which say something about time or duration

ante- 'preceding' as in *antechamber, ante-Norman*
fore- 'before' in time or space, as in *forecast, forefinger, foreskin*
neo- 'new, recent' as in *neonatal, Neolithic, neotype*
post- 'after, behind' as in *postpone, postnasal, postposition*

pre-, *pro-* 'before, in front of' as in *preconceive, preposition, progress, professor*

re-, *red-* 'anew, again, back' as in *regenerate, rehearse, reward, restore, redaction, redeem*

3.2   Suffixes

The last suffix of a word always determines what part of speech the word belongs to: i.e. whether it is a noun, verb, adjective, or adverb. Very often it seems that that is **all** the suffix is doing: just converting a noun into an adjective (*friend–friendly*) or an adjective into a verb (*final–finalize*). Some suffixes, then, have more specific meanings than others: in the list below, we have been as specific as possible, and some of the meanings are probably too highly specified. You should treat the meanings given as elastic and in need of fitting to any particular context.

Suffixes which form adjectives from nouns or verbs

-able 'fit for doing, fit for being done' as in *agreeable, comfortable, incalculable*

-al (-ial, -ical, -ual) 'having the property of' as in *conjectural, fraternal, dialectal, sensual, comical, analytical, ministerial*

-an, *-ian* 'belonging to, resembling' as in *reptilian, Augustan, plebeian, patrician*

-ary 'having a tendency or purpose' forms adjectives, and then secondarily nouns, as in *secondary, discretionary, rudimentary, tributary*

-ate 'full of' forms adjectives from nouns, pronounced [-ət], as in *passionate, affectionate, extortionate*

-ese 'belonging to a place' forms adjectives from locative nouns, as in *Japanese, New Yorkese, journalese*

-esque 'having the style of X' forms adjectives usually from nouns, as in *Romanesque, lawyeresque, statuesque*

-esc 'become' as in *tumescent, coalesce*

-ful 'full of X' forms adjectives from nouns, as in *peaceful, powerful, skillful*

-iac 'pertaining to the property X' as in *elegiac, hypochondriac, maniac*

-ic 'having the property X' forms adjectives, as in *alcoholic, atheistic, naturalistic, romantic, -ical* is an occasional variant, as in *comic/comical*

-ish 'to become like X' forms adjectives from nouns, as in *churlish, boyish, Irish, modish*

-ive 'characterized by' forms adjectives from most stems, especially verbs, as in *abusive, contradictive, retrospective*

-less 'without, free from' forms adjectives from nouns, as in *faultless, keyless, fearless*

-ly 'appropriate to, befitting' as in *friendly, timely, shapely, fatherly*

-oid 'having the shape of, resembling' as in *humanoid*

-*ory* 'connected with, serving for' forms adjectives as in *obligatory, inflammatory, illusory*; also forms nouns with the meaning 'place where,' as in *dormitory, lavatory, refectory*

-*ose* 'full of, abounding in' as in *verbose, morose, jocose*

-*ous* 'possessing, of the nature of X' forms adjectives, as in *virtuous, torturous, glorious, grievous*

-*some* 'like, characterized by, apt to' forms adjectives from almost any kind of stem, as in *cumbersome, awesome, bothersome*

-*y* 'full of, characterized by' forms adjectives from nouns, as in *mighty, moody, healthy*

Suffixes which form abstract nouns

-*asy*, -*acy* 'state or quality' as in *advocacy, intricacy, accuracy, ecstasy*

-*age* 'condition, state, rank, office of' as in *anchorage, postage, coinage*

-*ance*, -*ence* 'state, act, or fact of' forms abstract nouns from verbs, as in *repentance, perseverance, emergence*

-*ad(e)* 'general noun' as in *accolade, brigade, cannonade, ballad, salad, parade, lemonade, comrade, sonata, armada*

-*al* 'act of' forms abstract nouns from verbs, as in *renewal, revival, trial*

-*ation* 'state of being X-ed' forms abstract nouns from verbs of four types: those ending in -*(i)fy*, -*ize*, -*ate*, and a few without endings (like *damn, inform*), as in *purification, organization, contemplation, information*

-*ery*, -*ry* 'collectivity' forms abstract nouns from concrete nouns, as in *masonry, carpentry, slavery, savagery*

-*hood* 'state of, condition of' forms abstract nouns from concrete nouns, as in *childhood, womanhood, priesthood*

-*ia* 'condition of' as in *euphoria*

-*icity* 'abstract noun from -*ic*' as in *historic/historicity, electric/electricity*

-*ism* 'doctrinal system of principles' as in *communism, realism, romanticism*

-*ity* 'state, quality, condition of' forms abstract nouns from adjectives, as in *agility, diversity, actuality*

-*ment* 'condition of being X' forms abstract nouns from verbs and adjectives, as in *advancement, treatment, abandonment, aggrandizement, amusement, merriment*

-*ness* 'state, condition, quality of' forms abstract nouns usually from adjectives, but not verbs, as in *bitterness, fairness, idleness, deafness*

-*ship* 'state, condition' forms abstract nouns usually from concrete nouns, as in *dictatorship, trusteeship, workmanship*

Suffixes which form agentive nouns

-*ant*, -*ent* 'one who' forms agentive nouns from verbs, as in *agent, defendant, participant*

-arian 'member of a sect, holding to a doctrine' forms nouns or adjectives, as in *utilitarian, egalitarian, authoritarian, septuagenarian*

-ast 'one associated with X' as in *enthusiast, pederast*

-er 'agent' forms agentive nouns from verbs, as in *baker, thriller, worker, sweeper, retriever*

-eer 'agent', earlier *-ier* as in *grenadier, mountaineer, auctioneer, volunteer*

-ist 'one connected with, often agent' as in *socialist, perfectionist, dentist, pugilist, ventriloquist*

-ian 'one skilled in some art or science' as in *physician, musician, magician, mathematician*

Suffixes which form verbs from roots and stems

-ate 'cause X to happen' pronounced [-eyt], as in *create, contaminate, frustrate, terminate*

-en 'to become' forms verbs from adjectives, as in *darken, chasten, cheapen, deafen*

-(i)fy 'to cause to (be) X' forms a causative verb, as in *purify, satisfy, liquefy, sanctify, verify, amplify*

-ize 'to cause to be X' forms a causative verb from almost any stem, as in *popularize, legalize, miniaturize, weatherize*

Miscellaneous suffixes

-arium, -orium 'locative, a place for or connected with' as in *aquarium, vivarium, honorarium, auditorium, crematorium*

-ess 'feminine of X' as in *tigress, laundress, stewardess*

-let 'diminutive' as in *leaflet, driblet*

6   Replacement rules

This chapter and the next deal with rules that account for allomorphy, which can affect both the spelling and the pronunciation of a morpheme. The processes that can change the shape of a morpheme are covered by three types of rules:

replacement rules – replace one sound by a different sound in a certain position in the morpheme;
deletion rules – delete a sound, or sounds, from a morpheme;
expansion rules – expand a morpheme by inserting a new sound within the existing structure of the morpheme.

This classification exhausts the logical possibilities of what can happen to a phonetic segment. It can be replaced, deleted, or some sequence of sounds can be expanded.

1   Assimilation and types of assimilation

Assimilation rules are replacement rules which have the effect of making one vowel or consonant more similar to, or even identical with, another. In principle, assimilation can affect both vowels and consonants; most instances of assimilation discussed below, however, are cases of consonantal assimilation.

The process of assimilation can be described in terms of the **target**, the **direction**, and the **scope** of the resulting similarity. Assimilation can target some or even all of a sound's features: voicing, place, or manner of articulation. Depending on the direction of the influence between the sounds, we find **right-to-left** assimilation, when the influence is from the second to the first sound, i.e. A ← B, also known as *regressive assimilation*, and **left-to-right**, when the first sound influences the second, the A → B type, known as *progressive assimilation*. The majority of the consonantal assimilations presented here are instances of right-to-left assimilation. However, left-to-right assimilation is also a familiar process in English – some such instances will be mentioned when we come to the section on voicing assimilation. In terms of scope, assimilation can result in the replacement of a feature in one of the contiguous sounds by a feature of the sound with which it has come into contact (i.e. one gesture less). This kind of change is **partial** assimilation – the two consonants preserve their identity as distinct sounds, but become more similar to each other. The ultimate case of assimilation, **full or total** assimilation, involves the elimination of all differences between the contiguous sounds; full assimilation is in essence a replication of one of the sounds, also known as **gemination**. The types of assimilation that we will be referring to in what follows in this chapter are shown in Figure 6.1.

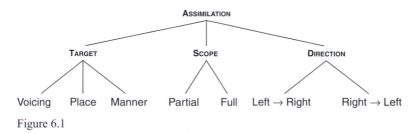

Figure 6.1

The principle which governs assimilation is the principle of ease defined in Chapter 5, Section 1.3. Stripped to their essence, assimilation rules simply say:

Prefer the easier articulation.

As a feature spreads from one sound to another, it replaces an existing feature in the assimilating sound. The two sounds end up sharing a gesture; the resulting articulation is easier because it eliminates one gesture from the overall articulatory process. The next two sections cover two types of partial assimilation; the target is either the place of articulation, or the voicing of adjacent segments.

2   Labial assimilation

The essence of labial assimilation is:

Prefer labials before labials.

```
-n + [p-, b-, m-, (f-)]

↓

-m
```

This formula is read, "When -*n* occurs at the end of a morpheme, followed by a morpheme beginning with [p-, b-, m-, f-], the -*n* changes to -*m*." The consonant [m] is labial, and therefore it is more similar to [p, b, m, f] than [n] is, since [n] is alveolar.

Labial assimilation affects the place, but not the manner, of articulation of the input consonant (the "input consonant" is the one in the top row: the "output consonant" is the one below the arrow in the second row). Although in principle labial assimilation may be a much broader process, we have limited it to the change of [n] to [m] because all morphemes affected by labial assimilation discussed in this section are prefixes which end in [-n]. Moreover, in many words showing adjacent labials, assimilation took place in the donor language, and not in English, and English borrowed the words wholesale. This is unsurprising in view of the naturalness of this phonetic change. All instances of labial assimilation in English are instances of right-to-left assimilation, i.e. a non-labial consonant becomes labial in anticipation of the "labiality" of the initial consonant of the second morpheme. Here is how it works:

in+ped 'foot'+e	impede
in+bib 'drink'+e	imbibe (but: inbred, inborn)[1]
en+bell 'beautiful'+ish	embellish (*en-* is intensifying)
en+ploy 'fold'	employ
en+pha 'speak'+t+ic	emphatic
pan+pleg 'stroke'+ia	pamplegia
pan+phag 'eat'+ous	pamphagous
syn+path 'feel'+y	sympathy
syn+bol 'throw'	symbol
syn+phon 'sound'+y	symphony

Labial assimilation affects the prefixes *in-*, *en-* from Latin and French and *pan-*, and *syn-* from Greek. The triggers of the change, the consonants [p-, b-] in the second morpheme, share the articulatory feature labiality.

Not all labial consonants have an equally strong effect on the preceding [-n]. The bilabial stops [p, b, m] are stronger in this respect, while the influence of [f] seems to be much weaker, hence our parenthesis in the definition of the rule above. In fact, Greek did not have a sound [f] which could have triggered assimilation. What English interprets as [f], spelled <ph> in formations with Greek roots: *symphony, pamphysic, pamphlet*[2] was a later development of a Greek aspirated stop [p^h]. The *n-* is preserved in the more recent formation *synfuel*, preserving the transparency of the blend of the first syllable of *synthetic+fuel*, a formation which entered the language in the early 1970s. The sound [f] does not cause assimilation of the prefix *in-* to *im-* either, compare *infant, infect, infinite, influence*.

The Latin prefix *con-/com-/co-* presents some difficulties. Its original form has the labial; it was *com-*, so words like *combat* and *compatriot* which surface with adjacent labials represent retentions of the older form, not assimilation of [n-] to [m-]. As for *com-* + [f-], the place of articulation of both [m] and [n] before [-f] was generalized to [n], in defiance of ease of articulation. Note, however, that the difficulty of pronouncing [n] before a labial fricative [f] is not nearly as great as the difficulty of pronouncing [n] before a labial stop [b] or [p], so the violation of articulatory ease is not as radical. Thus in all cases of nasal before [f], Latin had an [n], which was passed down to Old French, and thence into Middle English. To complicate the story

---

[1] The morpheme *in-* in **in**bred, **in**built, **in**most, is different from the negative *in-*. The adverbial *in-* has the status of a root morpheme, so that *inbred, input*, etc. are treated as compounds and the unassimilated prefix preserves its autonomy and transparency.

[2] The word *pamphlet* has an interesting history. The *OED* tells us that it comes, ultimately, from post-Classical Latin *Pamphilus*, a personal name based on ancient Greek, meaning 'beloved of all' (*<pan* 'all' + *phil-*us 'love' + Middle French *–et* 'noun, diminutive'), hence *Pamphilet*, the name of an amatory poem *Pamphilus*, very popular during the Middle Ages, and hence later, in an extended sense, any short piece of literary or political writing.

further, in the fifteenth and sixteenth centuries, there was a slight tendency to assimilate [n-] to [m-] before [-f], but it won out in only a few words. If you search for *comf-* in the *OED*, you find *comfit*, *comfort*, and *comfrey* and their derivatives. This is in contrast to the much longer list of words beginning with *conf-*. Barring these exceptions, therefore, we can generalize: *co*[n-]+[-f] is the expected sequence. We are not *con*fronted with *con*fusing and *con*founding patterns.

The effect of regular assimilation can be reversed by the need for greater transparency: the *OED* records a now obsolete form *pambrittanick*, but the same adjective today is *pan-Britannic*, the form *panpharmacon* is an undoing of the already assimilated Greek *pampharmacon*, again for the reason of transparency.

Our rule includes also the consonant [m] as a possible trigger of labial assimilation. The change of [-n] to [-m] before another [-m] is quite pervasive: earlier forms such as *inmaculate*, *inmaterial*, *inmovable*, *inmortal*, all on record in the *OED*, have changed to *immaculate*, *immaterial*, *immovable*, *immortal*. Such assimilation is both an instance of labial assimilation, and of total assimilation, discussed separately in Section 4 below. In pronunciation, one of the identical consonants may be lost if the word is perceived as unparsable, as in *immaculate*, where the rare adjective *maculate* may not be familiar to the speaker; obscuration of the morpheme boundary may result in a pronunciation with a single [m] and only the spelling preserves the trace of the total assimilation.

2.1   Blocking of labial assimilation

An apparent exception to the rule of labial assimilation is provided by the unchanged form of the native prefix *un-* meaning 'not' or 'reversal.' The alveolar nasal in this prefix does not change into a labial nasal in the environment of other labials, so: *unbridled*, *unbalanced*, *unmistakable*, *unmanageable*, *unprepared*, *unprofitable*, *unfair*, *unfathomable*. Although this prefix has been in the language since Old English times, and it has been steadily productive, the phonetic rules of relaxed spoken English have not produced forms with orthographic labial assimilation in such words. It must be acknowledged, of course, that connected speech combinations of [un-]+[p-, b-, m-, f-], as well as other apparently "unassimilated" sequences such as *inbred*, *inbuilt*, often show assimilation in casual or fast speech and sound like *umbridled*, *ummanageable*, *umplanned*, *imbred*, *imbuilt*. Labial assimilation occurs in rapid speech occasionally also when the final [-n] of one word is in contact with initial [p-, b-, m-] of the next word: *pen pal*, *ten boys*, *bran muffin* may change the [-n] of the first word to [-m], thus [pem-, tem-, bram-].

One reason for this stability of *un-* forms may be in the highly recognizable semantic individuality of this morpheme, which often correlates with stress, as in *unforeseen*, *unforgiving*, *unmistaken*, *unprepared*. Thus we can attribute the behavior of *un-* with respect to labial assimilation to the fact that among the prefixes likely to undergo this change, *un-* normally bears half stress, and is usually attached to free roots, unlike the prefixes listed above. It once carried main stress. It is the oldest negative prefix in the language: it was a very productive negative prefix in

4   Total assimilation

The transfer and replacement of features in adjacent sounds can alter completely the phonetic nature of the original consonant in a morpheme. When assimilation renders an input sound identical to the sound which follows it, we talk of total assimilation. The change of [-n] to [-m] before [m-] is due to labial assimilation, but it also represents a case of total assimilation:

in+mort 'die'+al	→ immortal
en+mesh	→ emmesh[4]
syn+meter+y	→ symmetry
syn+morph+ism	→ symmorphism

In these examples the labial gesture happens to be the only difference between the adjacent nasals [n] and [m]. In many other instances, however, total assimilation involves more gestures; it amounts to copying the second consonant over the first one. The word *assimilation* is itself an example of the process:

ad - simil - ate - ion → assimilation

4.1   Total assimilation of prefixes

Total assimilation occurs most frequently in borrowed words in which prefixes ending in consonants are attached to roots beginning with a non-identical consonant. To highlight the transparency of the root, its initial consonant was probably pronounced with sufficient force to trigger regressive, or right-to-left assimilation. Among the frequently used morphemes subject to total assimilation are the prefixes *ad-*, *sub-*, *ob-*, *in-*, *com-/con-*, *syn-*:

ad - 'to, towards, against':

ad - cur-ate 'care'	→ accurate	ad - note - ate	→ annotate
ad - brev-'short' (i)-ate	→ abbreviate	ad - lev 'light' (i)-ate	→ alleviate
ad - firm	→ affirm	ad - rive 'shore'	→ arrive
ad - grav 'heavy'- ate	→ aggravate	ad - sent 'agree'	→ assent
ad - pet 'seek' - ite	→ appetite	ad - tribute	→ attribute

A special case of total assimilation of the prefix *ad-* occurs before roots beginning with [st-, sp-, sk-]:

ad - spir - ation 'breathe'	→aØspiration
ad - string - ent	→aØstringent
ad - scribe	→aØscribe

The total assimilation of the [d] to the initial consonant of the following morpheme in these words results in both phonetic and orthographic deletion. Only a

---

[4] The unassimilated form *enmesh* is also standard in all varieties of English.

consultation with the dictionary and some semantic reasoning can help us recognize the compositionality of items such as *aspiration, astringent, ascribe.*

The [-d] in the prefix *ad-* is extremely susceptible to total assimilation when the base it attaches to is consonant-initial. The **only** consonants to which it does not assimilate are the voiced [m, v]; in front of these consonants the prefix keeps its shape.[5]

> ad - venture 'come, bring'   → **adv**enture
> ad - voc 'speak, call' - ate   → **adv**ocate
> ad - mir 'wonder' - e   → **adm**ire
> ad - mit 'send, go'   → **adm**it

The prefix *ad-* remains unchanged also if the morpheme following it begins with a vowel or <h->.[6] This pattern repeats itself: as noted in Chapter 5, vowels or initial <h-> frequently behave in the same way with regard to the operation of various phonetic rules.

> ad - ore 'speak'   →**ado**re
> ad - umbra 'shadow'+ate   →**adu**mbrate
> ad - here 'stick'   →**adh**ere

The final consonant of the prefix *sub-* 'down, under' undergoes total assimilation in more restricted environments: [-b] in *sub* is assimilated to [k, g, f, p, r, m]:

> sub - cumb 'lie'   →su**cc**umb   sub - mon 'warn'   →su**mm**on
> sub - fer 'bear, bring'   →su**ff**er   sub - port   →su**pp**ort
> sub - gest 'carry'   →su**gg**est   sub - rog 'ask'   →su**rr**ogate

Like *ad-*, the prefix *sub-* can lose its final consonant altogether before roots beginning with [sp-, st-, sk-]:

> sub - spect   →suØ**spect**
> sub - stenance   →suØ**st**enance

More often, however, we will find the <b> in this suffix intact in that environment: *subscript, substance, substratum, subspecies, subspecific.* These words preserve the components transparent mostly in writing; in relaxed pronunciation the [b] can be unvoiced to [p].

The prefix *ob-* 'to, towards' undergoes total assimilation only when followed by three voiceless consonants: [k, f, p], and sometimes when followed by [m] (when it undergoes orthographic loss as well):

---

[5] The [-d] of the prefix is assimilated also before labials in Old French, hence words borrowed directly from French do not preserve it, e.g. *avenge* (< Lat. *ad vindicare*), *avow* (< Lat. *advocare*), *avenue* (< Lat. *advenire*).

[6] Historically, examples of the type *advocate, advent* also belong here since <v> was an approximant in Latin.

ob - **c**ad-s-ion 'fall'   →o**cc**asion
ob - **f**er 'bring'   →o**ff**er
ob - **p**os 'place, put'   →o**pp**ose
ob - **m**it 'send, go'   →o**Ø**mit

We have already noticed that the prefixes *in-* (both with the meaning 'in' and with the meaning 'not'), *en-*, and *syn-* undergo total labial assimilation when followed by the labial nasal [m-]. The consonant [n-] in *in-*, *con-*, *syn-* is also fully assimilated to the liquids [l, r]:

in - **l**eg-al 'law'   → i**ll**egal
in - **r**eg-ular 'rule'   → i**rr**egular
con - **l**egt 'choose'   → co**ll**ect
con - **r**upt 'broken'   → co**rr**upt
syn - **l**og 'speak' -ism   → sy**ll**ogism

4.2   Double consonant spellings

Total assimilation is a very old change whose traces can often be recovered from a word's orthography. In such instances the spelling preserves the slot for the assimilated sound, so that there is a **double consonant letter** at the point of contact between the two morphemes: the word *assimilation* parsed above is an example of total assimilation with the input consonant position reflected in the orthography.

There is an important difference between doubling consonants in the spelling and pronouncing double consonants. English is a language which does not make use of long consonants in pronunciation within the boundaries of a single morpheme. Words like *furry* and *fury*, *masses* and *races*, *sappy* and *soapy*, *annotate* and *anonym*, *summon* and *lemon* have identical middle consonant sounds. We do get doubling of the consonants at the morpheme juncture in compounds and transparent derivatives: e.g. *pen-knife*, *lead-dancer*, *unnamed*, *midday*, *misspell*. Doubling is also quite audible within phrases, as in *big garden*, *some money*, *ten nights*, *lead down*, *stop pouting*. Although the sequence of identical consonants is pronounced with only one release and one onset, the actual duration of these "long" consonants may be as long as that of a cluster of two separate consonants. The extra length is useful because it identifies the boundary between the morphemes, which is immediately clear to any speaker of the language. This is not automatically true for words of classical origin whose components are not part of every speaker's basic knowledge of English. In spite of the spelling <-*ss*-> in *assimilation*, the pronunciation is as though it were spelled with a single <s> as in *aside*. The added knowledge from this chapter is that double consonant spellings such as <-*ff*-, -*ll*-, -*pp*-, -*rr*, -*ss*-> at the left edge of the root *can* be a very useful signal of the etymological composition of the word. We will return to the discussion of geminate consonants as boundary markers in the next chapter. For now, we summarize total assimilation as a two-step process:

(1)   the input consonant becomes identical with the contact consonant – the stage reflected by the spelling of the word, and

(2)   the "double" consonant is shortened phonetically to a single consonant. Step (2) involves the loss/deletion of the totally assimilated sound from the phonetic structure of the word.

5   Replacement by weakening or strengthening

Another set of morphological changes affects the sounds of morphemes without the clear and overt signals of labial and total assimilation. Some of these changes occur on consonants, some only on vowels. What the processes discussed in this section have in common is that they involve (a), a change in the level of sonority of the affected segment, and (b), a change in the amount of effort needed to produce the segment. When consonants rise in sonority, the process is called **lenition**, or weakening. The term is coined on the basis of the Latin adjective *lenis* 'soft, mild' (we also find the root in *lenient, leniency*). It refers to change in the stricture/opening and the glottal state/sonority of sounds: consonants are *lenited* when they involve less stricture and when they are voiced. The more *lenited* a consonant is, the more vowel-like it is. In terms of stricture, the strongest consonants are stops, and the weakest are the sonorants, and especially the oral sonorants [r, l, w, y]. For the vowels, the most open vowels are also most sonorous, while the high vowels are least sonorous – in that sense, they are more "consonantal." Bearing in mind that the numerical values for the sonority of English sounds shown in Figure 6.2 below are only an approximation, we can see how the scale of sonority is shaped:[7]

Voiceless stops	p, t, k	0
Voiceless fricatives	f, θ, h	5
	s, š	15
Glides and sonorants	w, y	70
	m, n, r	75
[l] and high vowels	l, i	80
	ɪ	85
Mid and low vowels	æ, ɔ, ou	95

Figure 6.2

[7] The hierarchy for English is based on the phonetic specification data in Peter Ladefoged, *A Course in Phonetics*, 2nd edn (San Diego: Harcourt Brace Jovanovich, 1982) Table 11.7, i.e. percentage values of the feature [sonorant], defined numerically in relation to the amount of acoustic energy measured during the production of the sound. The consonants are the allophones that occur before the vowel [ɑy] in a stressed syllable. The vowels are the allophones at the beginning of a stressed syllable.

The phonetic information for the segments can be represented as a sonority index in Figure 6.3:[8]

Sonority index:

Low sonority ⟶ High sonority

p, t, k	b, d, g	f, θ	v, ð, z	s	m, n	l	r	y, i, w, u	e, o	a
0.5	1	2	3	4	5	6	7	8	9	10

Figure 6.3

Looking at Figures 6.2 and 6.3, we see immediately that stops have more pronounced consonantal properties; they are "stronger" than consonants in which the airstream is modified in some way without actually being stopped. Single consonants produced without complete blockage of the air can also be interpreted as requiring less effort, though the correlation between lenition and decreased effort is less reliable than lenition and sonority.

The following two sections discuss lenition of the stops [t] and [d] before vowels; in both instances the stops are replaced by sounds whose consonantal properties are weaker.

5.1   T-Lenition

> t + {-y, -e, -is, -ia} (vocalic suffixes)
> ↓
> s

T-Lenition affects both roots and suffixes ending in [-t]. In the loan vocabulary it surfaces when a morpheme-final [-t] is followed by the suffixes -*y*, -*e*, -*is*, 'abstract noun,' and -*ia* 'condition.' Although all four suffixes causing T-Lenition begin with a high front or mid front vowel, that is not a sufficient condition for the operation of the rule, since other suffixes beginning with the same front vowels do not trigger the same change, e.g. *democratic, democratization, hypnotist, impor-ter, active*. Nevertheless, it is correct to think of the "frontness" and "closeness" of the following vowel as a facilitating factor since when [-t] is followed by a suffix beginning with an open vowel the rule never applies: cf. *important, auditorium,* etc. We will see below that the correlation of the lenition with the feature "front-ness" continues to be important after the initial change of [t] to [s], producing additional changes due to the principle of ease.

5.1.1   T-Lenition and spelling

T-Lenition may or may not be recognizable in the spelling. The [s] sound which is the immediate result from this change is spelled both <s> and <c>;

---

[8] Adapted from Elizabeth Selkirk's article "On the major class features and syllable theory," in M. Aronoff and R. Oehrle (eds.), *Language Sound Structure* (Cambridge, MA: MIT Press, 1994), pp. 107–36 at p. 112.

it can also remain unchanged, thus:

<-t-> + {-y, -e, -is, -ia}
- <s> stat 'stay' + is ⟶ stasis
- <c> grat 'kind' + e ⟶ grace
- <t> dict 'speak' + ion ⟶ diction

Unfortunately, there are no rules which can predict which of these letters will appear in the spelling of a particular form – it is a matter of orthographic conventions which started four centuries ago. Further examples of T-Lenition manifested in different spellings are:

Spelling change

<t> → <s>:	eu 'good'+thanat+ia	→euthanasia
	gen+et+is	→genesis
<t> → <c>:	in+port+ant+e	→importance
	demo+crat+y	→ democracy
<t> stays <t>	milit+ia	→militia
	in+tuit 'watch'+ion	→intuition

Note that in the subset of forms in which the letter <t> is preserved in the spelling, as in *militia* and *intuition* in the last row above, the consonantal change is not orthographically reflected. That subset behaves like the allomorphic variation discussed in Chapter 5 associated with vowel reduction and vowel shifting, where absence of stress or the change of a short vowel to a long one affects only the pronunciation.

5.1.2   T-Lenition, palatalization, and affrication

Historically, the [s] resulting from T-Lenition can undergo a second change called **palatalization**. This is an assimilation process which changes the alveolar consonant [s] to [š] or its voiced counterpart [ž] when the next morpheme begins with the historical palatal glide [y]. The appearance of the voiced palatal fricative [ž], probably through an intermediate [z] stage, is restricted to post-stress environments (immediately following a stressed syllable). Thus *station, minutia, euthanasia* show palatalization to [š] and [ž], but if the [s] is between two unstressed vowels, as in *genesis, ecstasy, democracy*, there is no palatalization. The place shift to a palatal shows up only in the pronunciation; the spelling remains <s>, <c>, or <t> as in other instances of T-Lenition.

In front of <-ure> [t] palatalization often goes a step further and produces the **affricate** [č]:

t- + -u(r)e [-yu(r)]
↓
č

This change, which is not inherited from the classical languages, but occurred after the borrowing of these words into English, has an easy parallel in our speech. We produce affricates in casual pronunciation of word sequences like *You betcha*, *I wancha to do it*. Affrication is another instance of palatal assimilation. Though the trigger, the palatal [y], does not appear in the spelling, it is nevertheless the correct basis for understanding why the <-t> is pronounced [č] in *bet you*, *want you* and in such Romance words as *culture, literature, mature, nature, statue, virtue*. (The vowel spelled <ue> or <eu> in Early Modern English words borrowed from French, as in *virtue, amateur*, was also understood as [yu] and had the same effect.) Affrication, too, is related to the presence of stress – historically the syllable in which the affrication occurred carried the main accent of the word (they were pronounced *literaTYUR, naTYUR*, etc.).

5.1.3   Summary of palatalization and affrication after T-Lenition

Four distinct changes can take place at the intersection of a morpheme ending in [-t] and a morpheme beginning with [i] or [y]. We can get simple lenition from [t] to [s], as in *secrecy, apostasy, genesis, importance*. In addition, within English, i.e. after the borrowing took place, we can get palatalization to [š] in addition to lenition, as in *patient, derivation, segregation, secretion, vacation, action*; or palatalization to [ž] as in *euthanasia, anesthesia*. Finally, we can get affrication to [č] as in *nature, literature*.

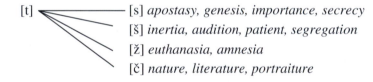

[t]   [s] *apostasy, genesis, importance, secrecy*
         [š] *inertia, audition, patient, segregation*
         [ž] *euthanasia, amnesia*
         [č] *nature, literature, portraiture*

5.2   D-Lenition

A pattern with a very different history, but with results quite similar to T-Lenition, turns the voiced alveolar stop [d] to [s] before the suffixes *-ive, -ion*.

```
d + {-ive, -ion}
↓
s
```

Like T-Lenition, D-Lenition can go through several stages. The simplest result is the one in the schema above: [d] changing to [s] as in:

     pen**d** 'consider' + ive   → pensive
     in + clu**d** 'close' + ive   → inclusive

In words ending in *-ion* and other [y-] suffixes borrowed from French, the lenited output [s] can undergo further palatalization to [š], palatalization and voicing to [ž], or affrication to [-ǰ-]:

pend 'pay'+ion   → pension [-š-]
ad+lud 'play, touch lightly'+ion → allusion [-ž-]
pend 'hang'+ulum   → pendulum [-ǰ-]

When affrication to [ǰ] takes place (as in *module*, *verdure*), the rule of D-Lenition is not involved, properly speaking. Affrication does not occur before *-ive*, *-ion*; it requires a following [yu-], which causes affrication of both [t] and [d] (*nature*, *verdure*). Moreover, like *pendulum* and *module*, the [-d] of *any* morpheme can become an affricate when followed by [-y] in the same word-like sequence. Here belong examples such as *mind you* with [-ǰ-] and even *bad year* coming out with the middle consonant of *badger*. Here is a summary of the various phonetic realizations of [d] in the relevant environments:

[d] ————— [s] *decisive, pensive, corrosive*[9]
         [š] *pretension, pension, session*
         [ž] *delusion, exclusion, corrosion, decision*
         [ǰ] *grandeur, verdure, assiduous*

5.2.1   Summary: palatalization and affrication of dental stops

Simple lenition of the dental stops [t] and [d] before suffixes beginning with a front vowel produces [s]. Further, in the environment of [-i, -y], [s] can develop into the palatal fricatives [-š-] or [-ž-]. In the narrower environment of the glide [-y-], affrication rather than palatalization is the more common result, with [t] developing into the corresponding voiceless affricate [č], and [d] developing into the voiced affricate [ǰ].

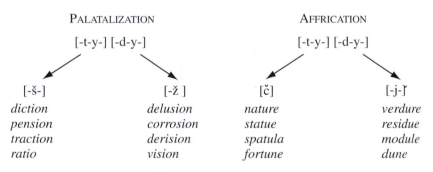

PALATALIZATION		AFFRICATION	
[-t-y-] [-d-y-]		[-t-y-] [-d-y-]	
[-š-]	[-ž]	[č]	[-ǰ-]
diction	delusion	nature	verdure
pension	corrosion	statue	residue
traction	derision	spatula	module
ratio	vision	fortune	dune

Some of the changes shown above are "young," historically speaking; they are not fully established in all words which contain the relevant phonetic sequences. There exist, therefore, alternative pronunciations, no doubt influenced by the spelling, as *amnesia* with [-z-], and not [-ž-], *habitual, fortune, literature* with [-ty-] and not [-č-], *grandeur, module* with [-dy-] and not [-ǰ-]. Although such pronunciations may appear to be more accurate representations

---

[9] From *rod* 'gnaw,' as in *rodent*.

of the spelling of the words, they violate the phonetic naturalness of the palatalized and affricated pronunciations, and can therefore sound pedantic and even affected.

5.3   [v]-Vocalization

The last consonantal replacement change is the most drastic example of consonantal weakening: it converts the voiced labio-dental fricative [v] into a vowel when another consonant, usually [t], follows it.

$$
\boxed{\begin{array}{l} v + C \\ \downarrow \\ u \end{array}}
$$

(Note that here the letter <v> is used in its normal alphabetical meaning, unlike capital V, which stands for 'any vowel sound.') Increase of sonority ultimately triggered by ease of pronunciation is the principle involved in [v]-Vocalization. Combining [v] with other consonants produces clusters which are difficult to pronounce: [-vt-, -vf-, -vs-]. The remedy is to convert the voiced labio-dental fricative [v] into a vowel when another consonant, usually [t], follows it. The rule of [v]-Vocalization is restricted to five morphemes which are all of classical origin: *av* 'bird,' *nav* 'sail, boat,' *salv* 'safe, healthy,' *solv* 'loosen, unbind,' and *volv* 'turn, roll.'

astro - na**v** - **t**	→astrona**ut**, but na**v**y, na**v**igate
a**v** - **s**pic- ious	→a**us**picious, but a**v**iator, a**v**iary
con - vol**v** - **t**ion	→convol**ut**ion, but re**v**ol**v**e, in**v**ol**v**e
sal**v** - **t**e	→sal**ut**e, but sal**v**ation, sal**v**age
sol**v** - **t**ion	→sol**ut**ion, but resol**v**e, sol**v**ent

The morpheme *eu* 'well, good' also shows two allomorphs. In *eugenics, euphony,* which were coined in Greek, the vowel is preserved, but in words in which the preservation would have resulted in two vowels in hiatus, the original <u> is realized as [v], as in *evangelical.*

There are some interesting possibilities for multiple replacements within this small group of roots. If the [-v] of the root is followed by a [-t], then the derived word may show more than one change, e.g. *salute,* with the [t] preserved, but *solution, convolution, revolution,* showing T-Lenition and palatalization. One set of words, namely *nausea, nauseous, nauseate,* show both [v]-Vocalization and a variety of options for T-Lenition: [s], [š], [z], and [ž].

6   Vowel replacement

Our final set of replacement rules covers changes of the vowels <a> and <e>, representing the short vowels [a] and [e] in Latin, when the morphemes containing them appear in the second syllable or later, never in the first syllable.

This kind of replacement is restricted to Latin loanwords – it does not affect the native vocabulary.

The vocalic changes discussed in the next three sub-sections are instances of vowel raising. Since higher vowels are less sonorous, the process can be described as a *weakening of the sonority* of the segments. Using the terminology usually applied to consonants, the vowels undergo *fortition*, because they are pronounced with increased constriction. In that sense, while the terms *weakening* and *lenition* used independently have overlapping meanings, *consonant lenition* means becoming less consonantal, while *vowel weakening* means becoming less vowel-like. The phenomenon of vowel weakening should be distinguished from **vowel reduction**, which turns vowels in unstressed positions to the neutral vowel schwa [ə]. Again, vowel weakening here is the progressive raising, or closing, of the affected vowel. Everything else being equal, low vowels have greater sonority than high vowels.

6.1   <a>-Weakening

The first type of weakening affects the vowel spelled <a> if it appears anywhere but in the first syllable:

$$\$\,a$$
$$\downarrow$$
$$e$$

The schema represents the change and the condition for it by the convention that "$" means 'any syllable.' By that convention, the <a> in the formula has at least one syllable to its left. If <a> were in the first syllable, it would not change. Examples:

art	→**art**istic	→in**ert** 'without skill'
cand 'shining white'	→**cand**id, **cand**idate[10]	→incend**iary**
cap 'seize'	→**cap**tive	→dec**ep**tive
fac 'make, put'	→**fac**t	→inf**ec**t 'put in'

This rule is very useful in explaining the morphological link between cognates. It is not an exceptionless rule, but, fortunately, the exceptions are words in which the original form of the root has been preserved intact; therefore the morphological relatedness between a root and its derivatives is transparent. Thus, the roots √*fac* in *manufacture*, or √*cap* in *recapture*, are easy to recognize although the words are technically exceptions to <a>-Weakening.

6.2   <e>-Weakening

A second rule of vowel lenition changes <e> to <i>, hence the name <e>-Weakening. In this instance, too, the decreased sonority, and therefore the

---

[10] In ancient Rome candidates for official posts wore white togas.

7 Deletion rules and other kinds of allomorphy

This chapter turns to deletion rules, as well as other kinds of allomorphy, some of which can be recovered only historically. The first set of changes to be considered produces allomorphic variation due to the dropping of one or more sounds from the edges of the original forms of roots or affixes. Like replacement rules, deletion rules must be defined in terms of both the phonological environment and the type, position, and number of morphemes involved in the change.

1 Consonant deletion

More on double consonants. The general principle which governs the simplification of double consonants to single ones, phonetically, is that English, unlike Italian, Finnish, and many other languages, does not allow "long" or "double" consonants within a word. Our discussion of double consonant spelling in Chapter 6, Section 4.2, pointed out the important distinction between double consonants in the spelling, which can arise as a consequence of total assimilation, and "long" consonants in the pronunciation. Morpheme-internal double consonant letters are not pronounced "long": *balloon* and *saloon* have only one [l], *lemma* and *lemon* have only one [m], and *peddle* and *pedal* have the same short consonant in the middle.

English allows real "long" consonants, but only at clear word and morpheme boundaries: *file log, big garden, roommate, bus-schedule, bookcase, sad day, unnoticed, dissatisfied*, etc. The phonetic nature of the abutting long consonants is not identical: the one to the left is "unreleased," because it is syllable-final, but the one to the right is fully released into the following segment in the syllable to the right. You can figure out what this means by repeating the phrase *big garden* while carefully monitoring the way you articulate the [g] sounds at the juncture of the two words.

The longer duration of double consonants is a phonetic phenomenon only; it is unrelated to spelling. Nevertheless, there is a parallel between real long consonants and the double letters resulting from the total assimilations covered in Chapter 6: both are signals of morpheme boundaries. The spelling of *accurate, affirm, arrive* indicates the historical point of contact between morphemes which have now merged. A double consonant at the left edge of a morpheme is also a boundary signal: thus, for example, the "long" consonant [s-s] marks the difference between *pass south*, and *pass out*, with a single [s]. Thus, when we hear long consonants, we know that they belong to two different morphemes: we are not likely to confuse *stop itching* from *stop pitching*.

Affixes which act like roots. In English the most common position for identical consonants to be realized is at the juncture of two independent words or roots: *car race*, *hip pain*, *roommate*. Some affixes, however, namely the affixes *-ful*, *-less*, *-ness*, *counter-*, *dis-*, *inter-*, *mis-*, *-un-* , and even *-ly* in careful speech, can show a strong degree of morpheme identity which is communicated through the phonetic length in *shelfful*, *soulless*, *sternness*, *counterrevolution*, *dissatisfy*, *interracial*, *misstate*, *unnamed*, *wholly* vs. *holy*. With respect to doubling of the consonants, these affixes are often treated as if they were independent roots. Consonant doubling with affixes is not obligatory, however: *dissident*, *dissent*, *interrogative*, *interrupt*, etc., are pronounced with single consonants. This is an indication that for the speakers of Present-Day English the etymological boundaries in these words have become obscure – the prefixes and the roots are treated together as base forms, not parsed further into their components. In other words, while *dissatisfy*, *interracial*, are immediately recognizable as compositional, the prefix-base juncture in *dissident*, *interrogative* is not activated, and we store them as single units.

We should also note that the boundaries in common compounds such as *home(-)made*, *bus stop*, *Van Nuys*, *grand(-)daughter* may be sufficiently fuzzy to justify pronunciation with a single [m], [s], [n], [d], respectively. The "unparsable word" treatment will also account for the lack of geminate consonants in *got to*, *ought to* in casual speech. Indeed, the realization of the long consonant often depends on the register and rate of speech: in slow and careful speech we are likely to prolong the [s] in *bus stop* and the [n] in *Van Nuys*, while the cluster will be simplified in fast and casual speech.

1.1   S-Drop

Naturalness. The simplification of consonant clusters across morpheme boundaries is a frequent and natural phenomenon: the unreleased first member of the potential geminate may be dropped altogether and the speaker may reinterpret the affixed word as a single unit. Our first instance of historical loss of length involves the voiceless fricative [s].

The process of S-Drop deletes the first [s] at the juncture between the prefix *ex-* 'out of, from, off' and a morpheme beginning with [s-]:

Orthographically: <ex-+ s> → <ex->
Phonetically: [eks+ **s**-] → [ekØ – **s**-]

Here are some examples illustrating **S-Drop**:

ex   +   spir 'breathe'   →   *expire*
         (cf. in+spir→*inspire*)
ex   +   sequ 'follow'   →   *exequies* 'funeral rites'
         (cf. con+sequ, as in *consequence*, *consecutive*)

> ex   +   sta 'stand'+nt   →   *extant*
> (cf. ob+sta, as in *obstacle*)
> ex   +   cep 'take, contain'+t →   *except*
> (cf. in+cep, as in *inception*)

Note that the last example does not have an orthographic <-s> in the second morpheme, *cep*, yet the principle of dropping the redundant consonant remains the same. This is also true of words such as *excess* < **ex**+ced 'go,' *excel* < **ex**+cel 'rise.' In some historical instances of S-Drop, the resulting single [s-] may get voiced to [z] as in:

> ex + sample   →   *example*[1]
> ex + sequ 'follow out' + ive →   *executive*
> ex + sud 'sweat'+e   →   *exude*

It is not just the [s] that gets voiced in these words: the whole sequence [-ks-] is voiced to [-gz-]. Often, the motivation for the voicing is the absence of stress in the first syllable, which weakens, or "lenites" the strongly consonantal voiceless [k] in [ek-] to [-g-], which then spreads its voicing forward to the following [s]. Phonetically, the causes of lenition can be very complex; among the triggers of the [k] to [g] voicing are drop in air pressure, the shorter duration and incomplete stop closure of the [k] in the coda of the unstressed syllable. The pattern is familiar from the pronunciation of pairs such as *Alex*, with [-ks], but *Alexander*, with the cluster split into two syllables and voiced: [-g-z]. Voicing of [-k-s-] to [-g-z-] is restricted to cases in which the cluster resulting from S-Drop is to the left of a vowel or a silent <-h->, as in *exaggerate*, *exaltation*, *exhaust*, *exhibit*, *exhume*, *exhort*. It should be noted that while roots beginning with <c-> + front vowel participate in S-Drop, the voicing in the resulting [ks] cluster in such words does not occur, e.g. *exceed*, *excel*, *except*, *excise*.

1.1.1   Spelling exceptions

S-Drop was an active process in Classical Latin. Later Latinate words, words which came into English through Neo-Latin, however, may appear to violate the rule. Words in which S-Drop occurs in the pronunciation, but does not affect the original spelling of the second morpheme, can be regarded as orthographic exceptions. Here, with dates in parentheses from the *OED*, are words which preserve both <-x-> and <-s>:

†*exsatiate* (1599)   *exsert* (1665) (also *exert*)
exsanguine (1661)   *exsiccate* (1545)

---

[1] Although *example* looks like the other words that undergo S-Drop, its history is different. The word *sample* is a case of historical mis-analysis. The etymology of this word goes back to ex-+em(p) 'to take,' thus an *example* is 'something taken out, a sample.' The [s] in *sample* appears in Middle English after the first vowel in *essample*, the French version of Latin *exemplum*, was dropped. We are grateful to Jared Klein for pointing out this etymological curiosity to us.

exsaturate (1623–6)	*exstipulate* (1793)
exscind (1662)	*exsudation* (1646) (also *exudation*)
exscribe (1607)	*exsurge* (1578)

These are all rare, obsolete, or specialized words, and keeping the original spelling of the second morpheme in them is clearly an attempt to safeguard the transparency of the two parts of the learned formation. Normally, they would be pronounced with a single [s], though some of them, e.g. *exsanguinate, exsolve, exstipulate, exsurge* allow the same "long" [s] at the morpheme boundary that exists in *mass suicide, crass sound, less salt.* Again, doubling of the consonant in the pronunciation calls attention to the morphemic composition of such words; the independent status of *ex-* remains transparent to the speakers who choose to use that pronunciation.

1.1.2   Exceptions to S-Drop

S-Drop does not apply when the morpheme *ex-* means 'a person out of a formerly held position or office' – a medieval Latin specialization of the spatial meaning of *ex-.* Originally, the prefix *ex-* in the meaning of 'former' was attached only to borrowed roots, but towards the end of the eighteenth century, it became a productive element within English: *ex-wife, ex-mate, ex-lord.* Orthographically the *ex-* in this meaning is distinguished by a hyphen between the *ex-* and the second root, and it leaves intact the phonetic shape of the second root, irrespective of the phonetic environment: *ex-convict, ex-president, ex-husband, ex-actress, ex-senator, ex-service, ex-spouse.* In these words, *ex* has a status closer to that of a free root than to a prefix, it is an ex-prefix. Since the nineteenth century, *ex* has been used colloquially as an independent noun, usually with reference to an ex-spouse, though it may be used for any person or persons who formerly held some contextually defined position or rank; the *OED* dates the first attestation of the noun *ex* to 1827.

The morpheme *ex-* triggers S-Drop only when it is used as a prefix and attached directly to a root to produce a derivative in which the prefix–root boundary is obscured. *Ex* does not participate in S-Drop when it is a preposition in borrowed phrases, or phrases coined on the Latin model, such as *ex officio* 'by virtue of the office,' *ex warehouse* 'sold directly,' *ex libris* 'out of the library.' Its status as an independent word is in accord with the cluster of identical consonants in *ex silentio* 'from silence, from absence of evidence,' as well as in the phrases of mixed etymological origin *ex ship, ex store.*

Having learned about S-Drop, one might be tempted to look for it in *any ex-* initial forms. To avoid overgeneralizations, one should establish the exact form of the root. By definition, the rule is triggered only by s-initial roots, and *consonant loss* implies the historical adjacency of two [s] sounds. Latinate words such as *expedite, exculpate, explicate, exquisite, extemporize* preserve the original forms of the adjacent morphemes, and though they may look like *expire, except,* their histories are different.

1.1.3   Other affixes in -*s*

The principle of S-Drop extends to two other affixes which end in [-s]: *dis-* and *trans-*. As with the prefix *ex-*, when they are combined with *s*-initial morphemes, the resulting "long" [s] is simplified. A blurring of the semantic morpheme boundaries can also occur in some cases, e.g. *disperse* (dis+sperse), *dispirited* (dis+spirit+ed), *distant* (dis+sta+nt), *distinct* (dis+sting 'to stick' +t). In these examples the rule is carried to its completion, both in spelling and in pronunciation. More frequently, however, our conservative spelling still preserves the clue to the composition of such prefixed words, as in:

dis+cern 'separate, decide' → *discern*
dis+cip (< **cap** 'take')+le → *disciple*
dis+ser 'join'+t-at-ion → *dissertation*
dis+sid (< **sed** 'sit')+ent → *dissident*
dis+son 'sound'+ant → *dissonant*

In these examples the etymological trace of the two [s]'s in contact is only orthographic, not phonetic or semantic; *discern*, *dissertation*, etc. are pronounced with only one [-s-]. When the meaning of the prefix *dis-* is recognizably negative, meaning 'reversal,' the cluster [-ss-] is still pronounced in American English: *dissatisfy*, *disservice*, *dissimilar*. The fuzziness of the morpheme boundaries may result in optional phonetic doubling: words such as *dissemble*, *dissociate* can be pronounced either way. Also, the prefix *dis-* displays a strong tendency to drop the [-s] when it abuts voiced consonants: [g, v, l, r, m]. Examples of this change are *digest* (dis+ges+t), *diverge* (dis+verge), *direct* (dis+reg 'lead'+t), *dimension* (dis+mens 'measured'+ion).

Occasionally, the [s] of *dis-* may be voiced to [z] under the influence of a following voiced sound: dis+aster 'star'> *disaster*, dis+ease > *disease*, dis+solve > *dissolve* all with [z]. Finally, the spellings *dissyllable*, and even *trissyllable*, were adopted from French where an unetymological second -*s* was added to the numeral prefixes. These spellings were frequent from the sixteenth century onwards, but are now only a historical curiosity.

The prefix ***trans-*** also triggers S-Drop:

trans+scend (< scand 'climb')   → *transcend*
trans+scribe 'write'   → *transcribe*
trans+sect 'cut'   → *transect*
trans+sept (< Lat. septum 'enclosure')   → *transept*
trans+spir 'breathe'+e   → *transpire*

Recent coinages such as *trans-sexuality* (first recorded 1941), or freely coined derivatives such as *Trans-Siberian*, *Trans-Silesian* (as in the railway lines), are pronounced with long consonants. The fate of some words is still being decided: the *Random House Webster's Collegiate Dictionary* (1991) records both *trans-sonic* and *transonic*, while the *American Heritage Dictionary*

(2000) has only *transonic*; *transship* and *tranship* are given as variants in both dictionaries. Notice also that in pronunciation most words with the prefix *trans-* allow its [-s] to change to the alveolar [-t] instead of being dropped, so that we pronounce it as if it was spelled <tran(t)->: [træn(**t**)sɛpt], [træn(**t**)spaɪr], etc.

As in the application of all other rules, overanalysis is a danger: while *transpire* undergoes S-Drop, a potential false cognate *transparent* (*trans+par* 'show' +*ent*), does not. Familiarity with the words' etymology, or a consultation with a good dictionary, will reveal that *disperse, distant* have undergone S-Drop, while *display, distort* preserve the original consonants at the juncture of the two morphemes. A good dictionary will also will also teach you that *dismantle, dismember* are composed of the prefix *dis* + the stems *mantle* and *member*, while *dismal* is not – it goes back to the Latin phrase *dies mali* 'bad days.'

1.2   X-Drop

More simplification. S-Drop simplifies the phonetic sequence [ks-+-s] to [ks], i.e. a potential "double-s" [ss] surfaces as a single [s]. Yet another process which can affect the phonetic [-ks] sequence of the prefix *ex-* is X-Drop, the complete disappearance of both consonants from the prefix *ex-* when it means 'out, out of.'

Unlike S-Drop, which affects also *dis-* and *trans-*, X-Drop is restricted to a single morpheme. When *ex-*, phonetically [eks-], is attached to a morpheme starting with a voiced consonant, the cluster [ks] is simply deleted. In the previous section we mentioned instances in which *dis-* can drop the [-s] when it precedes the voiced consonants: [g, v, l, r, m], as in *digest, diverge, direct*, etc. A similar phenomenon, only more pervasive, applies to *ex-*. Both the dropping of the [s-] in *dis-* and X-Drop are a consequence of avoiding phonotactically awkward consonant clusters. You will recall from Chapter 5, Section 1.3 that phonotactic constraints can block or inhibit the co-occurrence of certain sounds in sequence. A cluster of a voiceless stop followed by a voiceless fricative followed by a voiced consonant would be a highly unusual combination; it would be *marked*. In English, the clusters *-ksb-*, *-ksr-*, *ksl*, *-ksg-*, for example, are allowed across word boundaries: *likes **B**ob, lacks **r**igor, rock **s**lide, tax **g**oals, Thanksgiving*, etc. are all okay, but we cannot imagine packing these clusters within a single morpheme. Such "marked" clusters are unstable historically; already in Latin, if the [eks-] prefix was followed by a voiced consonant, and if the derivational history of the word became obscure, the speakers simplified the cluster by dropping the [-ks] and leaving just a trace of the original prefix.

Orthographically: **ex**-+voiced consonant   → <e->
Phonetically: [**ɛks**]+voiced consonant   → [ɛ-] ([ɪ-] or [i] if the
                                              prefix is unstressed)

Here is how X-Drop works:

$$[\text{ɛ}\underline{\text{ks}}\text{-}] + [\text{+ CONS, +VOI}]$$
$$\downarrow$$
$$[\text{Ø}]$$

X-Drop

ex+**b**ull 'boil'+ient	→ eØbullient	ex+**l**ev 'light'+ate	→ eØlevate
ex+**d**uc 'lead'+e	→ eØduce	ex+**m**erge 'dip'	→ eØmerge
ex+**g**es 'carry'+t	→ eØgest	ex+**r**as 'scrape'+e	→ eØrase
ex+**j**ac 'throw'+t	→ eØject	ex+**v**apor+ate	→ eØvaporate

The formulation of X-Drop implies that if the prefix *ex-* precedes a morpheme starting with a voiceless consonant (other than [-s] or [f], see below), or a vowel, it will be preserved. This indeed is the case; see *exhale, extol, expose, excursion, exit, exonerate*, etc. In this meaning of the prefix *ex-* too, in words in which the voiceless consonants [(k)s] precede a stressed syllable, voicing is likely to occur. Thus, with stressed roots which begin with a vowel (or *h*), we notice voicing of the [-ks] of the prefix to [-gz]: *exacerbate, exact, exaggerate, exalt, exhaust, exhibit, exhort, exist, exuberance, exude, exultation*. In all of these words the original [-k] of the first syllable is lenited to [g-], which then causes voicing of the [s-] onset of the syllable to the right. However, if the *ex-* is stressed, the cluster [-ks] may or may not be voiced: *exercise, exile, exit, exodus*. With some words in this group both [ks] and [gz] are acceptable: *exhume, exile, existential, exit*, etc.

1.2.1   Exceptions to X-Drop

Like S-Drop, X-Drop is blocked when *ex* preserves its status as an independent word, a preposition, as in the Latinate phrases ***ex gratia*** 'done by favor,' ***ex libris*** 'out of the library,' ***ex nihilo*** 'out of nothing.'

When it is attached to a root beginning with [f-], X-Drop commonly proceeds in a manner identical to the rule described above, namely the cluster [ks-] is dropped. In such instances the rule of X-Drop looks different because, in spelling, it leaves a trace – a doubling of the initial <f> letter of the root: *efface, effect, effeminate, effigy, effort, effusive*, etc. In words formed during the Renaissance and later, the prefix may be preserved: *exfoliate* (1612) alternates with *effoliate*, while late forms like *exfiltrate, exflagellation, exfodiate* (rare) show their composition both in spelling and in pronunciation.

1.3   N-Drop

Limitations. The rule of N-drop applies only to the *-n* of the negative morpheme *an-* 'not, without, -less' and to the English indefinite article *an* (originally meaning 'one' in Old English). The rule deletes the *-n* when the following morpheme (or word, in the case of the indefinite article) begins with a consonant. For both the negative morpheme and the indefinite article the rule operates without exceptions, so much so that in the case of the negative *an-*, the variant *a-* before consonants is described by the *OED* as a "living prefix of negation" in its own right. This is so because already in Greek, from where the "privative" **an-** was borrowed, the prefix appeared as **a-** before consonants, as in *amorphous*. The principle of alternating *a-* before consonants and *an-* before vowels is respected in Latin and French borrowings which use the same prefix; it carries through to modern learned and technical words, so *an-antherous, an-isomerous* vs. *asexual, aphemic*.

[n-] + [+CONS]

↓

[Ø]

N-Drop

an+	**chr**omat 'color'+ic	→	aØchromatic
an+	**m**or 'manner, custom'+al	→	aØmoral
an+	**gn**os 'know'+tic	→	aØgnostic
an+	**ph**a 'speak'+sia	→	aØphasia
an+	**p**ath 'feeling'+y	→	aØpathy
an+	**th**eo 'god'+ism	→	aØtheism

Phrasal scope of N-Drop. Unlike the other changes surveyed here, N-Drop does not occur only at morpheme edges in derivational processes, that is, within the confines of a single word. The dropping of *-n* in the indefinite article in English applies within a whole noun phrase. When a noun or its modifier is preceded by an indefinite article, the article carries no stress and is prosodically attached to the following word. The linguistic term for the unstressed satellite of a stressed host word is *clitic* (the morpheme *clit* means 'lean,' 'depend on'). Clitic and host together form a clitic group; a noun phrase containing an indefinite article contains by definition at least one clitic group. The noun phrase *a sore point* contains the clitic group *a sore* and it is within this group that the deletion takes place. Today, most speakers take the English indefinite article to be *a*, though the original historical form of this word is *an*. As with the *a-* of the negative *an-*, the allomorph *a* of the indefinite article is now considered an independent living form. Were it not for its history and the parallel between the two morphemes, we could consider the *an* form of the article as a synchronic variant of *a*, in which the consonant *-n* is inserted before vowels.

1.3.1   Pronunciation and boundaries

When the *-n* of the negative morpheme is deleted, the remaining vowel can be fully unstressed, pronounced like the indefinite article *a*, [ə] (schwa): *aphasia, amorphous*, etc. When the prefix is stressed, or when we want to emphasize the article *a*, the vowel is realized as the "named" and shifted vowel spelled <a>, namely, [e(y)] (the vowel of *late, they*): *asymmetry, atheist, apolitical*, or *Give me **a** [e(y)] coin, not the contents of your pocket*. In some rare instances, e.g. *apathy*, the vowel is stressed and therefore not reduced to schwa, but it surfaces as the lower front vowel [æ]. Yet another option is illustrated by *agnostic*, which can either have a fully unstressed initial [ə-], or [æ-] with some degree of prominence. In summary:

[ə] (unstressed): *aphasia, amorphous, agnostic*

<a> [æ] (stressed, short): *apathy, agnostic*

[e(y)] (stressed long): *asymmetry, atheist, apolitical*

The prefix *an-* remains unchanged before a vowel or *h-*:

an 'not' +	esth 'perceive' et+ic	→ anesthetic
an +	alg 'pain'+es+ic	→ analgesic
an +	hem 'blood'+ic	→ anemic (with drop of initial h-)
an +	hydr 'water'+ous	→ anhydrous
an +	onym 'name'+ous	→ anonymous

The preservation of [-n] in the indefinite article before <h->-initial words is subject to some variation and speaker uncertainty. This is due to the historic instability of initial [h-] in words borrowed from the Romance languages. In Late Latin and in Old French the [h-] sound was lost in the pronunciation of words such as *able* (compare to *habilitation*), *(h)istory, (h)erb, (h)onor*. The letter <h-> was frequently preserved, however, and under the influence of spelling and the model of native words such as *house, horse* which kept their first consonant, the [h-] was reinstated in many Romance loanwords in late Middle and Early Modern English. This accounts for the variant pronunciations of *herb, humor*, and for the allomorphy in pairs like *able–rehabilitation, heir–heritage, hour–horoscope, odometer–hodograph*. Therefore, for words borrowed from French (and ultimately "classical" sources), the drop of *-n* before *h-* is not fully established yet. It is acceptable standard English to say both *a historic event*, and *an historic event*, though the second choice sounds somewhat stilted and academic today, and is usually seen in writing, not heard in speech. For native words the rule of N-Drop operates without exception even before [h-]: *a house, a horse, a hot day*.

One curiosity of N-Drop is that it can reset the boundaries within a clitic group. Historically, when the numeral *an* began to lose [-n] before consonant-initial words, the largely illiterate speakers of the language had to make difficult decisions about the word boundaries in some clitic groups. The problem must have been similar to the problem we have in interpreting *an aim* vs. *a name, an ice* cube vs. *a nice cube* without reference to spelling or a larger context. Consequently, the boundaries within some such groups were misinterpreted: the Old English article–noun groups *a(n) napron, a(n) nadder* became *an apron, an adder*. Conversely, *an ewt* and *an eke name* 'substitute name,' became *a newt, a nickname*. Such resetting of boundaries gives rise to popular jokes: "Be *alert*: your country needs *lerts*!"

Finally, we should be careful not to overidentify N-Drop. The prefix *an-* 'not, without, less' should not be confused with *ana-* 'back, again' as in *anachronism* ('back in time'), *anapest* ('reverse, turned backward') referring to the fact that an anapest (*de-de-*DUM) is a reversed dactyl (*DUM-de-de*), as in *Cantonese* vs. *Italy*. Nor should the negative allomorph *a-* (after N-Drop) be confused with words containing initial morphemes which accidentally begin in *a-*: *apo-*, *ad-*, *ab-*, *ag-* – thus *agent* is not someone who does not belong to the *gentility*, nor is *account* the reverse of *count*.

1.3.2 Nasal Drop in other prefixes

While the more general rule of N-Drop before consonants affects only the two morphemes *an*, two other prefixes, *com-/con-* and *syn-* can also appear without their final nasal. The conditions for the loss of the nasal in these prefixes are different from the conditions for N-Drop in *an*; they are also different for the two prefixes.

The prefix *con-*, an allomorph of the prefix *com-* in Latin, regularly appears as <co-> if the following morpheme is vowel-initial, or if it begins with [h-]:

Realization of *co-* before a vowel or <h->:

co(**n**)+**ag** 'drive, do' + ulate'	→ coØagulate
co(**n**)+**erc** < arc 'keep in'+e	→ coØerce
co(**n**)+**it** 'go'+ion	→ coØition
co(**n**)+**oper** 'work'+ate	→ coØoperate
co(**n**)+**habit** 'abide'	→ coØhabit
co(**n**)+**hort** 'enclosure'	→ coØhort (> court)

In addition to the absence of [-n] regularly before vowels and [h-], the prefix *con-* is realized as *co-* before the root *gn* 'birth, origin,' as in *coØgnate*, or *gn* 'know,' as in *coØgnition*. Before the voiced labiodental fricative [v] the prefix behaves inconsistently: *con+ven* 'come' produces *convent*, *convention*, but the [n] is missing in *coØvenant* 'agreement,' *coØven* 'an assembly, gathering (especially of witches).' The *CoØvent* of London's *Covent Garden* retained the pronunciation of the word *convent* until the seventeenth century.

Like the post-N-Drop status of the negative *a-* and the indefinite article *a*, the allomorph *co-* has acquired independence and can now be freely attached to any roots or bases. A set of three cognate words: *consign* (1430), *coØsine* (1635), and *co-sign* (1900), illustrates the historical possibilities for the development of new meanings out of *con-* allomorphs. The Nasal-Drop variant *co-* is equally productive with borrowed and native roots: *co-owner*, *co-father*, *co-founder*, *co-driver*. Moreover, the *co-* can be prefixed to words beginning with *con-*: *co-conspirator*, *co-constituent*, *co-conscious*.

The situation with the prefix *syn-* is simpler. When not subject to labial assimilation, *syn-* surfaces intact: *synchronic*, *synergy*, *synthesis*. When it attaches to a morpheme which begins with [s] followed by another consonant, the [n-] is deleted:

syn+**st** 'stand'+(e)m	→ syØstem
syn+**stol** 'place, draw'+ic	→ syØstolic

The deletion in these examples, as well as the deletion in the only combination in English (borrowed from Greek) of *syn* followed by [-z]: *syzygy* 'conjunction' (syn+zyg 'yoke'), results in the simplification of consonant clusters which might have been hard to pronounce, another manifestation of the principle of ease.

2   Vowel deletion

This section describes processes which delete a vowel from a morpheme when that morpheme becomes part of a new word.

2.1   V-Drop in hiatus

Hiatus. The word 'hiatus' is a Latin borrowing meaning 'a gap, opening.' As a linguistic term, hiatus refers to a kind of phonetic opening which occurs when two vowels are directly adjacent across a syllable boundary, with no consonant in between. It is important to distinguish between vowel letters that are written next to each other, but belong to the same syllable, and phonetic vowels which are adjacent, but belong to two different syllables. The words *coat*, *sea-lant*, *prai-rie* have no vowels in hiatus, while *co-act*, *Se-attle*, *na-ïve* do.

Words like *reality*, *naïve*, *embryo*, which contain vowels in hiatus, are fairly rare in English. Hiatus within words or within clitic groups is disfavored in English and indeed in many languages; various "hiatus-avoidance" mechanisms are developed to repair hiatus. One such mechanism is the deletion of a vowel when the final vowel of a morpheme of more than one syllable is adjoined to a vowel-initial morpheme. We can call this **V-Drop**. (Read "vowel-drop"; we continue the convention of using a capital letter V to mean "any vowel.")

$$\$ \, V + \{V \ldots, h \ldots\}$$
$$\downarrow$$
$$\emptyset$$

V-Drop

an+theo 'god'+ism	→ atheØism, but theosophy, theology
dia+orama 'view'	→ diØorama, but dialysis, diagram
epi+en 'in'+thesis 'placing'	→ epØenthesis, but epigraph, epidermic
homo 'man'+age 'office of'	→ homØage, but *Homo sapiens*
homo 'same'+onym 'name'	→ homØonym, but homograph, homophone
hypo 'beneath'+alg 'pain'+ia	→ hypØalgia, but hypothesis, hypotoxic
meta 'beyond'+onym 'name'+y	→ metØonymy, but metabolism, metaphor
para 'beside'+en 'in'+thesis	→ parØenthesis, but paralegal, parameter
tele 'far'+ex(change)	→ telØex,[2] but telegraph, telephone, telescope

---

[2] The word is a blend of *tele(printer* + *ex(change*, n., first recorded in 1932 (*OED*).

As the examples show, V-Drop deletes the first of two consecutive vowels at the morpheme boundary. It affects both roots and affixes. The change can be attributed to the preference for an alternation of vowel – consonant – vowel across syllable boundaries rather than a sequence of two syllabic vowels appearing back-to-back within a word.

2.1.1   Exceptions

V-Drop is not an exceptionless change. The application of the rule before <h-> is inconsistent. The orthographic preservation of <h-> in Romance words often reinstated the [h-] in the pronunciation of these words in English, see Section 1.3.1. V-Drop before orthographic <h-> occurs in words such as *method* < meta+**h**od 'way,' *ephemeral* < epi+**h**emer(a) 'day'+al. Side by side with such forms, we find forms like *parhelion, telharmonium,* in which the V-Drop rule applies and [h-] is preserved phonetically. Finally, a third type of forms: *epihyal, homohedral, telehydrobarometer, parahypnosis,* all of them recent scientific coinages, preserve the [h-] and resist V-Drop. Many disyllabic morphemes, such as *anti-, poly-, semi-, neo-, macro-,* and *iso-,* tend to resist V-Drop altogether, as attested by words such as *antiemetic, antioxidant, polyandrous, semiautomatic, neoembryonic, macroanalysis, isoelectronic, isooctane,* etc.

Also, the V-Drop rule covers only the unstressed vowels in disyllabic morphemes; monosyllabic morphemes ending in a vowel are not subject to vowel drop. Thus *de-, bi-, re-* will not change their form, even if the morpheme attached to them begins with a vowel or h-: *deodorize, dehydrate, reinstate, rehabilitate, biennial.* Sometimes, however, V-Drop applies to the prefix *con-/com-,* after Nasal Drop has created hiatus conditions across a morpheme boundary:

Input	Nasal-Drop	V-Drop
con+ag 'drive'+ent	→ co+ag+ent	→ cogent
con+ag(it) 'put in motion'+ate	→ co+agit+ate	→ cogitate
con+hort 'enclosure, yard'	→ co+(h)ort	→ court

Finally, it should be noted that V-Drop within a clitic group is a change which accounts for the history of some Anglo-Saxon words, thus *no+one>none, do+off >doff,* and *do+on>don.* Hiatus avoidance accounts also for the contractions such as *she's, we're, I'm, we've.*

2.2   Syllable syncopation

Syllables are the smallest free-standing pronounceable units. When you say a word as slowly as possible, or when you yell it, you can count the syllables in it. Usually, there is a vowel at the nucleus of every syllable. However, the retroflex sonorant [-r-] is very commonly also the nucleus of a syllable, alternating freely with [ər], as in the unstressed syllable of *water, meter, matter, feather,* etc. The lateral [l] and the nasals [m, n] behave similarly: *little, rhythm, button.* In the case of [-r-], our spelling system usually represents syllabicity with the letters <e> or <o> in front of the <-r>. When the [r] becomes non-syllabic, the loss of syllabicity is accompanied by dropping the vowel in the spelling. We can think of the rule, therefore, as "Syllable Syncopation."

Syncopation is defined as "contraction of a word by omission of one or more syllables or letters in the middle" (*OED*). Like V-Drop, Syllable Syncopation requires that the morpheme (or stem) in which the omission occurs be at least disyllabic. When we attach a derivational morpheme to a morpheme or stem whose non-initial syllable is <-er> or <-or>, the unstressed vowel is lost from the pronunciation (and the spelling) of the word.

$$\$ \, [V] + r + \$$$
$$\downarrow$$
$$\emptyset$$

Syllable Syncopation

meter+ic	→ metØric	executor+ix	→ executØrix
cylinder+ical	→ cylindØrical	aviator+ix	→ aviatØrix
anger+y	→ angØry	actor+ess	→ actØress
equi+liber+ium	→ equilibØrium	bisector+ix	→ bisectØrix

However, Syllable Syncopation is not always reflected in the spelling. Consider the relaxed pronunciation of such words as *dangerous, federal, history, factory, natural, preferable*. The same type of syncopation in speech occurs with other syllabic consonants: consider the pronunciation of *bachelor, specialist, botany, scrivener*. The boldfaced unstressed vowels in these words are heard only in very slow and careful speech, probably only in citing the words in isolation, emphasizing them, or singing them so that each syllable corresponds to a separate note. Normally, however, the medial syllable in such words is not pronounced. The only difference between the spontaneous syncopation in speech today and the change occurring in historical derivational processes is that the historical syncopation of the sequence <-er> and <-or> is reflected in the spelling, while other syncopations are not.

2.2.1   Preservation of <-er> and <-or>

Syllable Syncopation affects only unstressed syllables. Syncopation is blocked if the derivation of a new word involves shifting the stress onto the syllable containing [-r-], e.g.: *victórious, metaphórical, matérial, supérior, ultérior*. Also, even without stress shift, the need for transparency of the root or stem can prevent the operation of orthographic Syllable Syncopation: *sorceress, motorist, mastery, liberate*, although these words will lose the [r-] syllable optionally in speech. The presence of an adjacent unstressed syllable is also a factor: in *caliber -calibØrate* the dropping of the internal syllable is prosodically harmless, the syllable *-lib-* separates the two stressed syllables, whereas in words such as *liberate*, v. and *operate*, syncopation would result in stress clash. Fortunately, non-syncopation will not create parsing problems: if the rule does not apply, we parse the word directly from the surface form, not worrying about undoing the rule to get to the original morpheme.

3   Expansion rules: vowel or consonant epenthesis

A third group of rules in which recognizable phonetic factors cause predictable allomorphic variation are the *expansion* or *epenthesis* rules. Epenthesis (*epi+en* 'in'+*thesis* 'placing') is the technical term for inserting a sound between two other sounds. Both vowels and consonants can be inserted within an existing morpheme. Unlike deletions, epenthetic processes occur less often, affect a relatively small number of morphemes, and show numerous exceptions. In principle, however, they are similar to the deletion rules in that both types have parallels in the spoken language, and in both cases the changes are triggered by the avoidance of phonetically undesirable sound sequences.

3.1   U-Epenthesis

U-Epenthesis affects clusters made up of a velar stop ([g], [k]), or a bilabial stop ([b], [p]), plus the sonorant [l] where it is syllabic. When a morpheme ends in a syllabic [l] and is followed by a suffix beginning with a vowel, the cluster is broken up by the insertion of [yu], (spelled <u>), which turns the original sequence of consonants into a clearly defined syllable.

```
{- gl-, -kl-, -bl-, -pl-} + V
    ↓     ↓     ↓     ↓
{-gul-  kul   bul   pul}
```

U-Epenthesis

single+ar	→ singular	angle+ar	→ angular
particle+ar	→ particular	oracle+ar	→ oracular
table+ate	→ tabulate	couple+a	→ copula

The final -*e* in words such as *single, particle, table, couple*, etc. merely indicates that the [l] is syllabic. In one exceptional case, namely the form *nucular (nuclear)*, the predictable, though not obligatory, U-Epenthesis has yet to achieve full respectability. U-Epenthesis occasionally appears in an environment not shown in our rule, as in *title–titular*. The pronunciation [nyu.kyə.lər] is described by the online *Merriam-Webster Dictionary* in the following terms: "Though disapproved of by many [… such pronunciations …] have been found in widespread use among educated speakers including scientists, lawyers, professors, congressmen, United States cabinet members, and at least two United States presidents and one vice president. While most common in the United States, these pronunciations have also been heard from British and Canadian speakers." There is no rational basis for the disapproval: the new pronunciation is a normal analogical development based on the model of U-Epenthesis found elsewhere in English. Actual usage by the majority of speakers is the only coherent basis for choosing one pronunciation over another.

A parallel to this change can be found in the alternative forms of pronunciation of words such as *athlete*. A widespread pronunciation, sometimes considered non-standard, has a schwa inserted between the dental and the liquid, [-θ(ə)l-]. A similar insertion of (parasitic) schwas can occur also between the sonorants in *film*, *firm*, etc. Not surprisingly, schwa insertion can be found in some varieties of American English in similar environments, i.e. before the syllabic sonorant [l] in a very wide range of environments:

ba**ffle**	→ baffling [f(ə)l-]	mu**ddle**	→ muddling [d(ə)l-]
ba**ttle**	→ battling [t(ə)l-]	o**gle**	→ ogling [-g(ə)l-]
bede**vil**	→ bedeviling [v(ə)l-]	to**pple**	→ toppling [p(ə)l-]
embe**zzle**	→ embezzling [z(ə)l-]	ti**ckle**	→ ticklish [k(ə)l-]
gar**ble**	→ garbling [b(ə)l-]	tu**ssle**	→ tussling [s(ə)l-]

The rule of U-Epenthesis does not apply to all potentially eligible words. Some exceptions are: *cycle–cyclical*, *single–singly*, *simple–simplex*, *bible–bibliophile*, etc. Non-morpheme-final velar-labial consonant clusters do not undergo U-Epenthesis: *diglossia*, *inclination*, *medulloblastoma*, *implication*.

3.2   P-Epenthesis

This change has very limited scope, since it covers the avoidance of only one specific consonant cluster, *-mt-*, which is not particularly common. P-Epenthesis resembles the other allomorphy rules in that it is phonetically motivated and can therefore also be observed in the spoken language. The effect of the change is to ease the transition between the voiced bilabial [m] and the voiceless stop [t]. The epenthetic stop [p] shares the bilabial articulation with [m], the first segment in the cluster, and has the same manner of articulation and the same voicing value as the following [t].

```
┌─────────┐
│ - m + t │
│    ↓    │
│  -mpt-  │
└─────────┘
```

P-Epenthesis

assume	→ assumption
tem-[3]	→ tempt
redeem	→ redemption

---

[3] **Tem** is an unpredictable allomorph of **ten** 'touch, try,' as in *tentacle*, *tentative*.

A parallel phonetic change occurs in the pronunciation of some native English forms, though in most instances the spelling does not reflect the epenthetic [p]. The Middle English adjective *emti* became our word *empty*. English speakers find the cluster *-mt-* difficult, even if the *-m-* and the *-t-* belong to separate morphemes. The borrowed word *controller* is recorded as *comptroller* since c. 1500 and that spelling (and the pronunciation with [-p-], according to the *American Heritage Dictionary*), is used for some special functions. The form *dreamt*, pronounced [drɛm(**p**)t] is unique; compare also *something*, often pronounced [səm(**p**)θɪŋ]. These examples mirror the historical process of P-Epenthesis in derivation, only the latter is reflected in the spelling. A similar phonetic phenomenon is observed in English in the sequence *n+s* which is broken up by an epenthetic [-t-], so that *prince, tense, mince* sound the same as *prints, tents, mints*.

8   Fossilized allomorphy: false cognates and other etymological pitfalls

1   Fossilized allomorphy

Unlike allomorphy resulting from phonetically motivated replacement, deletion, or epenthesis, the allomorphy discussed in this chapter cannot be attributed to the operation of an active and transparent phonetic rule. "Fossilized" allomorphs can be deceptively unlike each other in form, yet they are historically related – they *are* cognates. The morpheme variants in this group arose as a consequence of systematic changes in pre-Old English times, going all the way back to Proto-Germanic and even to Indo-European. Within English, i.e. after the fifth century, the conditions for these early changes became obscured, and their results can no longer be seen as regular or highly predictable. If we set up a scale of predictability for allomorphic variation, allomorphs due to assimilation or consonant and vowel loss will rank very high; mostly, the conditions for these changes are transparent and recoverable. At the low end of the scale would be the non-productive allomorphic variation described in historical terms, for which the conditions have ceased to exist. At the bottom of the scale are completely unpredictable alternate forms of cognates, the subject of Section 5 below. Historical, or fossilized, allomorphy tends to follow several general patterns; familiarity with these can help us discern etymological cognates in spite of their overt differences.

We will look at three fossilized processes: the *First Consonant Shift*, *Gradation*, and *Rhotacism*.

2   Consonant correspondences: the *First Consonant Shift* (Grimm's Law)

Recall from Chapter 2 that by being members of the same Indo-European family of languages, English, Latin, and Greek share deep historical connections. One of the many ways in which their common origin can be recognized is with reference to a set of changes called the *First Consonant Shift*, also known as *Grimm's Law* or *Rask's Law*.

The study of Indo-European sound changes in the various branches has a long history. The consonantal correspondences between Germanic and the parent language described below were discovered in the nineteenth century. As early as 1818, the Danish philologist Rasmus Rask observed the link between Latin words like *ager* 'field,' *pater* 'father,' *duo* 'two' and English *acre, father, two*. Some years later, Jacob Grimm, one of the two brothers Grimm who gained fame as collectors of folk songs and fairy tales, defined the regularities that relate the consonants of the Germanic and the other Indo-European languages of Europe and western Asia in his *Deutsche Grammatik* ("Germanic Grammar," 1819–37). Although the term "law" was not used by the discoverers of these consonantal changes, many philologists refer to them eponymously as *Grimm's Law* or *Rask's Law*. The great appeal of the discovery is that it accounts for the difference in the consonants in words that are clearly related, but have different consonants: *foot–podium, tooth–dental, heart–cordial*.

The historical span of time during which the First Consonant Shift occurred is reconstructed roughly between 750 and 250 BC. This coincides with the period when the Germanic branch gradually split from the proto-language, but before the evolution of the separate dialects of Germanic. The changes covered by the First Consonant Shift affected the Indo-European stops. They are summarized in Figure 8.1. below:

Indo-European		Germanic	Type of change
p t k	→	f θ h	(voiceless stops → voiceless fricatives)
b d g	→	p t k	(voiced stops → voiceless stops)
bʰ dʰ gʰ	→	b d g	(voiced aspirated stops → voiced stops)

Figure 8.1 *The First Consonant Shift*

The essence of the shift is as follows: the original voiceless stops [p, t, k] became voiceless fricatives [f, θ, h]. As shown in the second row, the voiced stops inherited from Proto-Indo-European, namely [b, d, g], became voiceless and filled the position of the shifted voiceless stops [p, t, k]. Neither Latin and its descendants, the modern Romance languages, nor Greek, were subject to the changes in the first two rows, so that in Latin and Greek words the Indo-European [p, t, k, b, d, g] preserved their quality, or a quality very similar to the original.

The situation with respect to the aspirated voiced stops of Indo-European [bʰ, dʰ, gʰ][1] is somewhat more complex: in Germanic their development was ultimately to voiced stops: [b, d, g], while Latin conflates [bʰ, dʰ] into the voiceless fricative [f] and changes [gʰ] to [h] in word-initial position.

Figure 8.1 presents a partial and simplified picture. We skip many details – what we want to emphasize is that the changes we are describing represent a "shift" of entire sets of consonants, hence the name *First Consonant **Shift*** mentioned earlier. It accounts for the consonantal differences in *cognate* words, i.e. words descended from the same etymological source. As the languages diverged from each other, the forms of the cognates also diverged: the consonants changed in Germanic, but

---

[1] Aspirated voiced stops in English can be pronounced in the borrowed Sanskrit words *bhakti* 'piety,' *dharma* 'decree, custom, law,' and Hindi *gharri* 'cart, carriage.'

in Latin, French, or Greek, the same consonants were either preserved (the original stops), or they underwent changes different from the changes in Germanic (the aspirated voiced stops). The relevant correspondences are shown in Figure 8.2:

Consonant set	IE	Germanic	Latin	Greek
Voiceless	p	f	p	p
Stops	t	θ	t	t
	k	h	k[2]	k
Voiced	b	p	b	b
Stops	d	t	d	d
	g	k	g	g
Voiced	b^h	b	f	ph
Aspirated	d^h	d	f	th
Stops	g^h	g	h	kh

Figure 8.2

It is important to realize that the operation of the shift is confined within a specific time-frame; it could not have continued beyond the beginning of the Christian era. Within Germanic, the results of the shift have survived in English, Dutch, other Low German languages, and the Scandinavian languages. The time-limit on the shift has allowed English to accommodate an original Indo-European root twice: first as a direct continuation of the Indo-European form into Germanic, Old, Middle, and Modern English. Then, independently, and after Grimm's Law had stopped operating, the language could borrow the same Indo-European root from Latin or one of its descendants. Such later borrowings are *not* subject to any "Germanic" changes: they are imported with their consonants as they appear in the non-Germanic branch of Indo-European. Here are some examples of these correspondences, where the numbers in parentheses indicate the first attestation of the Latinate loanwords in English (according to the *OED*):

Indo-European[3]	Germanic (English)	Borrowings
*pod-/ped-	**foot, fetter**[4]	**pod**ium (1743), **ped**al (1611)[5]
*ten	**thin**	**ten**uous (1597), **tend**on (1541)
*kerd-/kord-/kard-	**heart**	**cord**ial (1386), **card**iac (1450)[6]

---

[2] Note that the most common spelling for the sound [k] in Latin is <c>, as in *cado, cadere* 'to fall,' *circa* 'around,' *celer* 'swift,' *cursor* 'runner,' etc.

[3] As in the Appendix, the asterisks indicate a reconstructed form of the root.

[4] Old English *fōt* 'foot,' *feter* 'leg iron.'

[5] Other borrowings based on **ped-**, **pod-** are: *antipodes* (1398), **pod**agra 'gout in the feet' (1398), *expedite* (1471), *tripod* (1603), *impede* (1605) 'entangle the feet, hinder' (compare to English *fetter*), **ped**estal (1580), *millipede* (1601), **ped**estrian (1716), *podiatry* (1914), etc.

[6] Other forms showing the same root are ac**cord** (1297), *courage, concord, discord, misericord, record*. Here belong also the medical terms derived from *cardio-, -cardium*: *endocardium, epicardium, megalocardia, myocardium, pericardium*.

*leb-/lab	lip	labial (1650), labret (1857)
*den(t)-/odon(t)-	tooth	dental (1594), (perio)dontal (1899)[7]
*gen	kin	gender (c.1300), progeny (1330)

In matching native to borrowed pairs such as the ones shown above, recall that the Indo-European sets of voiceless and voiced stops continue unchanged in Greek and Latin, but the voiced aspirated stops in word-initial position change, as in the bottom three rows in Figure 8.2 above. Here is how the voiced aspirated stops develop in Germanic and in some borrowings:

Indo-European	Germanic (English)	Borrowing
*bher–	bear, bairn, barrow	fertile, infer, periphery[8]
*dhwer-	door	foreign, forest, forum[9]
*ghos-ti-	guest	host, hostile, hostel

The First Consonant Shift, described partially here, represents only one aspect in which the shape of the words we have inherited from Germanic and Old English differs from the Indo-European proto-form. We highlight these consonants because they make the association between numerous cognate pairs of words in English clearer without too much philological apparatus.

We now move to two other types of deeply buried allomorphy: gradation and rhotacism. Originally gradation and rhotacism affected root morphemes and occurred regularly in conjunction with specific grammatical changes within a *paradigm*,[10] e.g. the present vs. the past-tense form of one and the same verb, the nominative vs. the genitive case of the same noun. Thus generated, the allomorphy then carried over into various derivative words, where the selection of one or another of the alternative phonetic forms of the root became largely accidental. Gradation and rhotacism could accompany the formation of a noun from an existing verb root or vice versa, or in general could mark off one word class from another. Only a small part of the rich gamut of grammatical alternations and word-formation patterns of more than a millennium ago has come down to us, yet what remains is sufficiently coherent and interesting to make it worth understanding.

---

[7] Another cognate in Germanic is *tusk* from Germanic *tunth-sk > tusk*. Other post-Old English borrowings are *indent, indenture, dandelion* (Fr. *dent de lion*) (1513), and over 100 entries in *-odont* 'type of dentition' in the *OED*.

[8] Latin *fer-* (*confer, defer, differ, offer, prefer, proffer, refer, suffer, transfer, vociferate*) corresponds to Greek *phor- pher-*, e.g. *anaphora, euphoria, metaphor, paraphernalia*.

[9] Latin *foras, foris* 'out of doors' > prefix *for(e)-, foreclose, forfeit, forensic*, etc. Greek *thura* 'door,' produces *thureos* 'shield'; hence the seventeenth-century formation *thyroid* 'door/shield-shaped.'

[10] *Paradigm*: a set of inflectional forms, a conjugation, or a declension. Unlike the simple paradigms of Modern English, verbs, nouns, and adjectives in Indo-European, Latin, Proto-Germanic, and Old English had rich paradigms with different forms for different grammatical functions and meanings.

3   Gradation

Gradation, also known by its German name *Ablaut*, is a term characterizing the way in which the Indo-European vowels *e* and *o* once alternated with each other and with **zero** in different grammatical forms or word classes. Traditionally, the allomorph containing the vowel *e* is described as exhibiting the *e*-**grade**, the allomorph containing the vowel *o* shows the *o*-**grade**, and the allomorph with no vowel in it is labeled the **zero-grade**. Here are some examples of the alternations resulting from gradation:

Root	*E*-grade	*O*-grade	Zero-grade
kel 'hollow, cover'	**cel**lar	**col**or	**cl**andestine
gen 'birth, origin'	**gen**etic	**gon**orrhea	co**gn**ate
men 'think, warn'	de**men**ted	ad**mon**ish	**mn**emonic
pher 'carry, bear'	Christo**pher**	eu**phor**ia	–
gel 'cold, freeze'	**gel**atin	–	**gl**acier
sol 'whole'	–	**sol**id	**sal**ubrious[11]
ker 'mix, cook'	–	–	**cr**ater

The horizontal arrangement of the *e*-grade, *o*-grade, or zero-grade is simply alphabetical; the *e*-grade which appears in most of the entries in the first column has no special status in our context, though some grammars may refer to it as "the normal" grade. In many instances of historical gradation only two of the three possible qualitative allomorphs have survived and are attested in our vocabulary. The gaps indicated by the dashed line in the last three rows in the chart are accidental. Other roots in which gradation is incomplete are: *cere, cre* 'grow' (***cere**al, hypo**cor**ism*), *leg, log* 'gather, read, study' (***leg**ion, apo**log**y*), *sper, spor, spr* 'scatter, seed' (***sper**m, dia**spor**a, **spr**awl, **spr**out*), and *men, mon* 'lead, project, threaten' (***men**ace, **Mon**tana*) – many of them without a transparent zero-grade in English.

Another type of frequent Indo-European gradation is *quantitative* gradation, where short vowels alternate with long or reduced vowels to produce paradigmatic and derivational allomorphs. An example of fossilized quantitative gradation in English is the paradigm of the verb *stand* with its past-tense form *stood*; such is also the historical relationship between *sit* and *soot*.

3.1   Gradation in Germanic

The exact phonological and grammatical reasons for the existence of gradation are largely unknown. It is possible that the variation between *e* and *o* in the root is due to variation in the placement of the accent, while absence of stress correlates with the zero-grade. In the classical languages and in Germanic,

---

[11] The *sal-* of *salubrious* is a Latin development of the original zero-grade *sl-*.

gradation often signaled change from one word-class to another; it also regularly accompanied paradigmatic change. The major function of gradation within the Germanic languages was to mark person, number, and tense of a large class of verbs, traditionally referred to as *strong verbs*. Without familiarity with the phonetic changes from Indo-European to Present-Day English, through Germanic, Old, and Middle English, the original *e-*, *o-*, and zero-grades of the verbal allomorphs are not recognizable today; we have come to label these verbs "irregular."[12]

Gradation in word derivation was also a common Germanic pattern which became less and less productive in English, but not in the other Germanic languages. Still, there are some fossils of this pattern in Modern English, as in the verb–noun pairs: *do–deed, sing–song, break–breach, bind–bond, bundle.* Historical phonetic processes have changed the initial vowel grades beyond recognition, though the semantic relationship between the members of these pairs is obvious to every speaker of English.

Before leaving this topic we should also recall from Chapter 1, Section 3.7 that in the last three centuries English has started making use of a very different vowel gradation or *Ablaut*, producing words of the type *criss-cross, mish-mash, flim-flam, riff-raff, shilly-shally, tip-top.* In such forms the first and the second part of the word are linked by a special type of allomorphy involving both alliteration and the alternation of a high front vowel to the left with a non-high, non-front vowel on the right.

4   Rhotacism

Rhotacism is a philological term coined on the basis of the root *rho*, the Greek name of the letter and sound [r], Greek <ρ>. The term describes the change of the consonant [s] through its voiced counterpart [z] to [r] when paradigmatic alternations placed [s] between two vowels. Rhotacism is found both in words of Latin origin and in Germanic words, though the conditions under which it applies are slightly different.

4.1   Rhotacism in Latin

In Latin rhotacism accompanied the addition of vowel-initial suffixes (*-is, -a, -um, -ere*) to words ending in a vowel followed by [s], producing the sequence <-VsV->. Flanked by vowels, the consonant [-s-] was subject to weakening of its consonantal nature: first [-s-] was voiced to [-z-], and subsequently [-z-] developed into the sonorant [-r-]. The process accounts for the allomorphy in

---

[12] There are sixty-eight strong verbs in English, plus another thirteen which can be conjugated as both weak and strong (Baugh and Cable, *A History of the English Language*, p. 160). Strong verbs are, on the whole, frequently used verbs of native origin: *bite, choose, drive, eat, hang, lie, ride, run, see, write*, etc. Some verbs have alternative weak forms, though the strong forms are still used: *light, stave, thrive, wake.*

pairs such as *os* 'mouth,' gen. sg. *oris* 'of the mouth'; *rus* 'the country,' gen. *ruris* 'of the country'; *opus* 'work,' pl. *opera*; *ges* 'bear, carry,' verb *gerere* > *gerund*, but *gesture* 'bearing.' Historically, the appearance of a rhotacized or an unrhotacized form was predictable: [-s-] changed to [-r-] in <-VsV- > sequences, otherwise the [-s] remained unchanged.

$$\boxed{\begin{array}{ccc} V + & [\text{-s-}] + & V \\ & \downarrow & \\ & [r] & \end{array}}$$

Rhotacism

fl**os** 'flower'+**al**	→ flo**ra**l 'of or relating to flowers'
flos+**c**ule	→ flos**c**ule 'little flower, floret'
ges 'carry'+**t**+ure	→ ge**st**ure 'mode of carrying, way of action'
ges+**u**nd	→ ge**ru**nd 'carried, verbal noun'
op**us** 'work'+**c**ule	→ opus**c**ule 'small work'
opus+**a**te	→ ope**ra**te 'work, produce'
os 'mouth, speak'+**a**te+ion	→ o**ra**tion 'speech'
os+**c**it 'move'+ant	→ o**sc**itant 'gaping,' o**sc**itancy 'yawning'
rus 'open land'+**al**	→ ru**ra**l 'of the country'
rus+**t**ic+ate	→ ru**st**icate 'retire to the country'

In spite of the clearly defined conditions for the operation of rhotacism, some Latinate words appear to violate the above rule. Often an [-r-] or an [-s-] form will spread throughout the paradigm and will even be taken as the stem producing new words without further regard to the phonetic environment. Thus, we find an unchanged [-s-] allomorph between two vowels in the second words in pairs such as *adhere–adhesion, acquire–acquisition*. By the beginning of classical Latin, around 100 BC, rhotacism was no longer an active process; analogy from the more frequently used forms of the root and historical accidents have subsequently produced almost as many "irregular" pairs as there are regular ones. In order to recognize etymologically related sets, special note should be taken of both the unrhotacized *and* the rhotacized forms of the roots.

4.2   Rhotacism in Germanic

Voicing of [s] to [z] and a subsequent change to [r] in a vocalic environment could occur also in early Germanic, where there were additional prosodic conditions restricting the process. As with gradation, subsequent phonetic processes in English have eliminated, or greatly obscured, the results of Germanic rhotacism. Some pairs of cognate words which preserve traces of this ancient allomorphy are the past-tense forms of the verb *to be*: sg. *was* vs. pl. *were*, and the present tense and the adjectival participle of the verb *lose – (for)lorn* (from earlier *(for)loren*). The historical relationship between *rise* and *rear, sneeze* and *snore* can also be traced back to rhotacism, with some additional changes of the vowels.

5   Metathesis (transposition)

Metathesis (meta 'change, beyond'+the 'put'+(s)is 'process') is a term describing the transposition of sounds, and sometimes syllables, in a word. Although metathesis occurs commonly in many languages, the phonetic conditions for it can be identified only in very general terms: certain sound combinations, often involving [r], are more susceptible to metathesis than others. Metathesis is the fossilized residue of a rather erratic alternation; we separate it from the fully "unpredictable" allomorphy in the next section because unlike full unpredictability, the allomorphs resulting from metathesis retain the same consonants, only reordered, or scrambled. Metathesis may have originated in slips of the tongue; evidence of the process is found both in borrowed classical roots and in native roots. Some frequently quoted examples of metathesis are:

[ks] <–> [sk]:   mix – promiscuous
[nek] <–> [kep]: spectacle – skeptic
[rt] <–> [tr]:   nurture – nutrition

Sometimes metathesis combines with other processes and obscures otherwise transparent historical allomorphy. Thus the *o*-grade of the Indo-European root *ǝger-*, namely *ǝgor-*, is recognizably related by gradation to the allomorph *ǝgre-* only if we reverse the order of [-er-] to [-re-]:

Gradation:	*gregarious*	(ǝ)ger(g)	*agora*	(ǝ)gor
Metathesis:	*egregious*	(ǝ)gre(g)	*allegory*	–
	aggregate		*category*	

(Metathesis in pronunciation should not be confused with the alternative spellings for stem-final [(ǝ)r] written <-re> in British English vs. <-er> in American English as in *centre–center, litre–liter, lustre–luster, metre–meter, spectre–specter, theatre–theater*.) Finally, within the native vocabulary, Modern English dialect forms such as *apsen, waps, aks,* for *aspen, wasp, ask,* have their origin in an alternation which dates back to Old English: the Old English words were *æpse, wæpsa,* and *acsian*.

6   Obscure cognates: completely unpredictable allomorphy

Mastery of the rules of allomorphy still leaves a residue of obscure cognates. By "obscure" we do not mean words whose etymologies are "unknown" or "disputed" – those we can't even begin to discuss. By "obscure" we mean that the formal relationship between the allomorphs has become non-transparent, or that the semantic and logical link between the two allomorphs can no longer be reconstructed.

An example of phonetically obscure allomorphy comes from a small number of roots of classical origin: *spec, plec, fac, fid, neg, lig* which are historically related to *spy, ply, (petri)fy, (de)fy, (de)ny, (re)ly*. One of these obscured derivatives, *-(i)fy*, has developed into an extremely productive suffix in its own right: *signify, mortify, satisfy, terrify, typify*, to say nothing of more recent coinages such as *countrify, Frenchify, fishify*, even *speechify* and *happify*. Most dictionaries just list *-(i)fy* as a verb suffix based on the root *fac* 'do, make.' Similarly, the derivative of *plec, ply* 'fold, bend' has been quite productive: *apply, comply, imply, multiply, supply*. Notice also the productivity of *plex*, the past participle of the Latin verb with the root *plec*: *complex, duplex, perplex, simplex*.

The opacity of words which look and sound like Latin words has some interesting consequences for word-creation and spelling in English. The word *absquatulate* 'to scram, decamp,' is a nineteenth-century humorous pseudo-Latinism prompted by the existence in the language of words with *ab-* (**abbre**viate, **ab**dicate) and *-(ul)ate* (articulate, matriculate). The words *doubt, debt, advance, advantage, adventure* show what can happen when there is some real or putative discrepancy between the existing form of a word and its etymological history. *Doubt* and *debt* were borrowed into English from French at a very early date – between 1175 and 1225. The consonant <-*b*-> in these words (from Lat. *dub-* and *deb-* respectively) at that time had already been lost both in pronunciation and in spelling. This explains the absence of [b] in the pronunciation of these words. During the Renaissance, classical scholars became concerned about the "proper" form of these words and gradually reintroduced the *-b-* in their spelling on the analogy of newer borrowings and forms such as *dubious, debit*. *Advance, advantage, adventure* are examples of the *ad-* prefix resisting assimilation before [-v] (Chapter 6). This, however, was not true in Old French, from where these words were initially borrowed; loanwords such as **a**venue, **a**venge, **a**ver, etc. indicate that the combination of *ad-*+a [v-] initial root in French borrowings normally ends up as [av-]. In Middle English the words *advance, advantage, adventure* had no *-d-* in the prefix. The *-d-* came in later, reintroduced by overzealous classicists on the model of Latin; presumably it is here to stay in the pronunciation as well as in the spelling.

Examples of opaque etymologies are quite numerous: the very first root listed in the "Indo-European Roots" section of the *American Heritage Dictionary*, is the root *ag* 'to drive, draw, move.' The root is phonetically and semantically transparent in *act, agile, agitate, ambiguous, intransigent*. Somewhat more complex, but still possible, is the phonetic connection between *ag* and the derivatives *axiom* and *cogent*. However, without the help of the dictionary one could not guess that *essay, embassy*, and even *squat* (!!!) belong to that root phonetically. Nor is it in any way semantically possible to extract the wildly divergent current meanings of *ambassador, synagogue*, and *podagra* from the basic meanings of the morpheme *ag*.

Finally, there is some completely unpredictable allomorphy where the variation of sounds is apparently random and defies generalizations. The best we can do with these is to take notice of the variants and the words in which they appear. Specialized etymological dictionaries are quite helpful in this respect. Here are some examples of unpredictable allomorphy:

circ, curv, cor 'round, around': *circle, curvaceous, cornice*
cli, cliv, clin 'lie, bed, lean': *clinic, decline, inclination, proclivity*
cub, cumb 'lie, hollow': *incubate, recumbent, succumb*
dei, div 'god, augury': *deity, deism, divine, divinity*
don, dat, dot, dor, dos, dow 'give': *donor, data, anecdote, Dorothy, dose, dowager*
vac, van 'empty, vain': *evacuate, vacancy, evanescent, vacation, vacuum, vanish, vanity*

7   False cognates

Knowledge of allomorphic changes and the basic techniques of parsing will help you discover and verify the real identity of cognates. The misanalysis of unfamiliar material is always a danger, however. Homophony can lead to the wrong division of a word into its components; reconstructing a word's semantic history and associations is also treacherous. The following sections will alert you to some of the ways in which parsing and interpretation of the meaning of an unfamiliar word can go astray.

7.1   Boundary misplacement

New words. Our first concern when we encounter an unfamiliar word is to decide where exactly to draw the boundaries, if any, within that word. The decisions can be hard, especially in the context of exposure to so much new information about morphemes whose existence we had been unaware of. Often a string of morphemes or words can be interpreted in more than one way, especially out of context. The placement of boundaries then will depend on what is on our minds at the moment, or the greater familiarity of one interpretation over another. Parallels to boundary misplacement in borrowed vocabulary are found in the everyday errors, deliberate puns and *double entendres* we seek and hear in *syntax* vs. *sin tax, ice cream* vs. *I scream, sly drool* vs. *slide rule, fast ring* vs. *fa string*, and names like *Polly Glott, Eileen Forward, Sarah Bellum*; see also Chapter 9, Section 1.4.

Encountering a familiar-looking morpheme in a complex word can trick us into an erroneous parse. In the following example, an asterisk means that the analysis is wrong:

anathema: < **a(n)* 'not'+*nat* 'be born'+*hema* 'blood'

Though phonetically plausible, this misanalysis computes the meaning of *anathema* as some weird and absurd 'bloodless birth.' In fact, the real meaning of this word is a semantic extension of different components: 'back'+'place,' i.e. 'away (from mainstream society), and therefore accursed and loathed':

> *anathema*: < *ana* 'back'+*the* 'to place'+*ma* – noun suffix

Let us take another example. In the derivatives **mon***itor*, *premo****mon***ition*, etc., the root *mon* 'think' is the *o*-grade allomorph of *men*, *mn*, as in *demen*ted, ad**mon**ish, **mn**emonic. However, it would be wrong to parse the words **mon**arch, **Mon**day, **mon**th into *mon*+ the recognizable end of these words: a *mon+arch* is not a 'thinking ruler,' *Mon+day* is not a day (or at least *the* special day) for contemplation, a *mon+th* is not wisdom. **Mon**ster, on the other hand, is derived from the same root, where it has the meaning 'warn': a *monster* is something that you need to be warned against.

Predicting or memorizing all possible combinations of roots and affixes is an inhuman task, and over-enthusiastic etymologizing can lead to errors in boundary identification. Usually, the proper context will provide fairly reliable clues as to the correct parse. Imagine encountering the word *neotenic* in a biology book in the sentence "These animals are *neotenic* and retain their larval character throughout life." Technically, there are several ways to divide the word:

> neotenic < **ne* 'not'+*ot* 'ear'+*en* 'verb'+*ic* 'adj.'
> < **ne* 'not'+*ot* 'ease'+*en* 'verb'+*ic* 'adj.'
> < *neo* 'new, young'+*ten* 'hold'+*ic* 'adj.'

Since the word appears in a context describing the retention, the *holding* of larval, or *young*, *prior to maturity*, characteristics, logic dictates that only the last parsing will produce the combination of meanings that fit the context. Or, having just learned the root *via* 'way, road,' and knowing that *ad-* is subject to total prefixal assimilation (Chapter 6, Section 4.1), as in *avenge* (< Lat. *ad vindicare*), *avenue*, you want to know what the origin of the word *aviation* is. Since it has to do with transportation, one would be tempted to seek a connection with 'way, road.' Yet the word *aviation* is not composed of *ad+via+ation*. Its etymology is more poetic than that: *aviation* contains the root *avi* 'bird, fly'+*ation*. Parsing is useful and revealing, but it should be done with utmost care and regard for form and context; if in doubt, consult the dictionary.

7.2   Homophony in roots and affixes

The dangers of misanalysis persist beyond assigning the morpheme boundaries in the right places. Root and affix **homophony** ('sounding alike') is another potential source of confusion. Chapter 9 will discuss the phenomenon of word homophony – *caster–castor*, *seen–scene*, *sole–sole* – in greater detail. Misidentification due to root or affix homophony is easy to avoid if one is already familiar with the meaning of a parsable word: no one will associate **ped**iatrician with taking care of people's feet, or *biped* with a pair of children. We know that *genuflection* will not alter the hereditary features of an organism, and that *gene therapy* is not a procedure specific to injured knees. But then, most of us would be puzzled if some keen observer of the features of our language asked us why *invisible* should be something that cannot be seen, while *invaluable* is something *very* valuable. Is a *seditious* person really *sedentary*? (Actually it's one who 'goes apart.') If you are unduly doting or submissive to your wife, Latin *uxor*, you are *uxorious*, but does *nefarious* suggest that you are unquestioningly devoted to your nephew, Old English *nefa*?

Targeting the wrong association of identical or similar sounding words is the stuff **puns** are made of. The humorous exploitation of the ambiguity arising from homophony can be amusing and clever. The character in the daily cartoon BC, consulting *Wiley's Dictionary* for the verb *to deliberate*, came up with the meaning 'to throw a parolee back in the slammer,' capitalizing on the homophony of the roots *liber* 'free,' and *liber* 'weigh, scales.' Healthy lifestyles have rendered this familiar joke old-fashioned, but the pun: "Is life worth *living*? It depends on the *liver*," still evokes a smile. A famous pun, attributed to Dr. Johnson, is that when asked about the difference between men and women, he responded: "I can't *conceive*, madam, can you?"

On a serious note, before we can either parse or pun with confidence, especially on classical words, we must be alerted to the most frequently encountered homophonous morphemes. The rest of this chapter is intended to increase your awareness of root and affix homophony and help you avoid involuntary puns and socially embarrassing blunders.

7.2.1   Root homophony[13]

cap 'take, contain' as in *capture* vs.
cap 'head' as in *decapitate*

cit 'put in motion' as in *incite* vs.
cit 'civic' as in *city, citizen*

col 'filter' as in *percolate* vs.
col 'live, grow' as in *bucolic*

cur 'care' as in *curator* vs.
cur 'run' as in *recur*

dec 'ten' as in *decade* vs.
dec 'fitting' as in *decorum*

fer 'wild' as in *feral* vs.
fer 'bring, bear' as in *fertile*

fil 'offspring' as in *filial* vs.
fil 'thread' as in *filament*

gen 'origin' as in *genesis* vs.
gen 'knee' as in *genuflection*

ger(on) 'old' as in *geriatric* vs.
ger 'carry' as in *belligerent*

gn 'origin' as in *cognate* vs.
gn 'know' as in *cognition*

gon 'origin' as in *gonad* vs.
gon 'knee, angle' as in *orthogonal*

---

[13] Some of the homophonous pairs start out as semantic and morphological variants of the same root and are listed under the same head entry in *The American Heritage Dictionary of Indo-European Roots*, ed. Calvert Watkins (Boston: Houghton Mifflin Co. 1985). The semantic divergence in such instances (e.g. IE **ar* 'to fit together' producing both *artistic* and *arthritis*) is so extensive that it justifies the separate treatment under the rubric of "etymological pitfalls."

her 'inherit' as in *in**her**it* vs.
her 'stick, hold' as in *in**her**ent*

homo 'human being' as in ***homo**icide* vs.
homo 'same' as in ***homo**nym*

hum 'earth' as in ***hum**us* vs.
hum 'moist' as in ***hum**id*

lab 'seize' as in *syl**lab**le* vs.
lab 'lip' as in ***lab**ial*

lat 'carry' as in *col**lat**e* vs.
lat 'side' as in *col**lat**eral*

leg 'choose' as in *e**leg**ant* vs.
leg 'law' as in ***leg**al*

liber 'free' as in ***liber**ty* vs.
liber 'weigh' as in *equi**libr**ium*

lign 'wood' as in ***lign**eous* vs.
lign 'line' as in *a**lign***

med 'middle' as in ***med**iate* vs.
med 'attend' as in ***med**icate*

mel 'song' as in ***mel**ody* vs.
mel 'dark' as in ***mel**anoma* vs.
mel 'honey' as in ***mel**lifluous*.

men 'month' as in ***men**struate* vs.
men 'think' as in ***men**tal* vs.
men 'lead' as in *a**men**able*

mon 'think' as in *pre**mon**ition* vs.
mon(o) 'one' as in ***mon**arch*

mor 'custom' as in ***mor**ality* vs.
mor 'stupid' as in ***mor**on* vs.
mor(t) 'die' as in ***mor**ibund*

nat 'swim' as in ***nat**ant* vs.
nat 'be born' as in ***nat**ive*

nom 'law' as in *astro**nom**y* vs.
nom 'name' as in *ig**nom**iny*

od 'journey' as in ***od**ometer* vs.
od 'song' as in *pros**od**y*

or 'speak' as in ***or**acle* vs.
or 'appear' as in ***or**iginal*

ot 'ear' as in ***ot**ology* vs.
ot 'ease' as in ***ot**iose*

pal 'cover' as in ***pal**liate* vs.
pal 'pale' as in ***pal**lor*

par 'show' as in *ap**par**ition* vs.
par 'produce' as in ***par**ent* vs.
par 'setup' as in *pre**par**ation*

ped 'child' as in ***ped**iatrician* vs.
ped 'foot' as in *bi**ped***

pen 'tail' as in ***pen**is* vs.
pen 'punish' as in ***pen**alty* vs.
pen 'almost' as in ***pen**insula*

pha(n) 'show' as in *epi**phan**y* vs.
pha 'speak' as in *a**pha**sia*

pol 'pole' as in ***pol**ar* vs.
pol 'city' as in ***pol**ice*

prec 'pray' as in *de**prec**ate* vs.
prec 'worth' as in *de**prec**iate*

rad 'scratch' as in *ab**rad**e* vs.
rad 'root' as in ***rad**ical* vs.
rad(ius) 'ray' as in ***rad**ial*

sal 'jump' as in ***sal**ient* vs.
sal 'salt' as in ***sal**ine*

sen 'old' as in ***sen**ile* vs.
sen 'feel' as in ***sen**sual*

ser 'arrange' as in ***ser**ial* vs.
ser 'fluid' as in ***ser**um*

serv 'work for' as in ***serv**itude* vs.
serv 'keep' as in *con**serv**e*

sol 'sun' as in ***sol**arium* vs.
sol 'alone' as in ***sol**itude* vs.
sol (hol) 'whole' as in *con**sol**idate*

spir 'breathe' as in *re**spir**ation* vs.
spir 'coil' as in ***spir**al*

ten 'stretch' as in *ex**ten**d* vs.
ten 'hold' as in ***ten**ure*

ter 'frighten' as in *deter*rent vs.
ter 'earth' as in *terrestrial*

via 'way' as in *trivial* vs.
via 'live' as in *viable*

vent 'wind' as in *vent*ilate
vent- 'womb' as in *ventricle*

ver 'true' as in **ver**acious vs.
ver 'turn, roll' as in **ver**tigo vs.
ver 'spring' as in **ver**nal

vir 'male' as in *virility* vs.
vir 'poison' as in *virulent, virus*

The list is not exhaustive, but it provides a good start. It differs from all other published alphabetical root lists where only the homophony of invariable forms is evident, as *vir* 'male' and *vir* 'poison.' In many of the pairs collected here only one of several possible allomorphs is involved in the homophony, e.g. *cit* 'put in motion' has the allomorphs *kin/cin*, as in **kin**etic, **cin**ematography, and *cit* 'civic' has an allomorph *civ*, as in *civil*. Similarly, the allomorphs *men, mon* 'think' show homophony with *men* 'month,' *men* 'lead,' and *mon*(o) 'one,' but the allomorph *mn* 'think' has no homophone.

Awareness of the possibility that two or more identical forms may have different meanings should lead to more informed etymological guesses. The allomorphy information in the preceding chapters can be useful in keeping homophonous pairs apart. The root *ped* 'foot' has an *o*-grade allomorph *pod*: **pedal, pedestrian,** and **podium** are clearly related. The homophonous *ped* 'child' has no allomorphs, and it can be spelled *paed-*. The boundaries can blur, however. The word **pedology** is the 'study of what is under**foot**,' 'study of soil(s),' and it is also 'study of children.' Quite surprisingly, the word **pedigree** is **not** etymologically related to 'offspring,' but comes from the Old French *pie de grue* 'foot of a crane,' through its Anglo-Norman form *pe de grue*, used to denote genealogical branching by association with the branching / | \ mark left by the foot of a crane. The adjective *deciduous* parses correctly into *de* 'down'+*cad* 'fall'+*ous*, with multiple lenition of the root vowel. However, a parse such as *de* 'down'+*cid* 'cut'+*ous* would make equally good sense, and also be quite acceptable semantically. Knowing about homophony is only the first step; often there will be no sure and reliable way of disambiguating homophones except to check your derivations in a dictionary.

7.3   Affix homophony

Full affix homophony is rarer than root homophony. Nevertheless, homophonous affixes do exist, and awareness of the different meanings of one and the same affix can help us avoid misanalysis. For example, the most frequent meaning of the prefix *con-* is 'jointly, together,' but it also means 'altogether, completely,' and in that second sense it merely intensifies the meaning of the root to which it is attached. Thus **con**+*rupt* 'burst, become unsound' turns into **corrupt**, which does mean **very** unsound, but has nothing to do with 'togetherness.' Similarly, **com**fort goes back historically to the sense of having greater **fortitude**, greater strength; it is not derived from the 'togetherness' of *con-*, though perhaps in our understanding of human psychology the two notions can be related. A *complaint* comes from someone who is in a **very plaint**ive mood, but the 'togetherness' of a complainer and an audience is not required. The prefix *dis-* means 'apart, reversal, lacking' in *distend*, *disseminate*, *disallow*, *disrepute*. In *disannul*, *disgruntle*, *disturb*, however, the meaning of the prefix is simply 'more,' i.e. it is an intensifier. The prefixes *in-*, *for-*, *per-* can also be used as intensifiers meaning 'thoroughly, exceedingly, very': **in**candescent, **in**flammable denote objects that are **very** *candescent*, **very** *flammable*; similarly **in**scribe, **in**volve convey the sense of depth and thoroughness. The most **con**-*spicuous* examples of prefix homophony come from prefixes which have an intensifying meaning in addition to their other meanings.

7.3.1   Phonetic rules and homophony

Like root homophony, affix homophony can result from one of the phonetic changes discussed in the previous chapters. In the examples below, there are instances of N-Drop, Prefixal Assimilation, Vowel-Drop, as well as homophony without homography. The affixes to the right of the arrows in the following sets are homophonous:

an- 'not'	→ **a-** (**a**gnostic, **a**moral)
ad- 'to, towards'	→ **a-** (**a**scribe, **a**venue, **a**venge, **a**ver)
on- (Old English)	→ **a-** (**a**fire, **a**float)
an- 'not'	→ **an-** (**an**archy, **an**omaly)
ad- 'to, towards'	→ **an-** (**an**nihilate, **an**notate)
ad- 'to, towards'	→ **ap-** (**ap**posite, **ap**pease, **ap**pend)
apo- 'from, off'	→ **ap(o)-** (**ap**ogee, **ap**ology, **ap**oplexy)
bi- 'two, twice'	→ **bi-** (**bi**cycle, **bi**ennial, **bi**weekly)
by- 'near'	→ **by-** (**by**stander, **by**pass)
dia- 'through'	→ **di-** (**di**optric, **di**orama)
dis- 'apart, asunder'	→ **di-** (**di**ffer, **di**rect, **di**vide, **di**lapidate)
di- 'away from'	→ **di-** (allomorph of de-) **di**minish
di- 'two'	→ **di-** (**di**lemma, **di**syllabic)
dis- 'deprive, reverse'	→ **dis-** (**dis**robe, **dis**regard, **dis**establish)
dys- 'badly'	→ **dys-** (**dys**lexia, **dys**pepsia)
-oid 'like'	→ **-oid** (anthrop**oid**, human**oid**, ov**oid**)
-id 'noun'	→ **-(o)id** (fibr**oid**, polar**oid**, cellul**oid**[14])
par- 'thoroughly'	→ **par-** (**par**don, **par**boil)
para- 'along, beyond'	→ **par-** (**par**enthesis, **par**ody)

---

[14] *Polaroid* and *celluloid* are recent trademarks coined by analogy either to the *-id* in words such as *orchid*, or to the suffix *-oid*, as in *humanoid*.

Some affixes which are similar but not totally identical in form, may also be difficult to parse:

-(i)a 'plural of *-um*'	→ med**ia**, gang**lia**, rega**lia**, va**ria**
-ia 'condition'	→ ane**mia**, insom**nia**, pho**bia**[15]
hyper- 'over, above'	→ **hyper**critical, **hyper**tonic
hypo- 'below'	→ **hypo**critical, **hypo**tonic
infra- 'beneath'	→ **infra**red, **infra**sonic, **infra**structure
inter- 'between'	→ **inter**cede, **inter**lude, **inter**national
intra- 'within'	→ **intra**cranial, **intra**venous, **intra**uterine
per- 'through'	→ **per**ception, **per**secute, **per**chance, **per**fume
peri- 'around'	→ **peri**od, **peri**phery, **peri**scope

7.3.2   Homophony of suffixes

Suffixes can change both the lexical and the grammatical meaning of a word. The suffix *-ory*, for example, has two distinct meanings: one from the Latin *-orium* 'place where,' as in *auditorium*, which forms nouns, e.g. *conservatory, repository,* and an adjective-forming suffix meaning 'connected with, serving for,' as in *illusory, laudatory, mandatory*. Knowing this, we will not gloss *repository* and *dormitory* as 'inactive' and 'sleeping,' or *amatory* or *satisfactory* as the places where one finds love or satisfaction. The suffix *-ose* forms adjectives from nouns, and has the meaning 'full of,' thus *jocose, verbose*. In the specialized language of chemistry, however, the suffix *-ose*, which arose as a nineteenth-century *pseudo-suffix* (see below, Section 8) from a French pronunciation of the word *glucose*, is attached to a special group of carbohydrates: *fructose, dextrose, cellulose*. In its chemical function, *-ose* forms nouns.

Conversion from one grammatical class to another within English can create suffix homophony. In the nouns *dividend, reverend*, the *-end* started out as an adjectival suffix. A similar shift occurred with the suffixes *-ant* and *-ent*, as in *elegant*, adj., but *accountant*, noun. The dual nature of *-ant* and *-ent* is seen in adjective–noun pairs such as *consonant, irritant, migrant, vagrant, convalescent, crescent, patient*. The homophony of these suffixes is an accident of the way in which words of classical origin were adopted into English. In many words the duality never developed; there are two words each with the form *astringent, dependent, resident* in the language, while *client, ingredient, president, regent* are only nouns, and *evident, benevolent, urgent* are only adjectives. Some other suffixes used to derive words of different grammatical classes are:

---

[15] The suffix *-ia* is used also for plants, zoological classes, country names: *wisteria, amphibia, Rhodesia*. The suffix *-a* by itself is used in borrowed words to denote feminine gender – *alumna, Chicana*.

-al (adjective):	→ medicin**al**, semin**al**, torrenti**al**
-al (noun):	→ deni**al**, refus**al**, repris**al**
-ate (adjective):	→ delic**ate**, desol**ate**, Latin**ate**, orn**ate**
-ate (verb):	→ design**ate**, elong**ate**, intimid**ate**, neg**ate**
-ate (noun):	→ cogn**ate**, duplic**ate**, predic**ate**, prim**ate**
-esque (adjective):	→ gigant**esque**, pictur**esque**, statu**esque**
-esque (noun):	→ burl**esque**, humor**esque**
-ic (adjective):	→ kinet**ic**, patriot**ic**, pediatr**ic**, Socrat**ic**
-ic (noun):	→ col**ic**, heret**ic**, metr**ic**, rhetor**ic**, ton**ic**
-ite (adjective):	→ apposite, favor**ite**, contr**ite**, Clinton**ite**
-ite (noun):	→ paras**ite**, retin**ite**, gran**ite**
-ite (verb):	→ exped**ite**, ign**ite**, un**ite**
-ive (adjective):	→ deris**ive**, expens**ive**, oppress**ive**
-ive (noun):	→ execut**ive**, locomot**ive**, miss**ive**
-oid (adjective):	→ paran**oid**, fibr**oid**, tabl**oid**
-oid (noun):	→ alkal**oid**, cellul**oid**, ster**oid**, fibr**oid**
-ute (adjective):	→ abso**lute**, desti**tute**, mi**nute**
-ute (noun):	→ attri**bute**, insti**tute**, sta**tute**, substi**tute**
-ute (verb):	→ attri**bute**, insti**tute**, distri**bute**, substi**tute**

The original affix homophony can be obscured by changes in the pronunciation of nouns, verbs, and adjectives, as in *coordinate*, *delegate*, *duplicate*, *postulate*. The placement of stress can also serve as the marker of grammatical class, as in *present*, *attribute*, *minute*. When affix homophony persists, the context is usually sufficient to disambiguate the grammatical properties of the word.

7.3.3   Mixed homophony: affixes and roots

Some affixes and some roots may have the same form, either inherently, or accidentally, as a result of some derivational process. They may be pronounced and spelled in the same way (*id*, *it*, *par*, etc.), they may differ in the positions allowed for them in the word, as *id* 'that one, particular' vs. *-id*, a suffix for adjectives and nouns. Mixed homophony may involve different spellings, but identical pronunciation, as *poli* 'city' vs. *poly-* 'many.' We can't list all variant forms that might produce the appearance of root–affix homophony. The examples below are only intended to alert the reader to this source of potentially erroneous parsing.

id 'that one, same'	→ **id**entity, **id**em, **id**entify, ib**id**em
id(io) (Gk.) 'personal, private'	→ **id**iom, **id**iot, **id**iosyncrasy
-id 'adj., noun'	→ cand**id**, flu**id**, liqu**id**, orch**id**
it 'go'	→ **it**inerary, ex**it**, in**it**ial, trans**it**
-it 'adj., noun, verb'	→ pos**it**, Jesu**it**, aud**it**, herm**it**, also -ite

ot 'ear'	→ **ot**itis, **ot**ology, **ot**algia
-ot(e) 'noun, nativity'	→ idi**ot**, patri**ot**, Cypri**ot**
par 'give birth'	→ **par**ent, post**par**tum, multi**par**ous
par(a)- 'along, beyond'	→ **par**enthesis, **par**ody
par- 'thoroughly'	→ **par**boil, **par**don
poli 'city'	→ metro**poli**s, Minnea**poli**s, cosmo**poli**tan
poly- 'many'	→ **poly**clinic, **poly**gamy, **poly**morphous
re 'thing, affair'	→ **re**public, **re**alism, **re**ify, **re**bus
re- 'back, again'	→ **re**plica, **re**pose, **re**produce
sed 'sit'	→ **sed**entary, **sed**iment
sed- 'without, apart'	→ **sed**itious

8   Pseudo-suffixes

Burgers and the like. Misanalysis is bound to happen to the speakers of any language at some time, no matter how well educated they are. One of the interesting consequences of misanalysis is that it enriches the inventory of formative elements. The story of the *burger* is a famous example of how the composition of one eponymous word was misinterpreted. The ground-meat patty sandwich we all know as a *burger* was called originally a *Hamburger steak*, after the German city of Hamburg. For speakers of English the adjective *Hamburger* would have been unparsable, but the first syllable must have looked treacherously reminiscent of *ham*. Removing *ham* from *Hamburger* leaves the *-burger* part looking like a separate recyclable unit. And, indeed, *burger* did develop into a root meaning 'a sandwich,' now combining freely with adjectives and other roots that carry information about the ingredients: *double-* and *triple-burger, beefburger, cheeseburger, chickenburger, porkburger, steakburger, fishburger, jumboburger, oysterburger, veggieburger.*

The story of the *-buster* words is similar: it started out as a bound second element of a compound and became very productive in the twentieth century: *blockbuster, broncobuster, crime buster, doorbuster*, etc. – the *OED* lists over thirty words ending in *-buster*. Similar to *-buster* are the formations with *-cast* and *-caster*: *telecast, simulcast, sportscast(er)*. Less obvious are cases in which the wrong parsing of borrowed words has produced morphemes that are either non-existent in the source language: *-cade, -(a)thon*, or that have acquired a form different from that in the original language, as in *-(a)holic*.

-cade	→ aquacade, cavalcade, motorcade
-(a)thon	→ walkathon, telethon, jogathon, strollathon, bikeathon
-(a)holic	→ chocoholic, workaholic, sexaholic, shopaholic

When borrowed compounds are misanalyzed, one of the components can take a new life within English as a separate and productive root. In the late 1940s misanalysis gave us the word *copter*, where the first element of the word *helicopter* was wrongly associated with the sun, Greek *helios* (compare *helium*, *heliotropic*), rather than with *helix*, the spiral that keeps the flying object up in the air. The word *doxy* is a purely English creation based on borrowed items such as *orthodoxy* and *heterodoxy*. It still has a facetious ring about it, probably perpetuated by J. Q. Adams' famous 1778 quip that "Orthodoxy is my *doxy*, and heterodoxy is your *doxy*." This did not deter the *LA Times* from publishing a serious piece on religion which contained *flexidox* in its title. Clever misanalysis can be catchy, amusing, and useful: *prequel* is the opposite of *sequel*, and *prebuttal* is the opposite of *rebuttal*.

9   Semantic variation

The existence of different meanings for one and the same root (**polysemy**) sometimes results in the separation of homophonous roots, as in the case of *cap* 'take' and *cap* 'head,' but more frequently various related meanings continue to reside within the same form. A serious study of classical roots means also taking note of the possible range of meanings that they carry. The root *arch(aeo)* 'foremost, begin, rule' provides a good example of polysemy. The set of its derivatives includes words such as *archaeology*, *archbishop*, *archetype*, *matriarch*, *archipelago*, *architect*. On the surface, these are vastly different words. However, knowing the range of meanings of *arch(aeo)* helps us detect the common semantic denominator among them. The shift from 'beginning' and 'foremost' to 'rule' is logical, the semantic connections are transparent. Matching the right meaning to the right word is as important as knowing the range of meanings. *Archaeology* is not 'the study of ruling systems,' *matriarchy* is not 'the beginning of motherhood,' *archetype* is not 'a domineering type.' These glosses could make a good informed joke, but the analysis is useless if it does not reveal the overall meaning of the word.

Examples of the relevance of semantic variation in the analysis of words abound. The root *cast* means both 'purify' and 'fortify'; without knowing the two meanings we would not recognize that *castrate* and *castle* are cognates. The allomorphs *tag*, *tang* gloss as both 'touch' (concrete) and 'perceive, feel' (abstract); this semantic information is the essential link between the fairly concrete notion **contact**, and **tact**, the abstract perception of social propriety and respect for other people's feelings. The root *lev* 'rise' appears in the homophonous words **levee**. First, **levee** has the concrete meaning of 'embankment,' but the second word **levee** 'a reception, an assembly' is arrived at indirectly; it comes from the royal habit of receiving visitors after rising from bed, especially an afternoon siesta. It is a rather big jump from the **radish** in one's salad to the mathematical *radical*. Why would *regular* and *regal* mean such different things? What is the relationship between a *regent* and a *region*? No discussion of semantic pitfalls can supply all the answers. All we can do is flag the existence of variant meanings for one root and hope that etymological good sense and a good dictionary in hand will produce the right analysis.

10 Multiple derivatives – multiple meanings

Finally, we turn our attention to yet another pitfall – the shifting of the semantic focus, or the complete change of the semantic content of a root in derived words. This can happen either within the scope of a single root, as in *radish* and *radical*, or in the process of suffixation. This section addresses the possibility that two suffixes with the same grammatical meaning can attach to the same root and produce two different words.

Let us look at the two frequent adjective suffixes *-ic* and *-al*. They can be added to some roots twice, compare *diabolic* vs. *diabolical*, *problematic* vs. *problematical*, *rhythmic* vs. *rhythmical*. In these examples the stacking of suffixes with identical grammatical function does not seem to affect the meaning or usage of the words. In another set, the *-ic/ical* variants have the same meaning, but one of the forms is used more commonly: *academic, angelic, ethnic, iconic, semantic, symbolic*. On the other hand, *radical, conical, critical, logical, vertical* appear only in the form with *-ical*. Adjectives ending in *-ic* are easily converted into nouns: *academic, cynic, logic, tropic*, while the corresponding adjectives ending in *-ical* are mostly used as adjectives: *cynical, epical, logical, tropical*, etc. Finally, there are some word pairs in this set where the *-ic* vs. *-ical* distinction is both formal and semantic: *comic* vs. *comical, economic* vs. *economical, historic* vs. *historical*. Here are some more instances of multiple derivatives with different meanings:

-al (adj. /noun) vs. **-tion** (noun):
- → soci**al** vs. associa**tion**
- → propos**al** vs. propos**ition**

-al (adj.) vs. **-ous** (adj.):
- → factu**al** vs. fictiti**ous** (vs. fac**ile**)
- → offici**al** vs. offici**ous**
- → sensu**al** vs. sensu**ous** (vs. sensi**tive**, sens**ible**, sens**ory**, sensation**al**)
- → virtu**al** vs. virtu**ous**

-ic (adj.) vs. **-al** (adj.)
- → dialect**ic** vs. dialect**al**
- → gener**ic** vs. gener**al**
- → (geo)centr**ic** vs. centr**al**
- → ton**ic** vs. ton**al**

-**ity** (noun) vs. -**ness** (noun):
→ commun**ity** vs. common**ness**
→ enorm**ity** vs. enormous**ness**
→ nice**ty** vs. nice**ness**
→ gentil**ity** vs. gentle**ness**

Think further of *animosity–animation–animism*, *audience–audition*, *integrity–integration*, *variation–variance–variety*, and many, many more. These examples illustrate the incredibly rich gamut of possibilities that our language allows on the basis of a finite set of formative elements.

11   Multiple affixes – same meaning

As discussed in Chapter 5, the meanings that affixes carry are not specific; affixes are subject to semantic bleaching. The more general the meaning of a morpheme, the more likely it is to overlap the meaning of another morpheme. Thus, *ab-*, *cata-*, *apo-*, *de-*, and *ex-*, are all used with the meaning 'away.' Affixes from different classical sources may also be (near) synonymous, thus: *multi-*, *pan-*, *poly-*; *mono-*, *uni-*; *dys-*, *mal-*, *mis-*; *syn-, com-*; *meta-, trans-*; *bi-*, *di-*. Finally, there are synonymous pairs where one of the items is from Greek, while the other one comes from Latin: *hemi – semi-* (Latin), or *demi-* (Medieval Latin and French), *hypo – sub, hyper – super.*

9   Semantic relations and semantic change

1   Introduction and terminology

The meanings of words, and semantic analysis generally, can be discussed in terms of *sense variation* around a common core, and in terms of the kinds of *affinities* and *contrasts* we can discern between meanings.

1.1   Sense variation: homophony, homonymy, polysemy

In Chapter 8 we listed and commented on some roots and affixes that can easily be confused. We dealt with them under the umbrella of the neutral term **homophony** ('sounding the same'). All of the pairs below count as homophones:

chair: to sit on vs. *chair* of a department
corn: grain, seed vs. *corn* on toe
crane: a bird vs. *crane* a machine
ear: of corn vs. *ear* organ of hearing
load: of dirt vs. *lode* in a gold mine
meal: ground up vs. *meal* at dinner time
mettle: in the sense of courage vs. *metal* in the sense of iron, copper
pupil: of your eye vs. *pupil* a student
score: a notch, vs. *score* a game result, vs. *score* a group of twenty
sea: body of water vs. *see* verb of perception
seal: aquatic mammal vs. *seal* a device for making imprints
sole: fish vs. *sole* only vs. *sole* of a shoe, vs. *soul* in a religious sense
trip: journey vs. *trip* to obstruct, cause to fall
waist: of a person vs. *waste* squander

The term homophony, useful as it is, bundles together words of the type *chair* (to sit on) – *chair* (of a department) and *corn* (on the cob) – *corn* (on toe). Yet if you look these up in the *OED*, you will find the two meanings of *chair* under one single entry, while there are two separate entries for *corn*. The term *homophony* is thus used to cover two historically distinct types of semantic identity: **homonymy** and **polysemy**.

To be *homonymous* ('having the same name'), words that sound alike must have different meanings and different origins: thus *bear* 'carry,' *bear* 'grizzly,' and *bare* 'nude,' *corn* 'on the cob,' '*corn* on toe,' *riddle* 'puzzle' and *riddle* 'pierce with holes,' *rock* 'stone' and *rock* 'sway to and fro,' fit this definition. As noted above, homophony is the broader term, such that all homonyms are by definition also homophones. Dictionaries have separate entries for homonyms: thus *fast*, n. (1) is 'religious abstinence from some foods,' while *fast* (2) is a nautical term meaning 'rope'; *seal*, n. (1) means 'fish' and *seal* (2) is an 'imprint device.' Some homonyms are also *homographs* – spelled alike: *ash, corn, fast, pupil, sole, seal*.

Polysemy refers to a single word with several different meanings. The differentiation from one into several meanings is most commonly a consequence of the change, usually over long time spans, from concrete to abstract meaning – i.e. increasingly figurative use of language. If you think about almost any root whatever, you will probably find that it has several different meanings. This is typical of what is meant by the word *polysemy*. Over and over again, words which possibly started out with one coherent meaning develop new senses; these senses get differentiated and lose connection with each other. This would be the case with words such as *board, chair, crane, load–lode*. Dictionaries treat them differently depending on the spelling: *board, chair, crane* have their different meanings under single entries in the *OED*, but *load–lode*, and also such historically identical pairs as *flower–flour, metal–mettle* get listed separately.[1] Each of these pairs goes back to one single word, yet only etymologists would recognize them as going back to the same source. However, the histories of these words in any dictionary will indicate that they started out as the same word.

The difference between homonymy and polysemy is represented schematically below:

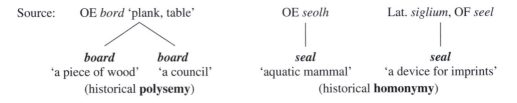

Source: OE *bord* 'plank, table'   OE *seolh*   Lat. *siglium*, OF *seel*

board   **board**   **seal**   **seal**
'a piece of wood'   'a council'   'aquatic mammal'   'a device for imprints'
(historical **polysemy**)   (historical **homonymy**)

Once again, bear in mind that polysemy differs from homonymy historically. Spelling is *not* a reliable cue to the type of relationship between two homophonous words. Many polysemous words are also *homographs*, e.g. *board, chair, crane*, but pairs such as *load–lode, flower–flour, metal–mettle* go back to the same historical source too, yet their different senses have been assigned different spellings. These are separate entries in the dictionaries now, but they started out as graphic variants of the same word. When the different senses of one word diverge *both* in spelling and in pronunciation, as in the pairs *gentle–genteel, petty– petite, person–parson*, such words are treated by all dictionary makers as

---

[1] The *OED*'s policy on homonyms is that "Identically spelt headwords that also belong to the same grammatical category are distinguished by following superior numbers ('*homonym numbers*') and are usually arranged in the order of their earliest occurrence" (Preface to the 2nd edition).

completely separate main entries; in spite of their shared origin, they have taken different routes of phonological change and they are no longer homophonous.

Spelling can be a false friend also when one tries to identify homonymy; as mentioned above, *corn*, *pupil*, *ash*, *sole*, *seal* are both homonyms and homographs, but the words in the homonymous pairs *foul–fowl*, *pale–pail*, *soul–sole*, *there–their*, *two–to*, *waste–waist* preserve the orthographic trace of the distinct origins of these words.

1.2   Diversity of meanings

In principle, the line separating polysemy from homonymy is clear, but in practice the criteria for identifying distinct senses can be problematic. Check in some dictionary the number of separate meanings it lists under everyday words like *about*, *beak*, *devil*, *eat*, *fine*, *go*, *happy*. It is not always easy to decide at which point two meanings of one polysemic word merit separate entries in the dictionary. Until the fifteenth century English had one word *hull* with two meanings; today *hull* 'husk, shell' and *hull* 'the hollow portion of a ship' are treated as two words. The *slice* of bread and the *slice* in tennis are both nouns based on the same verb borrowed from French, meaning 'to cut,' but the development of the tennis term since the end of the nineteenth century has earned it a separate entry in the *OED*. The semantic divergence between the adjective *continent* and the noun *continent* is about the same as that between the different meanings of *base*, *piano*, *volume*, *sensation*, *sentence*, and *solution*, but the decision on how to list these items in the dictionary is a matter of editorial judgment. The fourth edition of *The American Heritage Dictionary of the English Language* (2000) lists the different senses of *base*, *continent*, and *piano* separately, but *volume*, *sentence*, and *solution* are one entry each. For comparison, note that the online edition of *Webster's Third New International Dictionary* has two separate entries for *base* and *piano*, but only one entry for *continent*, noun, and *continent*, adj. These decisions reflect the editors' judgment on which of the senses is "central" and "most commonly sought" (p. xxv). That sense of the word is recorded first. We are all aware of the multiple meanings of *chair*, *club*, *honey* in our language, and more recently, with the computer, *load*, *mouse*, *window*, but these words are still single dictionary entries.

1.3   Similarity and contrast: synonymy, antonymy, hyponymy

Another way of looking at the meanings of words is by relating their meanings to the meanings of other words in the vocabulary, without reference to etymology, pronunciation, or spelling. The main criterion for grouping words together in this classification is the presence or absence of shared or contrastive meaning. The meaning relations we will discuss here are *synonymy*, *antonymy*, and *hyponymy*.

synonymy (**syn** 'with, together'+**onym** 'name' + **y**) is the approximate equivalence in meaning of two or more words: *quick*, *fast*, *rapid*, *speedy*; *search*, *seek*, *frisk, inspect*. Often the set of words that have similar or overlapping meanings is quite large. In addition to *quick, fast, rapid, speedy*, the *Merriam-Webster Online Thesaurus* lists *breakneck, breathless, brisk, dizzy, fleet, fleet-footed, flying, hasty, lightning, nippy, rapid-fire, rattling, snappy, swift, whirlwind*. The interesting question arising from such sets is whether the meanings of these words are fully equivalent. One can be happy to acknowledge a response to one's e-mail describing it as *quick, swift, rapid, fast, speedy*, but if the recipient describes the same response as *brisk, hasty, rattling*, or *snappy*, things are not so happy any more. Is *absolute synonymy* possible? It may be possible to have two different words with exactly the same meanings in all contexts, but this is extremely rare. Pairs often cited as exhibiting absolute synonymy are *anyhow–anyway, everybody–everyone*.[2] The avoidance of complete synonymy in language can be seen as the manifestation of a more general principle of identifying one form with one meaning. This principle counteracts absolute synonymy; therefore the most frequent type of synonymy we find is *near-*, or *partial synonymy*, the type of synonymy exhibited by the synonyms of *quick*, or by sets such as:

- *healthy, sound, wholesome, hale, robust, well, hardy, vigorous*
- *chink, cleavage, cleft, crack, crevice, fissure, rift, split*
- *expect, anticipate, hope, await*

Avoidance of absolute synonymy, in line with the principle of one form – one meaning, is at work also when native and borrowed words have approximately the same meanings. As we pointed out in Chapter 2, Section 2.2, native-borrowed pairs like *borough–city, deem–judge, red–rouge, wonder–miracle, room–chamber*, characteristically develop specialized senses in which each word is used. This is also typical in cases of re-borrowing of the same word, as was the case in sets such as *cattle–chattel–capital, warden–guardian*.

antonymy (**anti** 'opposed' + **onym** 'name' + **y**) is a term for words that have opposite meanings: *soft* vs. *hard, love* vs. *hate, early* vs. *late*. Antonym is the only technical term in this set that has a non-technical *synonym: opposite*. Within the broader umbrella of semantic opposites we can distinguish some subtypes: **contrary** (*hot–cold*), **complementary** (*alive–dead*), **gradable** (*hot–cold, warm–freezing, wet–dry, light–dark, full–empty*), and **non-gradable** (*male–female, married–single, alive–dead*).

hyponymy (**hypo** 'under' + **onym** 'name' + **y**) is a term for a word whose meaning is subsumed under the more general meaning of another word: *oak, beech, poplar* are types of *tree; spring, summer, fall, winter* form the subset for *season*. Hyponymy is a hierarchical relationship and we "file" hyponyms under the superordinate word – all we may remember about the words

---

[2] Cited in Kate Kearns "Lexical semantics" in Bas Aarts and April McMahon (eds.), *The Handbook of English Linguistics* (Oxford: Blackwell Publishing, 2006), p. 558.

caravel, *dinghy*, *junk*, *pirogue*, *skiff*, and *yawl* is that they are some kind of sailing vessel.

1.4   Some more -onyms

eponym (**epi** 'upon' + **onym**): using a proper name as a common noun, as in *sandwich*, *boycott*, *watt*, see Chapter 1, Section 3.6.

heteronym (**hetero** 'other, different' + **onym**): a word spelled like another, but having a different pronunciation and meaning: *bass* 'fish' vs. *bass* 'male voice,' *lead* 'metal' vs. *lead* 'to conduct,' *wind* 'to coil' vs. *wind* 'air in motion.'

meronym (**mero** 'part' + **onym**): 'A word denoting an object which forms part of another object' (*OED*), as the *lead* is of a *pencil*, a *page* is of a *book*, or a *seat* is of a *chair*. The notion is closely related to hyponymy.

metonym (**meta** 'changed' + **onym**): a word used for another with which there is some special association, as in space or time: "I always support the point of view of **Buckingham Palace**."

oronyms:[3] homophones based on misplacement of a word boundary, as in *I scream–ice-cream, sly drool–slide rule, fast ring–fa string*. In *The Language Instinct* (1994), Steven Pinker writes: "[In speech] it is impossible to tell where one word ends and the next begins. The seamlessness of speech is … apparent in 'oronyms,' strings of sound that can be carved into words in two different ways:

> The good can decay many ways.
> The good candy came anyways.
>
> The stuffy nose can lead to problems.
> The stuff he knows can lead to problems.

These are also called *mondegreens* from the name Lady Mondegreen, which is a mishearing of the phrase "laid him on the green" in the ballad "The Bonny Earl of Murray."

plesionyms (**plesi** 'close, almost, near, allied to' + **onym**): near synonyms, differing in the degree of the core property they share, as in e.g. *error* 'an act or thought that unintentionally deviates from what is correct, right, or true' (*AHD*), thus, *erratum, inaccuracy, incorrectness, lapse, miscue, misstep, mistake, slip, slip-up, trip*. These are clearly centered around the same basic meaning but their associations with the intentionality and seriousness of the error are different.

Finally, a small set of words, e.g. *cleave, ravel, oversight, sanction*, may have a pair of opposite meanings. There is no generally accepted term for such words, though the terms *fence-words, Janus-words, contranyms* or *antagonyms* have been proposed.

---

[3] The homophony may be imperfect in slow and careful speech. The term is not in the *OED*. According to Wikipedia, it was coined by Gyles Brandreth and first published in his book *The Joy of Lex* (1980), and it was used in the BBC programme *Never Mind the Full Stops*.

2   How meanings change ("semantic change")

> … Words strain,
> Crack and sometimes break, under the burden,
> Under the tension, slip, slide, perish,
> Decay with imprecision, will not stay in place,
> Will not stay still …
>
> T. S. Eliot, *The Four Quartets*: *Burnt Norton* (1936)

It is unlikely that scholars will ever be able to predict the directions in which particular words will change their meanings. Nonetheless, by looking at a wide range of examples of semantic changes that have happened in the history of the language, one can begin to develop a certain sense of what kinds of change are likely. Information about the original meaning of the morphemes and the intuition developed from observing various patterns of semantic change will help us make better-informed guesses about the meanings of unfamiliar words that contain familiar morphemes. We shall focus first on the **mechanisms** of change – what forces in our society, or what forces in our thinking, typically have brought about semantic change? Then we will turn to a classification of the **results** of semantic change: looked at in a long perspective, how do these changes affect the lexicon?

2.1   External forces

2.1.1   Technology and current relevance

The development of new material and social conditions may cause words or some of their senses to become unnecessary outside a specialized historical context. Here are some curious examples:

caboose meaning 'early nineteenth-century cast-iron cooking range used in ship galleys'
catasta 'a block on which slaves were exposed for sale'
caxon 'a kind of old, worn-out wig'
curtal 'an obsolete musical instrument, a kind of bassoon'
fletcher 'one who makes or deals in arrows'
guinea 'an English coin equalling 21 shillings'
merlon 'the part of a battlement between the crenels'
replevin 'restitution of cattle'
wimple 'a medieval head-covering'

Material obsolescence of the referent is only one of the forces behind the instability of words and meanings. When *new* technology changes the way we conduct our daily life, the words which refer to it change also. Consider the word *compute* and its derivatives – *computer, computation*. It used to mean 'to count, to reckon, to calculate.' Indeed the word *count* is a direct descendant (through French) of the Latin verb *computare* 'to count.' The first definition of *computer* in the *OED* is "One who computes; a calculator, reckoner; spec. *a **person** employed to make calculations in an observatory, in surveying*," with citations going back to 1646.

The computer, however, is no longer a 'person' or a 'counter': it has given its name to a new branch of science, *computer science*, we talk of *computer addiction*, *computer-aided design*, *computer ethics*, *computer literacy* (blended into *computeracy*), *computer viruses*, and even *computerese, computerholic, compusex*. Computers deal with text, graphics, images, symbols, music; the original meaning of 'counting' in computer language has been completely supplanted by the new associations of 'computing.'

As computers became common, many words changed their meanings because they could conveniently be used to refer to aspects of computing. For example, you can *customize* your *commands*, where *customize* refers to setting up specialized *function keys*. Think of the range of meanings that the word *custom* has outside the computer domain: *custom* as in 'characteristic behavior of a society,' *custom* as in 'to collect duty as you pass through customs at the airport,' *customer* as in 'one who shops at a store.' The word *command* in *customizing your commands* is a specialized sense of a word that once meant 'an order given by a person of higher rank to a person of lower rank' – now it means 'give a signal to the program by pushing a certain key or clicking the mouse on the right icon.' In defining *command*, we have introduced two new meanings: *mouse* and *icon*. Until the computer age, *icon* most commonly referred to pictorial representations of sacred personages in the Eastern Orthodox Church. The lively *mouse* is an input device, it can be *mechanical* or *optical*, it is connected through a *mouseport*, or is *wireless*, and it can cause *mouse elbow*. The computer revolution has given rise to new meanings for ordinary words. You can open two *windows* on your *screen*, select computing operations from a *menu*, use hyphenation *tools* from your *tools menu*, select a *hyperlink*, *paste* a section from one document into another, look at something called a *clipboard* which is neither "clipped on" nor a board, you find the *bug* in your program, you *surf* the *net*, and many more: *anchor* (1998), *application, back-up, Bluetooth* (1998), *bookmark, browse, bullets, cache, clip(art), close, crash, cookie, dashboard, drag, flaming, Firewire, floppy, formatting palette, function keys, gateway, hyperlink, icon, keyboard, load, lurk, mainframe, mailbox, memory, migrate, mount, navigate, net, nibble, off-* and *online, open, password, Powerpoint, surf, toggle, virus, widget, worm*.

The computer-related examples are numerous and striking, but the process they illustrate is neither new nor isolated. The word *shuttle*, whose original meaning is 'a device used in weaving,' is more frequently used today in its later, extended figurative meaning of anything that goes back and forth: a *shuttle bus*, a *shuttle flight, shuttle service, shuttlecraft*, the *space shuttle*, and, in politics, *shuttle diplomacy*. For some less-dramatic examples, think of the nineteenth-century meaning of *station wagon*, 'a horse-drawn covered carriage.' Going further back, notice the difference between the literal sense of *shepherd* vs. its meaning in a phrase like 'The Lord is my *shepherd*, I shall not want.' In many Christian denominations, *pastor* is the name for the leader or minister. Its original meaning is 'shepherd,' and of course it is cognate with *pasture*.

Another example comes from the history of the word *hierarchy*. Today it means 'a system of ranking,' but it started out as a term referring to the three divisions of angels and their ranking, from which it developed the meaning 'sacred rule,' used by the Church to describe the successive order of pope, cardinals, archbishops, bishops, priests, all arrayed from top to bottom in a branching structure of authority. Since it provided a natural model for the dissemination of authority, it spread to military and governmental structures as a superior model for organization, and from there, in a more abstract way, to the natural sciences. *Disaster* 'a bad, unfavorable, star or planet' refers to astrology, in which the future is supposed to be predicted by configurations of stars. Our faith in such predictions was shattered long ago, but the word maintains its meaning in a changed society. *Doctor* meant 'teacher,' and in that meaning it survives as an occasional title for professors. The medical sense, now the norm, was acquired gradually from the association with higher education that was characteristic of physicians.

2.1.2   Changing cultural relevance

As our world changes, we change the meanings of the words which refer to it. Consider the *default setting* of some parameter in a computer. *Default* means 'failure.' It stills refers to bank failures or individual failures to live up to financial obligations ('to default on a loan'). The current computer meaning does not appear even as recently as the first edition of the *American Heritage Dictionary* of 1973, namely 'the setting to which the program returns when no special setting is selected.' Computers have become widely used and understood subsequent to that date, and that fact has established very recently what is now one of the two principal meanings of the word, the computer sense. Thus, we can say that the cultural relevance of the word has changed.

One area in which we are keenly aware of the social significance of words is the naming of groups of people. A shift of attitudes often renders group labels socially unacceptable: *bohunk, Canuck, chink, coolie, frog, girlie, Jap, kraut, Paki, pansy, Polack*. Such words are considered so offensive that they are relegated to our "passive vocabulary" and may well be forgotten by the next generation of speakers. Others become highly fashionable or socially relevant: *cool, e-(lectronic), nine-eleven, ecology, ethnicity, hybrid, infomercial, outsource, sustainability*.

Changing cultural relevance is inevitable. All languages at all times reflect the needs, perceptions, interests, attitudes of their speakers. As the speakers and their social environment change, so do the words they use, both in form and in meaning. Our language is full of amusing examples of changing cultural relevance, most of which pass by without notice. Living in a *duplex* does not evoke the image of something folded twice. *Trivia* is transparently 'three ways' or 'three roads,' but that etymological sense is so far removed from the present meaning that we have to be told that in the Middle Ages, it was the lower division of the seven liberal arts, comprising grammar, rhetoric, and logic, eventually considered uninteresting, trifling, of little consequence. We do not think of the word *suffrage* in a phrase like *women's suffrage* as having anything to do with breaking, but it means literally 'broken under,' referring to the use of broken tiles for ballots in ancient Greece. During World War II, the word *axis*, a neutral geometric term, was adopted for the alliance of Germany and Italy in 1936, later including Japan and other nations. Subsequent history cast a blight on this word, and now it is a negative word, identifying those who were opposed to the Allies. The Allies, on the other hand, were "the good guys," from an anti-fascist perspective, though the word *ally* is a neutral word meaning 'associate, kinsman,' related to *alloy* 'something bound up.' More recently, the adjective *affirmative* in the phrase *affirmative action* has been interpreted to carry either positive or negative meaning depending on the context and the political views of the speaker and the audience. All such changes are of course unpredictable: they depend on changing technology, changing customs, even historical accidents of all kinds.

2.1.3   Other types of associations

Elegant means 'one who selects out,' based on √*leg*, i.e. someone who picks wisely. An elegant person, for example, is taken to be elegant because he or she selects clothes and accessories wisely. By association with the high price of quality goods, the word comes to mean 'exclusivity,' as in a phrase like 'the elegance of Rodeo Drive.'

What is the relation of *logic* to words? Logic has to do with the study of reasoning; and since reasoning is associated with language (√*log* means 'word,' originally), the association takes over the meaning and now logic is not thought of as having much to do specifically with words.

Consider *adore*. It means, literally, 'to speak to.' At some point in history, this kind of speaking came to be the speech of prayer, 'speaking to God.' Eventually the association went even further: looking heavenward, imploringly, would now be described as 'adoration.' Wordsworth has a wonderful line in a sonnet about a strikingly beautiful evening: "It is a beauteous evening, calm and free, The holy time is quiet as a Nun, Breathless with adoration." The point is, the root which meant 'speak' has come to refer to silent worship, a change brought about by association with prayer.

Scripture just meant 'writing,' but by association with religious writing, in particular the Bible (which itself just meant 'book'), it came to mean 'religious writing,' and not just any religious writing but that which is found in the Holy Bible of the Christian tradition. On the other hand, by a quite different association, the verb *prescribe* and its associated noun *prescription* are now limited almost entirely to what a physician writes out to allow one to obtain medication. The association with medicine is what has driven the particular semantic change we find in it.

The connection between *amble* and *ambulance* is an accident of war: *ambulance* comes from a longer phrase, *hospital ambulant*, a 'moveable hospital,' one which could be present on the battlefield to tend to the wounded. It was merely shortened to the second part of the phrase, giving us *ambulance*.

Metonymy (see Section 1.4 above) is an association of a particular type, usually accidental association in space or time. The real referent and the transferred referent are associated by virtue of being in the same place, as when we speak of *Hollywood* standing for the US film industry, or *The White House* when we are referring to the current President of the United States and his staff (association of both place and time, since *The White House* can only refer to the president identified with a particular period of time); *pigskin* 'football' is an example of association through material, and so is *rubber* in the expression 'burn some rubber.' Metonymy can be extended to cover changes resulting from other associations such as part and whole – *drink the whole bottle, give me a hand, live by the sword*. From the classical vocabulary of English, an example is *exposition*, which meant 'putting things out.' Now the event at which new cars are displayed, or new computer technologies or whatever, is called an exposition. Another classical example is *commissary*, which in America means a place where food and other supplies are dispensed in the military. Its meaning still, in Britain, and its only meaning earlier in history, was an officer of the law or of the military forces to whom responsibility was assigned for – among other possibilities – the supply storehouse. The association is between the person (to whom the term originally referred) and the place of their work.

2.2   Internal forces: analogy

The association covered by the notion of metonymy is due to a more general cause: analogy. Analogy involves the perception of similarity between some concrete object or process and some abstract concept or process. The basic meaning of a word is related to another meaning in such a way that by analogy there can be a transfer or extension of meaning from one to the other. This implicit comparison is known also as **metaphoric** extension, and the resulting new word is a **metaphor** (*meta* 'beside, after' + *phor* 'carry'). For example, if someone is the *head* of a department, the relationship of the head to the body – the **literal** sense – is being used in an **extended** or **figurative** sense, in which there is an analogical ratio set up: *head* is to *body* as *head* (= *leader*) is to *department*. It can be seen as an equation:

```
                meaning
            /            \
     literal            extended
    head/body     =     leader/group
```

Thus if we say that "The population is *mushrooming* all over the world," we are comparing the rapid growth of population to the unmanageable fecundity of a mushroom. If we say, "The New Hampshire primary will be the acid test of this candidacy," we are metaphorically comparing the ability of a politician's campaign to survive the results of close scrutiny in New Hampshire with the well-known test for genuine gold by means of using nitric acid. If we speak of "The strong arm of the law," we are comparing an individual's strong arm and the abstract notion of law enforcement. If we speak of a "traffic bottleneck," we are comparing some narrowing of traffic flow with the neck of a bottle where the contents flow more slowly (think about getting ketchup out of the bottle!).

Virtually any perceived similarity can be the basis of analogical change and the source of a new meaning. Thus √*cad* means 'fall,' and the analogy in *recidivism* is between returning to crime and falling backwards – returning to crime is like falling backwards. All analogies can be stated in a similar manner: some abstract relationship reminds one of a concrete relationship. The concrete relationship may be topological (*above, below, behind, in front of, inside of, beside*), or it may be temporal (*before, after*), or it may be a matter of experiential similarity (*smell–hear–feel–touch–taste*).

The analogy can be quite remote and even unlikely, but if it catches someone's fancy it may easily stick in the language. Here are some examples in which the etymology depends precisely on analogy of the type seen in the phrases above. In each example we try to formulate the basis for the comparison, even though it is sometimes tediously obvious:

companion: *con* 'together' + Lat. *panis* 'bread' → 'any partner, comrade, associate' (basis: sharing bread, i.e. eating together)
construct 'piled up together' (like stones forming a house)
    → construct a sentence (piling up words like stones)
culminate 'reach the top of a hill'
    → 'to reach a decisive point, after struggling as if climbing'
dependent 'hanging from something'
    → 'supported by virtue of someone else's money or power'
educate 'to lead forth, to bring up'
    → 'to make competent, to raise to a higher social or cultural level'
illustrate 'to purify, to give physical light to, to throw light on'
    → 'to make clear, demonstrate visually or by reasoning'
offend 'strike against'
    → 'create bad feelings'
precipitate 'head in front, falling forward'
    → 'to behave in a manner that lacks forethought'
progress 'to step forward'
    → 'to improve, to move toward a better existence'
provoke 'call forth, summon'
    → 'to incite with anger or desire, to irritate'

The role played by analogy cannot be overestimated. It is fair to say that the mind looks for concrete ways of representing abstract concepts, and the concrete meanings clarify the intended abstract relationships. Analogy is the most frequent and most important source of semantic enrichment of the language.

2.3   Internal forces: semantic nativization

One of the most remarkable characteristics of the English vocabulary today is the diversity of its sources. Our survey of borrowing at the beginning of this book revealed that about two-thirds of the most frequently used 10,000 words in the language are non-Anglo-Saxon. In addition to adapting the new loan-words phonologically, as in the application of vowel reduction and vowel shifting (Chapter 5) and palatalizations and affrications accompanying dental stop lenition (Chapter 6), borrowings frequently undergo semantic change. The most obvious trigger of meaning change in the loanword is the pre-existence of a word, or words, with similar meanings in English. Following the principle of avoidance of synonymy (see Section 1.3 above), loanwords may lose some of their original senses or develop new senses within English: *infidel* is not the same as *unfaithful*, although their components correspond directly to 'not'+ 'belief' + adj. Adaptation occurs without regard to, or knowledge of, the original meaning(s) and grammar of the word. Here are some more examples of words whose meaning in the donor language is the same as the meaning of the native word, but after "nativization" in English, the loanword meaning has changed because of new associations:

babushka (Russ.) 'grandmother'	*babushka* (PDE) 'head covering'
bonus (Lat.) 'good'	*bonus* (PDE) 'extra payment'
credo (Lat.) 'I believe'	*credo* (PDE) 'a set of beliefs'
diet(a) (Gk.) 'way of life'	*diet* (PDE) 'food regimen'
ego (Lat.) 'I'	*ego* (PDE) 'self, self-esteem/consciousness'
macho (Sp.) 'male'	*macho* (PDE) 'aggressively virile'
rouge (Fr.) 'red'	*rouge* (PDE) 'cosmetic aid'

3   The results of semantic change

We turn now from the mechanisms of change to the consequences of change. Traditionally, the results of semantic change are described and classified in terms of two properties: (1) scope, and (2) status. Other categories of traditional classification, like relation to culture and technology, have been considered above, because they are part of the causes of change.

3.1   Scope change

How broad is the range which the meaning of a word covers – how much does it include? A familiar example will illustrate this property: *meat* used to mean 'any kind of solid food,' as in the familiar expression 'meat and drink,' and now it means only a particular kind of food, namely the flesh of animals. The scope of the word has been **narrowed**. The scope of a word's meaning can, of course, change in the opposite direction: originally the word *escape* meant 'to get out of one's clothing, lose one's cape while fleeing' (*ex* 'out of'+ Medieval Latin *cappa* 'cloak, cape'). Today we could escape and keep our cape on, if we wore capes any more. Moreover, we can escape our daily worries by sitting on the couch and watching a movie at home. The scope of the word has been **widened**.

Another type of scope change is **semantic bleaching**, where the original meaning of the word has been eroded away and generalized by heavy usage, as in words like *very* (originally 'true'), *awful* ('full of awe'), *terrible* ('able to cause terror'). The ultimate examples of bleaching are the words *thing*, *do*, *nice*, and *okay*, and of course the more a word is bleached the further left it moves on a scale of hyponymy. *Thing* originally referred to a sort of parliamentary town-hall meeting, hence *affair*, *act*, any kind of *business*. The bleaching of this word is so complete that people have come up with variations such as *thingum(a)bob*, *thingummy*, *thingamajig*, possibly in the desire to restore some of the "lost color" of *thing*. *Nice* (ultimately from Lat. *ne* 'not' + *sci* 'know,' *nescius* 'ignorant') was used in English until the thirteenth century only with the meaning 'foolish, stupid,' then in the fifteenth century it developed the meaning 'coy, shy,' and from that, in the sixteenth century, it changed into 'dainty, fastidious, accurate' (as in the derivative *niceties*), 'delightful' in the eighteenth century, and a very loose positive adjective today. And *okay*, though there has been debate about it, seems to have started as a sort of joke, an acronym for 'Oll Korrect,' attributed to President Andrew Jackson. It was probably distributed widely also as an abbreviation of 'Old Kinderhook,' Martin van Buren, who followed Jackson in the presidency and whose supporters formed "OK clubs" to solicit money for his campaign. This very general affirmative word was apparently needed and has been borrowed into virtually every language in the world whose speakers have had any significant amount of international contact.

Semantic bleaching is a necessary part of the process known as grammaticalization, whereby a content word becomes a grammatical word. *Do* meant 'to put, lay, cause' – "I did him (to) cry" meant 'I caused him to cry' and gradually started replacing *any* verb; when used as an auxiliary today, *do* has no lexical meaning – it has been grammaticalized and is functionally equal to an inflection. Similarly the verb *go* in "I am *going* to submit the application" is no longer associated with walking, ambling, shuffling, or striding – its completely bleached version (*gonna*) is a new entity in the language. Note that we cannot say, "I'm gonna a movie tonight," though "I'm going to a movie tonight" is fine.

3.1.1   Loss of specificity

Loss of specificity is another outcome of scope change. This process could equally well be called **over-generalization**, but loss of specificity has the slight advantage of reflecting a common human tendency. All of us are prone to generalizing, prone to failures of specificity. One of the techniques we study when we are learning to write acceptable prose is how to be more specific, how to provide details and examples, how to find the right word for the meaning we have in mind. Nonetheless, in everyday speech and casual writing we choose the more general meaning because most of us have no particular talent for words. This tendency shows up historically when words acquire broader and more general meanings. A word like *docile*, from the same root as *doctor*, originally meaning 'teachable,' has developed the sense of non-resistant, pliable, a kind of over-generalization of the notion 'teachable.' *Guy Fawkes'* infamous first name lost its specificity with the proliferation of November 5th effigies of the criminal; then *guys* began to be used of males of strange appearance, then it was broadened to refer to any males, and now it is generalized (especially in the plural) to any group of people, including groups of females. Let us examine this notion of overgeneralization more deeply.

All the words of a language can be arranged in **hyponymic sets**, see above, Section 1.3. How does a relation of hyponymy help us understand the notion of overgeneralization in historical semantic development? A hyponymic relation exists between two words when one can replace the other without changing the reference, but not vice-versa. Thus *scarlet* is more specific than *red*: if one can say, "Her face was scarlet," one can always say "Her face was red." Here is a hyponymic diagram which helps make the notion clear (the symbol [⊃] 'is the superset of, or contains as a subset' means the term to the right is a hyponym of the term to its left, and the leftmost one is the most general word; two terms on the same level, not hyponyms of each other, are separated by a comma):

> *go* ⊃ *walk* ⊃ *amble, shuffle, stride, …*

What this says is, "*Go* is the most general and least specific of these words; *walk* is a type of *going* but not all going is walking; *amble, shuffle, stride* are types of walking but not conversely." When, as in this example, there are several equally good hyponyms and none of them is a hyponym of the other (e.g. *shuffle* is not a hyponym of *amble*), we call them **co-hyponyms**. Now, when we say that language tends toward loss of hyponymy and favors the more general category – the one at the head of such a hyponymic diagram – it is somewhat clearer what it means to lose specificity.

Where would one look for examples? Answer: that is what a thesaurus is about. A thesaurus lists vocabulary under a small number of the most general categories, the ones that are most likely to come to mind when one is formulating a concept. Peter Mark Roget, the Frenchman who constructed the first useful thesaurus, in the middle of the nineteenth century (1852), called the most general term the "key word," and he tried to compress the language to just one thousand such key categories, which were in turn grouped into a small number of logical categories: abstract relations, space, matter, intellect, volition, and affections. These days nearly all computer word-processing programs include both a dictionary and a thesaurus. A thesaurus is about the same as a dictionary of synonyms. Both are arranged with a keyword that the editors hope we will think of as the general category for an idea, and we will follow from there to more and more specific words with the special senses that we are looking for. Here are some typical sequences available from the *Merriam-Webster's New Dictionary of Synonyms*:

expert ⊃ *adept* ⊃ *artist* ⊃ *virtuoso* – note how the items on the right necessarily imply the meanings of the ones to the left, but not conversely. You cannot be a virtuoso without being an expert, but the converse is not true at all.

honor ⊃ *glory* ⊃ *renown* ⊃ *fame* ⊃ *celebrity*
likeness ⊃ *similarity, resemblance, similitude* ⊃ *analogy*
limp ⊃ *floppy* ⊃ *flaccid, flabby* ⊃ *flimsy*
lure ⊃ *entice, inveigle* ⊃ *decoy, tempt* ⊃ *seduce*
mistake (v.) ⊃ *confuse* ⊃ *confound*
parsimonious ⊃ *miserly* ⊃ *penurious* ⊃ *niggardly* ⊃ *penny-pinching*
partiality ⊃ *prepossession* ⊃ *prejudice* ⊃ *bias*
enthusiasm ⊃ *fervor, ardor* ⊃ *passion* ⊃ *zeal*
small ⊃ *petty* ⊃ *puny* ⊃ *trivial* ⊃ *trifling, paltry* ⊃ *measly* ⊃ *picayune*

We can now define the notion "loss of specificity" with some precision: the more the words on the right side of these hyponymic rankings approach in meaning the ones on the left, the more general they have become and the more they have lost specificity.

3.1.2 Narrowing/specialization

Narrowing is an unnatural change in that it requires moving to the right on a hyponymic scale – we have already seen that the natural change is to the left, toward greater generality and less specificity. But narrowing takes place quite frequently when common words with non-specialized meanings are borrowed into some scientific field where they are given a highly specialized meaning within the context of one area. The transfer from one area of human experience to another is frequently accompanied by a figurative shift from the more concrete to the more abstract. We have noted recent examples where technology has given specialized meanings to ordinary words: recall terms like *bootstrap, clipboard, desktop, icon, software, style, toggle, tools, vaccine, virus, window* in the analogical and specialized sense we use in reference to our computers. In television, an *anchor* is primarily a 'newscaster,' and only secondarily a nautical object. In linguistics, a syntactic or prosodic *tree* can have *nodes* and *branches*; in these words the analogical transfer is also accompanied by narrowing. The *crescent* of the moon has a very specific shape, but the adjective from which the word is derived, √*cre(s)* 'grow' + *ent* means simply 'waxing, on the increase.' The words below are transparent examples of narrowing:

acquiesce 'become quiet' (general)
    → 'agree without further comment' (narrow, specific)
actor 'one who does something' (general)
    → 'one who has a role in a dramatic production' (specific)
ammunition 'military supplies of all kinds' (general)
    → 'bullets, rockets, gunpowder' (military supplies which explode)
biblical 'relating to a book'
    → 'relating to a particular book'
hound 'dog'
    → 'type of hunting dog'

liquor 'beverage, including water'
>   → 'alcoholic beverage of certain types, excluding wine'

science 'knowledge of any kind'
>   → 'knowledge acquired through controlled experimentation'

3.2   Status change: amelioration and pejoration

Has the reference of the word gone up, or down, in its social status and content? Rising in status is called **amelioration** (from Lat. *melior* 'better'). One classic example of a word that has risen in status is *knight*, which used to mean, quite simply, 'boy, manservant.' Some roots and words are better "social climbers" than others – from a neutral, or even negative original meaning they have attained an improved "social" status. Instances of this type of upwards semantic shift are not as frequent as instances of the opposite development; for some reason words are more likely to lose their status and respectability in the language than to "go up in the world." Note the social unacceptability, or near unacceptability, of *poor, cripple, idiot, stewardess* – we have replaced them with *underprivileged, disabled, mentally challenged, flight attendant*. However, examples of **amelioration** do exist, as the more recent uses of the adjectives *hopping, designer, cool, awesome* testify. The words listed below are instances of amelioration:

dexterity 'right (handedness)'
>   → 'skill'

knight 'stable boy'
>   → 'feudal warrior'
>   → 'lower rank nobility in Britain'

mellifluous (*mel* 'honey' + *flu* 'flow') 'flowing like honey'
>   → 'smooth and melodious,' especially of voice, tune, etc.

meticulous 'fearful, timid'
>   → 'very careful and precise in performance'

pastor 'one who tends sheep'
>   → 'one who ministers to the religious needs of people'

pedagogue 'a slave who takes the children to school'
>   → 'any teacher'

sensitive 'capable of using one's senses'
>   → 'perceptive, keenly observant, responsive'

The main driving force behind amelioration is the social prestige and relevance of the new meaning. Some interesting recent instances of amelioration are associated with our increased awareness of the need to preserve the ecological balance on our planet. The word *sustainable*, borrowed in English in the early seventeenth century, originally had the meaning of 'capable of being borne or endured,' but the *OED* 2001 entry adds the meaning 'relating to, or designating forms of human economic activity and culture that do not lead to environmental degradation, esp. avoiding the long-term depletion of natural resources.'

Pejoration/degeneration. A development of the meaning in the opposite direction, which is perhaps more frequent, is called **pejoration** (from Lat. *pejor* 'worse'). *Hussy* used to mean 'housewife.' *Demagogue* in ancient Greece meant 'a leader of the people,' completely lacking the negative connotations it has today (Hitler and Mussolini were demagogues). The Latin adjective *praeposterus* describes a 'before–behind' relationship, a typical 'cart-before-the-horse' situation. Such situations are undesirable; such inversion is illogical and contrary to reason. The English word *preposterous* now has a strong pejorative meaning and can be used in much broader negative contexts. In one sense, status change is also a scope change. The scope that changes, in both pejoration ('getting worse') and amelioration ('getting better'), is **social** scope. When we focus on status, we ask whether the things these words refer to are higher or lower in the social scale. The examples below give the earlier higher-class or neutral meaning first, and then one or more of the lower-scale meanings the word has acquired in the course of pejoration:

aggravate 'add weight to'
    → 'annoy'
animosity 'high spirits, courage'
    → 'strong dislike'
artificial 'skillfully constructed'
    → 'fake'
brutal 'animal, non-human'
    → 'extremely cruel, ruthless'
censure 'judgment, estimate'
    → 'blame, severe criticism'
chaos 'chasm, gulf'
    → 'total disorder'
obsequious 'following along'
    → 'groveling'
officious 'hard-working in carrying out one's duties'
    → 'over-zealous and offensive in carrying out one's duties'
pretend 'to stretch forth, to assert'
    → 'to feign'

3.3   Mixed examples

We classified the various types of semantic change above according to the factors that set change in motion and the consequences of the change, but in reality most individual instances of semantic change can be seen as examples of two or more of these types simultaneously. The word *vixen* is clearly an instance of figurative use (analogical extension – it used to mean only 'female fox' and now means both the animal, and, you might say, 'foxy female'); it has also undergone generalization of meaning (i.e. the scope of the word has been widened to include not only foxes but also humans). It has furthermore undergone a change in status, namely pejoration (i.e. its associations have become negative). The word *offend* is an example of widening of meaning, analogical extension, and pejoration. Since the late 1970s psychologists have been using the word *bonding* in a highly specialized manner (scope change), extended from its original context, and positive with respect to social values (status change); this is especially obvious if you note the cultural associations of the two cognate nouns: *bonding* vs. *bondage*. *Nepotism*, although historically related to the word *nephew*, is favoritism no longer restricted to one particular family member; its scope has been widened and at the same time its status has gone down. It now refers to any hiring or other practice of favoritism in the workplace which gives an advantage to one's relatives or friends. Our simple everyday phrase *goodbye* is a contraction of the phrase *God be with you*. The change involves both semantic bleaching and a shift in cultural reference (it no longer refers to God).

4   Semantic guesswork

Parsing. The first step in figuring out what an unfamiliar word means is to parse it – that is, divide it into morphemes. We have seen many examples of this and need not go over it again. Given a correct parse, the question is how to go about figuring out the meaning. First we **gloss** it morpheme by morpheme, dividing the surface form into its meaningful components, then showing the basic forms of the morphemes, then the meanings. At this stage of the exercise the result may look dangerously like gibberish. In these examples, the parse is marked by hyphens and the morpheme-by-morpheme gloss is given to the right in quotes:

homeo-stas-is < *homeo-stat-is* 'same' - 'stay' - 'abstract noun (AN)'

To make sense of this, we have to try reading the gloss in both directions to see which makes more sense (usually right to left works better). In this case, a right-to-left reading produces something like 'state of staying the same.' So our full analysis looks like this:

homeo-stas-is < *homeo-stat-is* = 'same' - 'stay' - 'AN'
                                                   'state of staying the same'

Another example that works well in the same direction:

necrophobia < *necro-phob-ia* = 'dead body' - 'fear' - 'condition'
                                               'condition of fear of corpses'

With the word *hieroglyphic*, on the other hand, the easier reading goes from left to right: 'sacred' + 'carving' + adj., that is, 'having the properties of sacred carvings,' though in this case, too, the last morpheme in the string determines whether we are dealing with a verb, a noun, an adjective, or an adverb. The gloss 'having the properties of sacred carvings' is not very helpful: the problem is to figure out what those properties might be. In order to understand what *hieroglyphic* really means, you have to deduce that the carvings are ancient, that they are like letters cut into stone, and that they are hard to read, or at least that it caused a lot of trouble to decipher them. Only in that way can you discover that in addition to referring to the sacred writings on the temples of Egypt, the word can mean simply 'hard to read.'

Consider a word like *supererogation*.

$$super\text{-}ex\text{-}rog\text{-}ate\text{-}ion = \text{'above' - 'out of, beyond' - 'ask, payout' -}$$
$$\text{'V' - 'AN'}$$

If we leave off the *super*, we get 'paying out beyond' or 'something which is paid beyond what was asked for' (no way to know which, in this case: the first is active, the second passive, and either is possible). When we add *super* to the first guess, the meaning is sensible enough: 'something which is far beyond asking.' It could mean, therefore, a really nice favor you might do for someone, something that no one would ask for. That is roughly what it means: 'something which is above and beyond what was asked for.' It refers to the behavior of people who go that extra mile, but it can also mean 'superfluous, unnecessary.'

Now consider the word *apheliotropism*:

$$ap - heli\text{-}o\text{-}trop\text{-}ism < apo\text{-} = \text{'away' - 'sun' - 'turn' - 'state, condition,}$$
$$\text{process'}$$

To produce a good reading for this word, we have to supply a sensible relationship between 'away,' 'sun,' and 'turn'; the *-ism* is the easy part. Starting from the end, first we get 'the state of turning' and then, left-to-right, 'away from the sun.' As soon as we see that, the full reading is obvious, 'condition or state of turning away from the sun.'

One really acquires the ability to make such guesswork come out right only after looking at hundreds of examples, guessing, and not being afraid to be wrong: guess, then check the dictionary, and after a while you get the knack of it.

10   The pronunciation of classical words in English

1   Unassimilated classical words

English contains classical words and phrases of two types:

(1)   Those that have been assimilated into English, and have simply
        become English words: all the early borrowings, also most borrowings
        during and before the Renaissance and most scientific words coined
        recently from Latin and Greek bases. These words follow the phono-
        logical patterns of English, and frequently show semantic *nativization*
        (see Chapter 9, Section 2.3): *abbot*, *circus*, *comet*, *cumulus*, *delta*,
        demon, *locus*, *psyche*, *tunic*, *system*.

(2)   Classical words that are either recognizably recent borrowings, or
        words and phrases fossilized in legal or scientific language. These
        words and phrases are commonly italicized in print: *casus belli* 'rea-
        son for war' (Lat. *casus* 'case' + *belli*, gen. of *bellum* 'war'), *panta
        rhei* 'everything is in flux,' *sensu stricto* 'in the strict sense,' *viva voce*
        'with a living voice, by speaking.' The *OED* editions prior to the current
        New Edition uses the parallel symbol ‖ for a "non-naturalized" or
        "alien" entry.

The bulk of this book has been concerned with the former group, the words of
classical origin that are now fully assimilated into English, and this chapter will
be no exception. Before turning to the main topic, however, it may be useful to
deal with the **second** group and recount briefly how **un**assimilated classical words
and phrases are pronounced in English. The issue with these is: to what extent
does one try to reproduce or simulate "authentic" Latin pronunciation? There
are five traditional systems of Latin pronunciation found in modern times: (1) the
classical Ciceronian,[1] (2) the Italian, (3) the continental, (4) the British, and (5) the
American. The British system, though the one most commonly recorded in
dictionaries, including some American dictionaries, is not in fact the one most
commonly used in American English. It is, however, strongly favored in Britain.
The essence of the British system is that not only the consonants but also the
vowels are pronounced as they would be in a similar English word. Thus even *a*

---

[1] Named after Cicero, the Roman philosopher and politician (106–43 BC).

priori, which is almost universally pronounced so that it rhymes with "I'm sorry" in America, is pronounced in Britain to rhyme with "say pry oh rye." As we will point out below, neither the British nor the American system is thoroughly consistent. For unassimilated words and phrases in America the most acceptable approach is to follow one fairly easy rule: English consonants, continental vowels.[2] And before reading further here, it would be well if you were to review the phonetic explanations and special symbols found in Chapter Five.

1.1   The pronunciation of consonants in unassimilated classical words

It is now generally accepted that the consonants of any classical words in English should be pronounced in accord with the standard values associated with those letters in **English** orthography. In most cases, of course, the values of the consonant letters in Latin and in English have remained the same. In other words, treat the Latin consonant letters in the way that they would most commonly be pronounced in English orthography. Take a phrase like *prima facie*. In ancient Rome, it would have been something like [pri ma ′fa ki e]. In modern English, however, it is generally pronounced [prai ma ′fe ši i]. Other examples of familiar words: *ex officio* would have been something like [ɛks o ′fi ki o] in ancient Rome, but it is now pronounced [ɛks o ′fi š i o]. *Ceteris paribus* would have been [′ke te ris ′pa ri bus], now [′se te ris ′pa ri bus]. *Sui generis* would have been [su i ′ge ne ris] but is now pronounced [swi ′ǰe nə rəs]. The consonant spelled <v> was pronounced [w] in Classical Latin; only classical scholars today are aware of this fact. For this consonant, too, it is best to follow an anglicized pronunciation, so that an expression such as *volenti* 'to a consenting person' which used to be pronounced [wo len ti] is now pronounced [vo ′len ti]. If you want to warn your friends that wine will loosen their tongue, *in vino veritas* is pronounced [in ′vi no ′ve ri tas] and not with [w].

The table summarizes the main differences between the classical and the anglicized pronunciation of consonants:

Letter	Classical Sound	Anglicized Sound	Example
c	[k] always	[s] before i, e	*pace, et cetera, Cicero*
g	[g] always	[ǰ] before i, e	*ab origine, cum privilegio, gemini*
t	[t] always	[š] before i, e	*ab initio, in absentia, ratio*
v	[w]	[v]	*verbatim, vox populi, (modus) vivendi*

---

[2] In this section we follow closely two articles by H. A. Kelly which from their titles and place of publication ("Pronouncing Latin words in English," *Classical World* 80 (1986–87), 33–37, and "Lawyers' Latin: *loquenda ut vulgus?*," *Journal of Legal Education* 38 (1988), 195–207) might appear to be too formidable for the general reader, but which in fact are accessible and strongly recommended.

1.2   The pronunciation of vowels in unassimilated classical words

While we can treat the consonants in unassimilated words and phrases as if they were just unfamiliar English words, the vowels can be pronounced in accord with two quite different systems:

(1)   as normally pronounced in English in that position in the word, the system most favored in Britain, or

(2)   roughly, as normally pronounced in other European languages such as Spanish, German, French, the system used in America.

In either case the consequence is that they are not pronounced in the way they would have been in classical times, though the European-American tradition is much closer.

European values. It is indeed easiest to be consistent in the pronunciation of the vowels of classical words if one simply follows the European values of the vowels given below. The angle brackets < > enclose the letters with which a word is spelled, the square brackets enclose our representation of the pronunciation of the letters when they appear in stressed syllables.

<a> or <au> as in *father, nausea*, represented as [ɑ] in our pronunciation guides: *magna, paribus*[3]

<e> as in *fiancé*, represented as [e]: *ceteris paribus, ad quem*

<i> or <y> as in *machine*, represented as [i]: *Cicero, vino*

<o> as in *hope*, represented as [o]: *locus, opus*

<u> as in either *boot* or *cute*, represented as [ʊ] or [yu]:[4] *summa, urbi (et orbi), tempus fugit*

<oe> like [i] if long, but [ɛ] or [ɪ] if short: *Oedipus, poena*

<au> like [ɑu] in *bout, noun*: *causa, gaudeamus, cum laude*

The letter <a> is not treated consistently in anglicized Latin pronunciation, even though the value [ɑ] is generally favored. The options for the letter <a> in stressed syllables are:

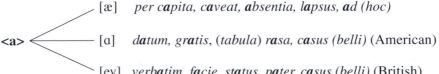

<a>

[æ]   *per capita, caveat, absentia, lapsus, ad (hoc)*

[ɑ]   *datum, gratis, (tabula) rasa, casus (belli)* (American)

[ey]   *verbatim, facie, status, pater, casus (belli)* (British)

---

[3] About half of all American English speakers – roughly speaking, eastern New England, western Pennsylvania and those who live west of the Missouri River – have this vowel in both *father* and *nausea*. In other eastern areas and in the South, the two words will have two somewhat different vowels, but there is little uniformity about *which* two different vowels.

[4] These are not the same; both pronunciations are widely used, even though the latter is actually the English version rather than continental, e.g. *humanum est errare* 'to err is human,' would have [hu-] in the continental version, [hyu-] in the English version.

The letter has three main values in English: the vowel of *cash* [æ], the vowel of *father* [ɑ], and the vowel of *hate* [ey]. The first of these does not correspond to any Latin sound spelled with <a>, and should not, speaking from a technical view, be used in pronouncing unassimilated Latin words, though in practice it is the sound you will hear in *caveat, magnum (opus), lapsus, status,* etc., a spontaneous and natural assimilation of the classical [ɑ] to the English [æ]. The last one, [ey], is the "name value" (you will note that wherever it appears, it has undergone the long-vowel shift, Chapter 5, Section 2.6) that we commonly find in (*prima*) *facie, status, pater,* because the <a> appears before a single consonant, one of the positions favoring the "name vowel." This is the preferred British pronunciation of the "long" <a>. But except for that situation and a few others that cause the same choice to be made, the letter <a> is usually pronounced as indicated above, [ɑ], in the proper circumstances or by people who want to preserve more of the authentic classical flavor of the word or phrase they are using. Thus the expressions *tabula rasa* 'scraped tablet,' *pater familias* 'father of the family,' and *alma mater* 'the nourishing mother,' are pronounced ['tɑbyulə 'rɑs/zə] (British ['tæbyulə]), ['pɑtər fə 'miliəs], and ['ɑl mə 'mɑ tər], respectively.

Fossilized pronunciations. One should make the point once again that our recommendations here would be more straightforward were it not for the considerable diversity of pronunciations inherited from the past. We have to take into account the fact that many Latin words and phrases (though not fully integrated into the language) have a well-established and widespread pronunciation that follows the patterns of phonological nativization generally accepted in Britain. For instance, our recommendation for the phrase *prima facie* would have to be ['primə 'feyši] if we followed our rules exclusively; but this phrase is so well known in the British pronunciation ['praymə …] that we think that that variant is perfectly acceptable in North America also. The famous opening of the student merry-making song, *Gaudeamus (igitur, juvenes dum sumus)*, 'Then let us be merry while we are young,' would be ['gɑude 'ɑmʊs] in the continental pronunciation, but in Britain the pronunciation is ['gɔ:di 'eyməs], identical with "gaudy Amos." Vacillation may occur even with relatively well-defined patterns. An example of this is the pronunciation of <-i> at the end of borrowed words. It is very likely to be pronounced [-ay], as in *alumni, a priori, loci,* yet while most borrowed Latin nouns whose plurals end in <-i> do indeed follow that model, e.g. *gemini, magi, nuclei,* all with [-ay], the <-i> in phrases such as *advocatus diaboli* 'devil's advocate,' *anno Domini* 'in the year of the Lord,' *memento mori* 'remember that you will die,' *modus vivendi* 'a way of living,' or *vox populi* 'voice of the people', *casus belli* 'a case of war,' both [-ay] and [-i] are freely used, while in *lapis lazuli* the most common pronunciation is with [-i].

Our discussion of this particular pattern is strictly confined to Latin borrowings. Thus the plural of *alumnus* 'male student' is alumni, with [-ay], but non-Latin loanwords: *salami* and *tutti frutti* from Italian, *corgi* from Welsh, *yogi* from Sanskrit, *colibri* from Caribbean via Spanish, *pastrami* from Yiddish, *hara-kiri, kabuki, tsunami* from Japanese, all have *only* [-i]. In summary, the value of the word-final letter <i> in non-Anglo-Saxon words can be one of the following:

Latin borrowings:
[-ay]: *alumni, a priori, Gemini, loci, magi, nuclei*
[-i] or [-ay]: *anti, anno Domini, memento mori, modus vivendi, vox populi, stimuli, a fortiori, casus belli*

Other borrowings – always [i]
Italian: *salami, tempi, spaghetti, tutti frutti*
Japanese: *hara-kiri, kabuki, tsunami*
Arabic: *mufti*
Sanskrit: *yogi*
Swiss German: *muesli*
Turkish: *effendi*
Welsh: *corgi*
Yiddish: *pastrami*

2   More on consonant spelling and pronunciation in non-native words

By definition "fully assimilated" is a qualification which suggests that words in this category are treated exactly like English words. There are some peculiarities of pronunciation, however, which are specific to the classical, and more broadly, to the non-native vocabulary of English. This section will address the pronunciation of the letters and diagraphs <x>, <ch>, <g>, and initial <ng->. The first three are used for native words too, while <ng-> is used exclusively in borrowings.

In classical words, the pronunciation of the consonant spelled <x> varies depending on whether the source of the word is Greek or Latin.

	Latin	Greek
<x>	[ks/gz]	[z]
	expel, vortex, examine, anxiety	*xylophone, Xanadu*

The letter <x>, named *ix* by the Romans, was adopted by them from the Greek alphabet. In words of Latin origin, <x> is normally pronounced [ks], as in *cortex, dexterous, expert, sextet*. In some cases the sequence [k]+[s] can even be reconstructed: *flec* 'bend' + *s* (<-*t*-) + *ible* becomes *flexible, para* + *dog* 'teach' + *s* becomes *paradox*; notice that there is no change of pronunciation in such cases; the only change is in the spelling, a change that has not been fully agreed upon on the two sides of the Atlantic. The accepted British spelling for the historical phonetic sequences of [k]+[s] is <-x->, while the most widely used spelling in the US is <-ct-> as in *connexion, inflexion* vs. *connection, inflection.* Both traditions have only *complexion* and *crucifixion.* The Yiddish word *laks* 'salmon,' German *Lachs*, has now been re-spelled as *lox*, and Americans are familiar with spellings such as *thanx, (White) Sox*, and the clever attention-getter *truxtop.* Another alternative, already discussed in Chapter 7, Section 1.2, is the voicing of [ks] to [gz] when the cluster precedes a vowel-initial stressed syllable: *examine, exact, exasperate, luxurious, anxiety.*

The [z] pronunciation of <x>, according to the *OED*, arises from "a reduction of (gz)." In English it is the most common pronunciation of initial <x->; it is also the case that most words with initial <x-> are of Greek descent. Spelling alone may be an unreliable guide to the source of a word, of course. Even in a word for which one *does* know the origin, as in the Greek name of the letter *xi*, the *OED* records four pronunciations: [s-], [z-], [ks-], [gz-], though only [z-] is common in Modern English. It is nevertheless fairly safe to assume that if the initial <x> in a word is not capitalized, or hyphenated as in *X-rated, x-ray*, the word is Greek and its first consonant is [z].[5] In transcriptions from non-classical alphabets <x> can be [s] or [š] as in *xu* [su], 'a Vietnamese monetary unit,' and in the place names *Xian* [šian], *Xin-xiang* [šin šiaŋ], except in the transcription of *Xosa*, also *Xhosa*, the people and the language of the Eastern Cape in South Africa, in which <x> stands for a sound similar to [kh]. Adding these additional values produces a rather complex picture for the pronunciation of the letter <x> in English:

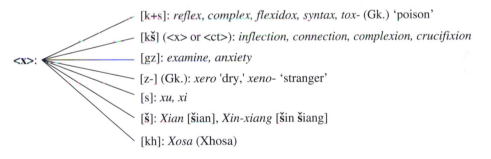

<x>:
- [k+s]: *reflex, complex, flexidox, syntax, tox-* (Gk.) 'poison'
- [kš] (<x> or <ct>): *inflection, connection, complexion, crucifixion*
- [gz]: *examine, anxiety*
- [z-] (Gk.): *xero* 'dry,' *xeno-* 'stranger'
- [s]: *xu, xi*
- [š]: *Xian* [šian], *Xin-xiang* [šin šiang]
- [kh]: *Xosa* (Xhosa)

Another potentially confusing orthographic difficulty may arise from the use of the digraph <ch>. The sequence <ch> was foreign to native Roman spelling; it was introduced to represent the Greek aspirate or affricate [x]. In words derived from Latin its value is what you would expect, namely the sound that <ch> has in native words and in words like *channel, chart, chapel, chisel.* If an etymologically Latinate word was borrowed into English not directly from Latin, but via French, the <ch> may represent [š]: *chammy < chamois, chute, cliché, douche, machine, moustache.* Note that in the latter group – words which are etymologically Latinate, but come to English through French – there is a tendency for the

---

[5] This convention is quite well established. A *Los Angeles Times* story about Xena, the "Warrior Princess" of TV, was cleverly headlined "Princess of the **X**eitgeist," punning on *Zeitgeist*, with an initial [z-], a word borrowed from German meaning 'spirit of the time' and pronounced [tsait gaist] in German.

replacement of the [š] by [č], as in *avalanche*, *niche*; clearly the innovative pronunciation with [č] is due to the influence of spelling. Yet a third way of pronouncing <ch> is found in words derived from Greek. These are consistently [k], as in:

archangel	Achilles	chi	stomach
chaos	chronology	character	echo
chimera	technology	charisma	machina

Some familiar roots with this pronunciation are *choros* 'dance,' *chem* 'alloy,' *chir* 'hand,' *chlor* 'green,' *chrom* 'color,' *mechan* 'device,' *tachy* 'speed,' *machy* 'battle.' In summary, then, <ch> can have the following pronunciations:

           [č] Latin via (S)French: ***channel, chart, chapel***

<ch>:   **[š]** French: *cliché, douche, machine, chef* (1842) *crèche, panache, quiche, pastiche, douche*

           [š] or **[č]**: *avalanche, niche, (carte) blanche*

           [k] (Greek): *epoch, monarch, chorus, chi, echo, chimera*

When **the letter <g>** is followed by a front vowel, *i, y,* or *e,* it is normally pronounced as the first sound in *gem, gin, gym,* i.e. [ǰ]. This is generally true of both Latin and Greek words (though, notice, there are exceptions to the rule in the **native** vocabulary: *gear, geek, geezer, geld, get, gill, gimmick, giggle*). One Greek root, *gyn* 'woman' has an interesting history: in some derivatives the consonant appears to contradict the rule, so we have *gynecology, gynecocracy, gynecoid, gynogenesis* pronounced with initial [g-], a pronunciation which was probably artificially introduced and is now maintained by the professional community. Notice that both [g] and [ǰ] are allowed by the *American Heritage Dictionary*. Inside the word, -*gyn*- is always [ǰ]: *androgynous, heterogynous, protogynous*. In summary:

           + front vowel → **[ǰ]**: *genesis, legitimate* (**Latin** and **Greek**)

<g>   (**[g]** *gear, geek, get, gill, gimmick, giggle*) (**native**)

           + cons./back vowel → **[g]** *magnum opus, gaudeamus*

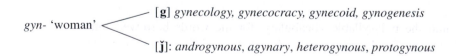

gyn- 'woman'   **[g]** *gynecology, gynecocracy, gynecoid, gynogenesis*

           [ǰ]: *androgynous, agynary, heterogynous, protogynous*

The clustering of [n] + [g] in word-initial position is phonotactically constrained in English. There are no [ng-] words in Latin and its descendants either. Yet the *OED* lists more than twenty <ng-> words all of them first recorded in the last two centuries: *ngaio* 'evergreen shrub,' *ngaka* 'doctor,' *ngapi* 'Burmese pressed fish,'

Ngbandi, *ngiru-ngiru*, etc. The accommodation of the initial cluster in such words can result in three different pronunciations:

In borrowings from Maori, British and American English favor simplification to [n-]. Occasionally, the dictionary records unassimilated pronunciations, as in *ngapi* [ŋəˈpiː], also NZ *ngaio* [ŋaio], *ngawha* [ŋafa]. By far the most common strategy, shown in the bottom row, is the insertion of a schwa to the left of the cluster, making a new unstressed syllable, so that the cluster appears in its coda and is therefore within the pattern of the native [-ŋ] syllable codas. A similar strategy of schwa insertion can be observed also with the <mb-> initial cluster, so that *mbongo* 'a political stooge' (from Zulu and Xhosa) is pronounced [əm-], *mbari* 'an extended family unit' (from Swahili) is also pronounced [əm-].

These minor complications are predictable in a language which is constantly expanding its vocabulary. Putting the inconsistencies aside, and looking at the vast body of loanwords in English, we can say that the consonants and vowels of the borrowed vocabulary are well on their way to becoming fully assimilated into the corresponding English values: the one-time loanwords are English words now, and both vowels and consonants should be treated in standard English ways.

3   Finding the main stress[6]

There is one respect in which words from classical sources can catch us by surprise: which syllable gets the main stress? This is not always obvious because it depends on some information which does not show up in the spelling, namely whether certain vowels were long or short in Latin. The importance of this question is developed below. But this chapter makes no attempt to deal with the rules of stress placement in general. To deal with the full lexicon, the rules are numerous and complex, with many exceptions to any formulation. The stress placement for words which have been in the language since Anglo-Saxon times presents no serious problems and we hardly need "rules" to describe the situation: it is the first syllable of the root that is stressed, e.g. *blóssom*, *bódy*, *hóly*, *néver*, *súmmer*, *unpáck*; these are mostly mono- or disyllabic words anyway. However, once we look into the polysyllabic vocabulary, for the words borrowed into English from Latin and Greek or formed by the addition of foreign suffixes, the rules can become fairly intricate. Knowing them will usually enable us to

---

[6] For a comprehensive description of stress on words and affixes, see Eric Fudge, *English Word Stress* (London: Allen and Unwin, 1984). A good accessible introduction to the linguistic principles governing word stress in English can be found in chapter 7 "Word stress" in Heinz Giegerich *English Phonology: An Introduction* (Cambridge University Press, 1992).

pronounce correctly a long classical word even if we don't know all the details of its meaning or how to parse it.

First, what is meant by "stress"? A syllable is said to be stressed if it is given more prominence than the syllables on at least one side of it, commonly both; if it is the most prominent syllable in the word it is said to carry the **main stress**. If you can figure out where the main stress is, then all the subsidiary stresses will fall into place automatically. Some people have trouble identifying the stressed syllable in a word; one way of training yourself to hear which syllable in a word is the most prominent is by pronouncing the word in a loud, emphatic manner: imagine a fiery speaker addressing a large audience: "I say de-MOcracy … we want edu-CAtion … let's give every child the oppor-TUnity …" Try yelling a word across a noisy room – soon you will develop the knack of recognizing stress.

Stress is not normally orthographically marked on the printed page, though sometimes authors will insist on italicizing a particular syllable or word for special effect. In dictionaries and philological descriptions such as this one, it is common to indicate the prominence of the main-stressed syllable by the use of capitalization, thus: *capitaliZAtion, PROminence, unaccountaBIlity, dicTAtorship, senSAtional, aristoCRAtic, arisTOcracy, TElegraph, teLEgraphy*. There are various other, equivalent, systems of notation found in dictionaries and in text-books, employing stress diacritics, accent marks before, over, or after the stressed syllable. They are usually explained in the front matter. Here is a sample of stress marking on the word *poster* in some of dictionaries we have been recommending:

The Oxford English Dictionary: ˈpoʊstər
Merriam-Webster Online: ˈpōs-tər
The American Heritage Dictionary: pō´stər

We find the system which uses capital letters for the most prominent syllables most readily recognized, and we will therefore use it here.

Stress is always associated with a particular syllable; you will recall from Chapter 4, Section 1.2 that the syllable is the smallest independently pronounce-able unit into which a word can be divided. Since both the position of the syllable in a word and its composition are important in the determination of stress-placement, we need to go over some principles of syllable division and define the properties of a syllable that will make it eligible to receive stress.

3.1   Syllable structure, syllable division, and syllable weight

Not every string of sounds can form a syllable: *skd* is not a syllable, but *a, I, skid* are syllables. The simplest way to identify a syllable is to assign a syllable to every vowel in a word. Vowels, and sometimes the sonorants [r, l, m, n], are the single obligatory component of a syllable. Structurally, that part of the syllable is known as the **syllable peak**. The syllable peak is the location where the most sonorous sound of any syllable is placed. Syllables have to have a peak. In addition, a syllable can have an **onset**, a consonant or a cluster of consonants to the left of the peak, and a **coda**, the position which is filled by any consonants following the peak. Thus, in the syllable *I* only the peak is filled by the diphthong [ay], while in *skid* [sk] is the onset, [ɪ] is the peak, and [d] is the coda.

Another important piece of preliminary information related to the composition of syllables has to do with syllable division. Some principles of syllable division are universal. Any two consecutive vowel sounds in a word form independent adjacent syllables, i.e. the sequence –VV- syllabifies as -V – V-:

> **VV → V – V**: *Se-a-tle, ide-a, Le-o, fi-as-co, Mi-a-mi, bi-o-logy, I-o-ni-an*

Note that the definition "any two consecutive vowel sounds" includes the combination of a diphthongal vowel plus a simple vowel, as in *Mi-a-mi, bi-o-logy*, and the sequence of two diphthongal vowels as in *I-o-nian*. A rather unusual case is the borrowed four-syllable word *ooaa* 'an extinct Kauaian bird', pronounced [ow-ow-a-a].

A single consonant between two vowels becomes the *onset* of the second syllable:

> **VCV → V – CV**: *fa-vor, po-tent, ra-ther, psy-chic, ci-vi-li-an*

This approach to syllabification ignores complications due to the nature of the medial consonant, the nature of the flanking vowels, and the effect on the perception of the syllable breaks after the assignment of stress. In effect, we take <C> to refer to a letter or letters representing a single consonant.

A sequence of two consonants flanked by vowels is usually split, so that the first consonant forms the coda of the syllable to the left, while the second consonant becomes the onset of the syllable to the right:

> **VCCV → VC – CV**: *fic-tion, sub-merge, prag-ma-tic, com-pul-sion, fer-tile*

The syllabification VCCV → VC – CV is not the only way two consonants behave between two vowels. The composition of the cluster and its distribution in the lexicon is very important. The clusters [kš] as in *fiction*, [bm] as in *submerge*, [gm] as in *pragmatic* do not occur at the beginning of any words in English. Splitting those clusters between two syllables is obligatory. Other clusters which are common word-initially may resist splitting. Thus, sequences of a stop [p, t, k, b, d, g] + a liquid [r, l] are frequent word-beginnings: *prom, tree, clasp*, etc. If such sequences are flanked by two vowels, they can remain cohesive and jointly serve as the onset of the syllable to the right, as in *re-prieve, pa-tristic, re-cline*. Interestingly, in Latin, the clusters *sp, st, sk*, which behave cohesively in English, are split in syllabification: *mo-des-tus* 'moderate,' *o-le-as-ter* 'olive tree,' *re-si-pis-co* 'come to one's senses.'

Sequences of three consonants are syllabified depending on the cohesiveness of the consonants.

VCCCV:
  VC – CCV: *al.tru.ist, An-glo-phone, in-clu-sive, tem-plate*
  VCC – CV: *func-tion, gaunt-let, sump-tuous*

The relevant functional aspect of this syllable division is that the syllable to the left always has a coda. Similarly, in sequences of four consonants, as in *instruct*, *excrescent*, *obstruction*, the syllable to the left always has a coda, and the syllable to the right has an onset.

Once we have divided the unfamiliar words into syllables, we have another important thing to discover about them, namely their **weight**. Syllables are **heavy** or **light**. A **heavy** syllable consists either of a long vowel or of any vowel, long or short, plus at least one consonant following it in the same syllable. Consonants in the onset, i.e. consonants which precede the vowel, do not count in determining weight. A **light** syllable has a single short vowel in the peak and no coda. Since coda-less syllables are also known as *open*, it follows that all light syllables are also open.

The syllable whose weight is crucial in determining stress in the Latinate vocabulary is the penultimate syllable (the **penult**). The penult is the next-to-last syllable (*pen* 'almost' + *ult* 'last'). The penults in these words are heavy: *recruit-ment*, *confronta-tion*, *deter-gent*, *extre-mely*, *esca-pist*, *abys-mal*. The penults in these words are light, because in each instance the consonant after the vowel of the penult belongs to the next (final) syllable: *a-ve-rage*, *bun-ga-low*, *re-gi-ment*, *ulti-mate*, *re-so-lute*.

3.2   The role of final syllables

Stress neutrality. The determination of stress placement depends on certain facts about the last two syllables on the right-hand edge of the word. However, not all such syllables affect the location of the stressed syllable. Inflectional suffixes, whether they are separate syllables or not, remain invisible to the stress placement rules. Certain final syllables which happen also to be suffixes are **stress-neutral** too. You can add them onto the stem to which stress has already been assigned, and that stress does not change. Most of these suffixes are from earliest English times, even though, as you can see below, they combine freely with familiar classical roots. There are also historically non-native suffixes which belong to this set: *-ist* and *-ize*. The following suffixes are stress-neutral:

-dom as in *MARtyr – MARtyr-dom*
-en as in *forGIVE – forGI-ven*
-er as in *inTERpret – inTERpre-ter*
-ess as in *PROphet – PROphe-tess*
-ful as in *reGRET – reGRET-ful*
-hood as in *GRANDfather – GRANDfather-hood*
-ish as in *FEver – FEve-rish*
-ist as in *perFECtion – perFECtio-nist*
-ize as in *CApital – CApita-lize*
-less as in *comPASSion – comPASSion-less*
-ly as in *MAtron – MAtron-ly*

-**man** as in *FOrestry – FOrestry-man*
-**ness** as in *inVINcible – inVINcible-ness*
-**some** as in *adVENture – adVENture-some*
-**ward(s)** as in *HEAven – HEAven-ward(s)*
-**wise** as in *WEAther – WEAther-wise*

It should be noted that while the borrowed suffixes *-ist* and *-ize* are normally stress-neutral, they remain so only if the form they attach to is a free-standing form as in *perFECtion–perFECtionist, ACtive–ACtivist, CApital–CApitalize, Union– Unionize*, but when attached to non-free forms, they require stress on the third syllable from the end as in *reCIdivist, anTAgonize*, or on the preceding syllable, if there is no third syllable from the end, as in *BAPtist*.

The most common stress-neutral suffix, not listed above, in classical vocabulary is the noun-forming suffix **-y** as in *Animate–Animacy, TEnant–TEnancy*. We list the examples with it separately; unlike most of the other stress-neutral suffixes above, *-y* can affect the phonetic shape of the word but not its stress: it changes [k] to [s], it triggers T-Lenition as described in Chapter 6, and it changes the [g] to [ǰ] in the derived suffixal form *-(o)logy* from the root *log* 'speak, write' + *y* as in *morphology, musicology*, etc., and in stems ending in *-agog* 'teach, induce' as in *demagog–demagogy, pedagog–pedagogy*. Also, since *-y* is frequently added to words which contain three or more syllables, nouns formed in this way can have a rather exceptional main stress position – four syllables from the right-hand edge. Except for examples with a stress-neutral suffix, it is extremely rare to have the main stress appear further than the third syllable back from the right-hand edge of the word:

Accuracy	efFEminacy	INtricacy
CElibacy	imMEdiacy	leGItimacy
deGEneracy	inDElicacy	LIteracy

Other suffixes are **stress demanding**. When you add them to a stem, they always steal the stress away from the stem and require that it be placed on them. Some standard examples of these appear below:

-aire as in *doctriNAIRE*	*-ese* as in *CantoNESE*
-ee as in *absenTEE*	*-esque* as in *araBESQUE*
-eer as in *auctioNEER*	*-ette* as in drum majoRETTE*
-elle as in villa*NELLE*	*-oon* as in *balLOON*
-esce as in *acquiESCE*	

More **final stress**. Some word-endings, which may or may not be productive suffixes, behave in the same way: they demand main stress. You will recognize the stress-demanding elements in the following words:

cruSADE	*kangaROO*
promeNADE	*shamPOO*

canTEEN	*techNIQUE*
velveTEEN	*uNIQUE*

Furthermore, a significant number of words take main stress on the final syllable, like the stress-demanding suffixes, usually because they were borrowed from some other language in which they already had final stress. They simply count as exceptions to the general rules of stress placement, and they include examples like these:

aBYSS	*guiTAR*
baROQUE	*hoTEL*
baZAAR	*inTRIGUE*
caNAL	*masSEUSE*
craVAT	*miNUTE*
cuLOTTES	*personNEL*
doMAIN	*raVINE*
gaLORE	*terRAIN*

3.3   Steps in determination of main stress placement

To determine main stress placement, follow these steps:

STEP ONE: Remove inflectional suffixes and stress-neutral suffixes.

All inflectional suffixes in English are stress-neutral, as discussed above – they never affect the position of stress in the word. By "remove" these suffixes, we simply mean "treat them as invisible in calculating the stress placement."

absenteehood	*(-hood)*	– stress as *absentee*		
contortionist	*(-ist)*	– stress as *contortion*		
defenselessness	*(-ness)*	– *defenseless*	*(-less)*	– stress as *defense*
demagoguishly	*(-ly)*	– *demagoguish*	*(-ish)*	– stress as *demagogue*

STEP TWO: If the word has two syllables, stress the first one.

Step two will assign the stress to the first syllable in words like *ANxious*, *COMmon*, *Exit*, *VERdict*. This general pattern goes back to Old English, where non-prefixed words were always stressed on the first syllable of the root. This is a very pervasive and resilient stress pattern – it is commonly referred to as the *Germanic Stress Rule*, though it also applies by default to disyllabic words borrowed from Greek and Latin: *delta, drama, datum, duo.*

The rule should not be overgeneralized. For verbs, it applies only to verbs whose final syllable is of the type -V̆C, a short vowel followed by a single consonant, as in *GALlop, PAMper, FURnish*. It does not apply to verbs whose final syllable contains a long vowel or ends in -VCC: *aMEND, reMARK, supPLY, surPRISE.*

Even if we set the verbs aside, we will find exceptions such as the ones listed above, the type represented by *craVAT, guiTAR, hoTEL*, all of which "feel" foreign, because they run against the stress pattern of native English nouns. There is also one completely native and entirely systematic set of exceptions: pairs of words, one of them **a verb** and the other the corresponding **noun**, where only the nouns follow STEP TWO:

Verb	Noun
esCORT	*EScort*
ferMENT	*FERment*
fragMENT	*FRAGment*
perVERT	*PERvert*
preSENT	*PREsent*
reBEL	*REbel*
segMENT	*SEGment*
surVEY	*SURvey*
torMENT	*TORment*

In some cases the pairings involve an adjective which has the same structure as a verb, but differs from it in the placement of stress. If there is a corresponding noun, adjectives and nouns pair together, while the verbs remain end-stressed:

Verb	Noun	Adjective
abSTRACT	*ABstract*	*ABstract*
freQUENT	–	*FREquent*
preSENT	*PREsent*	*PREsent*
perFECT	–	*PERfect*
susPECT	*SUspect*	*SUspect*

There are about 150 pairs in English in which the difference in stress is based entirely on whether they are verbs or nouns. The systematic character of the examples listed above has wider implications: even outside these homographic pairs, disyllabic nouns in English have stress on the first syllable, while verbs are more likely to frustrate the expectations of our STEP TWO. In addition to verbs ending in a long vowel or VCC, this is true of verbs, either of Anglo-Saxon origin, or later fully naturalized loans, which contain a recognizable prefix as their first syllable:

beGRUDGE	*proPEL*
comPEL	*reSIGN*
eJECT	*subTRACT*
exPLODE	*transCEND*
forGET	*unDO*

With these exceptions and the ones noted above, it is generally true that the first syllable of disyllabic words is stressed: *anxious, bias, bonus, carnage, common, current, donkey, ethics, exit, famous, finger, govern, horror, pepper, person, verdict, weather.*

A large number of the words we analyzed in the central chapters of this book, however, are words which contain more than two syllables. The next three steps will help decide where the main stress should be in such polysyllabic words.

STEP THREE: In words of three syllables or more, determine whether the penult is heavy or light.

Recall from Section 3.1 above that a **heavy** syllable consists either of a long vowel or of any vowel, long or short, plus at least one consonant following it in the same syllable. A **light** syllable consists of a single short vowel and nothing else following it in the same syllable. Note also that a fair number of words have penults that are **spelled** as if they were heavy, and therefore they count as heavy for stress assignment even though we pronounce only a single consonant and they are, strictly speaking, phonetically light: *baccillus*, *compassion*, *dilemma*, *discussion*, *dismissive*, *falsetto*, *occurrence*, *rebuttal*, *spaghetti*.

STEP FOUR: If the penult is heavy, stress it.

In Chapter 5 we covered the differences between **short** and **long** vowels. Finding out whether the penult is heavy or not depends on these notions. Recall that the labels "long" and "short" have mostly historical relevance – a genuine quantitative distinction between longer and shorter vowels once existed in English, as it did in Latin, but now the vowels of English are not always clearly different with respect to "length" but rather only with respect to quality (i.e. they sound different, but not in terms of actual duration). "Long" and "short" should therefore be thought of mostly as convenient labels. A long vowel, which always makes a syllable heavy, is one which corresponds in sound to the "name" of the vowel – A, E, I, O, U. In addition to these five, the diphthongs OU as in *house* and OI as in *noise* count as long. Thus the stressed syllable of each of the following words contains a long vowel, in the order just named:

spAcious
spEcious
spIcy
Ocean
mUtant
profOUnd
rejOIce

On the other hand, the stressed syllable of each of the following words contains a **short** vowel:

fAbulous
respEct
tItillate
harmOnic
profUndity

Here are some more examples which behave in accord with STEP FOUR, i.e. they have heavy penults:

confronTAtion   eLECtric
encycloPEdic   eNORmous
innuENdo   proFESsion
pronunciAtion   repliCAtion
spaGHEtti   verANda

STEP FIVE: If the penult is light, stress the antepenult.

"Antepenult" is a word which is etymologically fairly transparent. Here is how it parses:

> ante 'before' + pen 'almost' + ult 'last' – that is, 'before the almost last syllable,' therefore the third-from-last syllable.

Some examples in which the stress is assigned correctly by STEP FIVE (notice that it does not matter whether the final syllable is light or heavy, only whether the penultimate syllable is light or heavy) are as follows:

aSPAragus   MElody
CInema   MULtiply
comPArison   non SEquitur
eMEritus   phiLOlogy
encycloPEdia   PLEnary
eSOphagus   syLAbify
hyPOthesis   TElephone

The difficult examples are those where the spelling system does not reflect whether the penultimate syllable is light or heavy; that is, our spelling system does not indicate whether vowels are long or short (or were in Latin or Greek). Consider examples like these:

caesura – if light, stress CAEsura; if heavy, caeSUra (it's heavy)
corona – if light, stress COrona; if heavy, coROna (it's heavy)
detritus – if light, stress DEtritus; if heavy, deTRItus (it's heavy)
integer – if light, stress INteger; if heavy, inTEger (it's light)
stamina – if light, stress STAmina; if heavy, staMIna (it's light)

In a significant number of words, English speakers have not been able to make up their minds (or they had some misinformation when the word was first borrowed). Words like these can go both ways:

abdomen – either ABdomen or abDOmen (penult vowel is long in Latin)
acumen – either Acumen or aCUmen (penult vowel is long in Latin)
Caribbean – either CaRIBbean or CaribBEan (Sp. caribe, no vowel length)
cerebral – either CErebral or ceREbral (penult vowel is long in Latin)
choleric – either CHOleric or choLEric (penult vowel is long in Greek)

decorous – either *DEcorous* or *deCOrous* (penult vowel is long in Latin)
quietus – either *QUIetus* or *quiEtus* (penult vowel is long in Latin)
vagary – either *VAgary* or *vaGAry* (penult vowel is long in Latin)
vaginal – either *VAginal* or *vaGInal* (penult vowel is long in Latin)

And in a small number of words, the rules above make the wrong predictions (figure out why, in each case).

deCREpit	*COventry*
deVElop	*eLEven*
eNAmel	*soLIcit*
disPArage	*INterval*
iMAgine	*CAlendar*
INtegral	*deLIver*
apPArel	*PArallel*
caDAver	*CYlinder*

You should have concluded that the rules predict STRESSED + unstressed + unstressed for *decrepit, deliver, develop, eleven, enamel, solicit, disparage*. For *integral, calendar, Coventry, interval*, they predict stress in the middle. It should be easy to figure the reason why the rest of the words: *cadaver, cylinder, apparel, parallel, imagine* can be labeled "irregular."

4   Stress-changing affixes

Words which contain borrowed stress-changing affixes are regular in their own way, though they often appear to violate the general rules. You can think of the effect of the affix as a sort of override effect: no matter where the stress would be fixed by the general rules, the general rules are overridden by the special affix effect. We will not be able to cover the entire set of affixes in any depth; what follows is only a sample of the most frequent ways in which some affixes influence stress.

4.1   Affixes which attract the stress to the syllable on their left

With a small number of exceptions (*arithmetic, choleric, heretic, lunatic, politic, rhetoric, arsenic, Catholic, choleric, Arabic*), the suffix *-ic* and its extension *-ics* attract the stress to the penultimate syllable even if it would not normally be entitled to get the stress. When *-ic* itself is the penult, as in *-ical*, stress falls on the immediately preceding syllable, the antepenult:

genetic	*encyclopedic*	*acoustics*	*calisthenics*
orthopedic	*demonic*	*mathematics*	*robotics*
telepathic	*hygienic*	*athletics*	*poetics*
algebraic	*telephonic*	*hysterical*	*political*
Cyrillic	*Pacific*	*microscopical*	*ideological*

The suffix *-id* also attracts stress to the penult, but it is not so common a suffix:

arachnid	*intrepid*
carotid	*pellucid*
insipid	*perfervid*

The nouns *invalid* and *pyramid* are exceptions. The suffix *-ity* behaves in the same way, whether alone or in combination with other suffixes: it attracts stress to the syllable immediately preceding it: *divinity, masculinity, authority, vulgarity*. In a string of suffixes as in *-id* + *-ity* as in *frigidity, liquidity, morbidity, stupidity* and *-ic* + *-ity* as in *authenticity, infelicity, periodicity, specificity*, the stress is controlled by the rightmost suffix, the one that also determines the part of speech, while the stress-attracting properties of *-id* and *-ic* remain invisible.

Stress in long words of non-classical origin. On a final note, it may help to understand the stress rules in classical words if you recognize that the same rules work even for the many words, such as names of places, that we have borrowed from other sources like American Indian languages. Consider these words: *Chattanooga, Winnebago, Minnesota, Nebraska, Oklahoma, Okeefenokee*. All have a heavy penult, and the stress falls there. On the other hand, these all have a light penult, and so the stress falls one syllable earlier: *Potawatomi, Michigan, Oregon, Temecula, Canada, Tehachapi*.

We conclude this brief survey of the stress-placement rules with some caveats: our description was intended as a guide to the placement of primary stress only. Many polysyllabic words in English, as well as the place names in the previous paragraph, may have additional stresses, so that we do not get sequences of three unstressed syllables within a word. Another area that has not been explored here is the interaction between prefixes and stress. With the knowledge you have acquired in this chapter, you can try and figure out for yourself what happens when we attach prefixes to words, and how the stress of prefixes affects their morphological status. Happy searching.

Appendix

This list includes *all* morphemes[1] cited and glossed in the Root Exercises of the *Workbook* (Part B in each chapter), plus the affixes cited in Chapter 5 of the *Textbook*. The numbers in parentheses correspond to the chapter of the Workbook in which the morpheme is introduced for study or memorization.

This appendix does *not* include many other morphemes introduced as examples in the textbook.

Notation: In the list of examples, Latinate words, if any, are listed first. If words of ultimately Greek origin exist, they follow, separated by a semicolon. Unless otherwise noted, Greek words can be assumed to have been borrowed through the medium of Latin. In the rare cases where a word was borrowed or coined directly from Greek, the word is italicized. If only Latinate or only Greek words are present in the examples, the source is marked as respectively "L" or "G." If both are present, the Proto-Indo-European root, marked with an asterisk, is given where transparent. Otherwise the Latin and Greek derivatives are listed separately. Hybrid words are not marked. The connecting vowel and thematic vowel -*o*-, if it appears in any of the examples provided, is given in parentheses for Proto-Indo-European and Greek forms. In Latin the connecting vowel underwent vowel weakening to -*i*- but the thematic vowel to -*u*-, and very often neither is found in any of the examples, so no vowel is listed for the sake of simplicity.

---

[1] We have chosen base morphemes which are, with a few exceptions, near the top of the text-frequency and list-frequency counts found in E. L Thorndike and I. Lorge, *The Teacher's Wordbook of 30,000 Words*, 3rd edn (New York: Columbia University, 1959). We gratefully acknowledge the assistance of Sherrylyn Branchaw in correcting mistakes and omissions of the Appendix in the first edition.

	MORPHEME	MEANING	EXAMPLES	SOURCE
1.	a- or an-	'lacking' (5)	amoral; asymmetric, atonal	G a/an-
2.	ab-, a-, abs-	'from, away' (5)	abnormal, abstinence, abjure	L ab-
3.	-able	'fit for' (5)	agreeable, comfortable, incalculable	L -abil-
4.	ac, acer, acerb	'sharp, tip' (10)	acumen, acrid, acerbic, exacerbate; *acme*	*ak-
5.	-acy	'state or quality' (5)	advocacy, intricacy, accuracy	L -atio
6.	ad-	'toward' (5)	admit, advance, admonish	L ad-
7.	-ade	'an action done' (5)	fusillade, tirade, masquerade, arcade	Fr. -ade
8.	ag, act	'act, drive' (9)	agent, act, agile, ambiguous, litigate, navigate	*ag-
9.	-age	'condition, state' (5)	anchorage, postage, coinage, leafage	Fr. -age
10.	agog	'teach, induce' (4)	pedagogue, demagogue, synagogue	G ag- (*ag-)
11.	agon	'struggle' (11)	antagonize, protagonist	G agon- (*ag-)
12.	agr	'field' (11)	agriculture, agrarian; agronomy	*agr(o)-
13.	-al	'act of' (5)	renewal, revival, trial	L -al-
14.	-al (-i(c)al, -ual)	'with the property of' (5)	conjectural, fraternal, dialectal, sensual	L -al-
15.	al(i), ol(t)	'grow, nourish' (11)	adolescent, adult, alimentary (canal), coalesce	*al-¹
16.	al, all(o)	'other' (5, 7)	alien, alibi; allegory, allomorph	*al-²
17.	alg	'pain' (11)	analgesic, analgesia, algolagnia	G alg(o)-
18.	alt	'high' (7)	altitude, altimeter; alto	L alt- (*al-¹)
19.	ambi, amphi	'both, around' (5, 6)	ambidextrous, ambivalent; amphiarthrosis	*ambhi-
20.	ambl, ambul	'walk' (5)	ambulance, perambulate, preamble	L ambul-
21.	ampl	'large' (10)	amplify, amplitude	L ampl-
22.	-an	'of, resembling' (5)	reptilian, Augustan, plebeian, patrician	L -an-
23.	ana-	'up, back, again' (5)	anatomy, analogy, anachronism	G ana-
24.	-ance, -ence	'state, act, or fact of' (5)	repentance, perseverance, emergence	L -anti-, -enti-
25.	ander, andr	'male' (6)	android, androgynous, polyandrous, philander	G andr-
26.	ang	'constrict' (7)	angst (Ger.); anxious, anxiety, anguish; angina	*angh-
27.	anim	'mind' (3)	animate, animosity, animadversion, animal	L anim-
28.	ann	'year' (2)	annals, annual, superannuated, annuity	L ann-
29.	-ant, -ent	'one who' (5)	agent, defendant, participant	L -ant-, -ent-

	MORPHEME	MEANING	EXAMPLES	SOURCE
30.	ante-	'preceding, old' (5)	antenuptial, antechamber, ante-Norman	L ante < *anti-
31.	anth	'flower, collection' (11)	anthology, *anthophore*	G anth(o)-
32.	anthrop	'man, human being' (6)	*anthropology; anthropoid, anthropolatry*	G anthrop(o)-
33.	anti-	'opposed, instead' (5)	antidote, antisemitic, antacid, anti-Christian	G anti- < *anti-
34.	apt	'fit, capable' (3)	aptitude, ineptitude, inept	L apt-
35.	arch(aeo)	'begin, foremost' (2)	archaeology, archaic, archaism	G archai(o)-
36.	arch-	'chief, principal, high' (2)	archbishop, archduke, autarchy	G arch-
37.	-arian	'member of a sect' (5)	utilitarian, egalitarian, authoritarian	L -arian-
38.	art	'skill'	artful, inertia	OFr. art
39.	-ary	'having a tendency ' (5)	secondary, discretionary, rudimentary, tributary	L -ari-
40.	aster	'star' (2)	asteroid, astronomy	G aster, astr(o)-
41.	-ate	'cause X to happen' (5)	create, contaminate, frustrate, terminate	L -at-
42.	-ate	'full of' (5)	passionate, affectionate, extortionate	L -at-
43.	-ation	'state of being X-ed' (5)	purification, organization, contemplation	L -ation-
44.	aud	'hear' (4)	audit, auditory, auditorium, audience	L aud-
45.	aug	'increase' (7)	auction, augment, augur, august, August	L aug-
46.	auto-	'self, same' (3, 5)	automobile, automaton, autobiography	G aut(o)-
47.	av(i)	'bird, fly' (11)	aviary, aviation, aviator	L avi-
48.	barbar	'uncivilized' (12)	barbarian, barbarous	G barbar(o)-
49.	bell	'war' (8)	bellicose, belligerent, antebellum	L bell-
50.	bene, bon	'good, well' (8)	benefit, beneficent, bonus, bonanza	L ben-, bon-
51.	bi-	'twice, double' (5)	bifocal, biennial, bipolar, bisulphate	L bi-
52.	bio	'life' (6)	*biology, biogenic, biography, biogenetic*	G bi(o)-
53.	bol, bl	'throw' (10)	symbol, *hyperbole, metabolism, parabola, parable*	G -bol-, -bl-
54.	brev	'short' (2)	abbreviate, breve, breviloquent	L brev-
55.	burs	'pouch, money' (9)	bursar, bursa, bursitis, disburse, reimburse	L burs-
56.	cad, cas	'fall' (5)	cadaver, cadence, decadence, case, casual, occasion	L cad-
57.	camp	'field' (11)	camp, campaign, campus, decamp, encamp	L camp-
58.	cant	'sing' (4)	incantation, incentive, enchant	L cant-

#	Root	Meaning	Examples	Etymology
59.	**can, cyn**	'dog' (11)	canaille, canary, canine, cynic	L can-, G kun(o)-
60.	**cap(it)**	'head' (3)	cape, capital, capitol, capitulate, recapitulate, captain	L caput
61.	**cap, cup, ceiv**	'to take, contain' (9)	capsule, captive, accept, occupy, anticipate, receive	L cap-
62.	**car(n)**	'flesh' (3)	carnal, carnage, carnival, carnivore, carrion, incarnate	L carn-
63.	**card, cord**	'heart, agree' (3)	accord, accordion, concord, record; cardiac, cardiology	G kardi-, Lat. cord-
64.	**cata-**	'down, away, back (5)	catapult, catastrophe	G kata-
65.	**cast**	'cut off, removed' (3)	caste, castigate, castle, castrate, chateau, chaste	L cast-
66.	**ced, ceed**	'go, let go' (7)	concede, precede, proceed, access, accessory, ancestor	L ced-
67.	**cele(b)r**	'swift, frequent' (2)	celerity, accelerate, celebrate, celebrity	L cele(b)r-
68.	**cer(t), cre, cri**	'separate, judge, settle' (9)	certain, certify, crime, excrement, secret; critic	L cert-, -cre-^{1}, cri-, G kri-
69.	**cere, cre**	'come forth, grow' (7)	accrue, create, decrease, recruit, cereal	L cer-, cre-^{2}
70.	**chrom(at)**	'color, embellishment' (10)	chromatic, chromatophilic, chromosome	G khromat(o)-
71.	**chron**	'time' (12)	chronology, chronic, chronicle, anachronism	G khron(o)-
72.	**cid, cis**	'cut, kill' (11)	decide, fratricide, genocide, concise, incisor, precise	L -cid-
73.	**circum-**	'around' (5)	circumnavigate, circumspect, circumcise	L circum-
74.	**cit**	'set in motion, summon' (9)	cite, excite, recite, solicit, resuscitate	L cit-
75.	**civ, cit**	'city, refined' (8)	civic, civil, civilian, civilization, citadel, city	L civ-
76.	**clar**	'clear' (12)	clarity, declare, clarify	L clar-
77.	**class**	'group' (8)	classic, classical, classicism, classify, déclassé	L class-
78.	**clam**	'call out' (12)	exclaim, declaim, exclamatory, proclamation	L clam-
79.	**cli, cliv, clin, clim**	'lean, lie, bed' (5)	client, climate, climax, clinic, decline, proclivity	L, G kli-
80.	**clud, claus, clos**	'close' (2)	conclude, exclude, claustrophobia, closet, disclose	L claus-
81.	**co-, con-, com-**	'together, jointly' (5)	coexistence, cooperate, concur, compete, college,	L com-
82.	**col, cult**	'live, inhabit, grow' (11)	bucolic, colonial, cultivate, culture, horticulture	L col-
83.	**com**	'comic, comedy' (12)	comic, comedy, comedian	G kom(o)-
84.	**contra-**	'against, opposite' (5)	contradiction, contrary	L contra-
85.	**cor, curv**	'round, around' (10)	curve; corona, coroner, coronary, corolla, corollary	L curv-, G. koron(o)-
86.	**corp**	'body, flesh' (3)	corporal, corporale, incorporate, corporeal, corpse	L corp(us), corpor-
87.	**cosm**	'universe, order' (4, 12)	cosmic, cosmology, cosmos, cosmetic, microcosm	G kosm(o)-
88.	**counter-**	'against, opposite' (5)	counterfeit, counterbalance	L contra-
89.	**crat**	'rule' (8)	autocrat, aristocracy, bureaucracy, democracy	G krat-

	MORPHEME	MEANING	EXAMPLES	SOURCE
90.	cre, cred	'believe, trust' (8)	credence, credential, credible, credit, credo, creed	L cred-
91.	crypto-	'secret, hidden' (5)	cryptography, cryptoanalytic	G krupt(o)-
92.	cub, cumb	'lie (5)	concubine, cubicle, incumbent, succumb	L cu(m)b-
93.	cur, car, cor, cour	'run' (9)	current, incur, corsair, car, career, courier	L curr-, carr-
94.	de-, di-, dis-	'away from, down' (5)	decay, debase, digest, divert, disjunct, dismiss	L dis-, de-
95.	dei, div	'god, augury' (2)	deify, deism, deity, divine, divinity	L de(us), div
96.	del	'erase, wipe out' (11)	delete, indelible, deleterious	L del-
97.	dem	'people' (8)	demagogue, democracy, endemic, epidemic	G dem(o)-
98.	dent, odont	'tooth' (3)	dent, dental, indent, indenture, dandelion, mastodon	L dent-, G odont(t)
99.	dexter	'right hand, adroit' (3)	dexterity, dextrorotatory, dextrose, dextrous	L dexter
100.	di-	'two' (5)	dioxide, ditransitive, dichloride	G di-
101.	dia-	'across, through,' (5)	diameter, diachronic	G dia-
102.	dic(t)	'speak, give' (4)	dictate, edict, verdict, benediction, contradict, addict	L dic-
103.	dis-	'apart, reversal, lacking' (5)	displease, disallow, distaste	L dis-
104.	dis-	intensifier (5)	disturb, disgruntle, disannul	L dis-
105.	doc, dog	'teach, praise' (4)	doctrine, indoctrinate, doctor; document; dogma	*dok-
106.	dol, dolor	'suffer' (11)	condolence, doleful, indolent, dolorous	L dol-
107.	dom, domin	'control, lord, master' (8)	domestic, domicile, domain, dominate, domineer	L dom-
108.	don, dat, dot, dor, dos, dow	'give' (7)	donate, data, addition, editor, endow; antidote, dose, Theodore	*do-, L da- (zero grade)
109.	du-, dubi, doub	'two, double, doubt ' (5, 12)	dubious, dubiety, indubitably, doubt, double, duple, duplicate, duplicity	*du-
110.	duc(t)	'lead, pull' (8)	abduct, aqueduct, conduct, deduce, educate, induce	L duc-
111.	dur	'hard, lasting' (11)	durable, duration, duress, endurance, endure, obdurate	L dur-
112.	dys-	'bad, badly' (5)	dyslogistic, dyspeptic, dyslexia, dystrophy, dysentery	G dus-
113.	eco	'environment' (12)	ecosystem, ecology	G oik(o)
114.	-eer	'one who deals in X' (5)	auctioneer, balladeer, mountaineer, profiteer	Fr. -ier
115.	ego	'self' (3)	ego; egocentric, egoism, egoist, egomania, egotism	*ego
116.	electr-	'electric' (12)	electricity, electrode, electron (Gk. root = 'amber')	G elektron

#	Root	Meaning	Examples	Source
117.	**em(p)**	'take' (7)	exempt, exemplary, preempt, redemption, example	L em(p)-
118.	**-en**	'to become' (5)	darken, chasten, cheapen, deafen	OE -en
119.	**en-**	'in, into' (a form of in-) (5)	encapsulate, enclose	L in-
120.	**epi-**	'on, over' (5)	epiglottis, epidermis, epicenter, epicycle	G epi-
121.	**equi**	'even, level' (10)	equanimity, equator, equilateral, equinox, equity	L aequ-
122.	**-er, -eer**	'agent' (5)	baker, thriller, sweeper, retriever, volunteer	OE -ere, L -ari-
123.	**erg, urg, org**	'work' (9)	energy, erg, synergism, metallurgy, organ	G erg-, org-
124.	**ero**	'physical love' (6)	erotic, erogenous	G ero(s)
125.	**err**	'wander, go wrong' (12)	aberrant, err, errant, erratic, erratum, erroneous, error	L err-
126.	**-ery, -ry**	'collectivity' (5)	masonry, carpentry, slavery, savagery	L -ari-
127.	**-esc, -escent**	'become, becoming' (5)	tumescent, coalesce, pubescent	L -esc-
128.	**-ese**	'belonging to a place' (5)	Japanese, New Yorkese, journalese	L -ens(is)
129.	**-esque**	'having the style of X' (5)	romanesque, lawyeresque, statuesque	Fr -esque
130.	**-ess**	'feminine of X' (5)	tigress, laundress, stewardess	Fr -ess
131.	**esth**	'feel' (11)	esthetic, phonaesthetic	G aisth-
132.	**etym**	'true, source' (4, 12)	etymology, etymon	G etum(o)-
133.	**eu**	'good, well' (8)	eucalyptus, evangelist, *eugenics*, eulogy, *eupeptic*, *euphony*	G eu-
134.	**ex-, ec-, e**	'out from, away' (5)	exconsul, exwife, educate, eradicate, emit; eccentric	G ek-, L ex-
135.	**extra-**	'outside the scope of' (5)	extraordinary, extramarital	L extra-
136.	**fa, pho, phe, pha**	'speak, spoken about' (4)	fable, affable, infant, phonology, blaspheme, aphasia	*bha-
137.	**fac**	'do, make' (7)	fact, affect, infect. office, suffice	L fac-
138.	**fem**	'effeminate, female' (12)	feminine, female, effeminate	L femin-
139.	**fend**	'strike, ward off' (8)	defend, defence, fence, fend, fender, offense	L -fend-
140.	**fer, pher, phor**	'bear, carry, send, bring' (5)	circumference, conifer, defer, differ, fertile, infer; semaphore, phosphorus, periphery, *pheromone*	*bher-, *bhor-
141.	**fess**	'admit, acknowledge' (12)	confess, confession, profess(or), profession(al)	LL -fess(us) (*bha-)
142.	**fid, feder**	'trust, persuade' (8)	affidavit, *bona fide*, confide, federation, infidel	L fid-, foed-
143.	**fig**	'form, build' (10)	figure, figurative, effigy, fiction, figment	L figur-
144.	**fin-**	'end' (12)	final, finish, define, definite	L fin-
145.	**firm**	'strong' (12)	affirm, affirmation, affirmative, infirm	L firm-

MORPHEME	MEANING	EXAMPLES	SOURCE
146. flec	'bend, turn' (2)	flexible, reflect, reflex, deflect, circumflex	L flect-
147. flict	'strike' (12)	inflict, conflict, afflict	L flict-
148. flu, fluc, fluv	'flow, river' (5)	fluent, fluid, influence, affluent, fluctuate, fluvial	L flu-
149. fore-	'before' (5) (time or space)	forecast, forefinger, foreskin	OE fore
150. form	'shape' (12)	conform, uniform, formation, formal	L form-
151. fort	'strong' (12)	comfort, effort, fortification	L fort-
152. frag, frang	'break, deflect' (7)	fragment, fraction, fracture, refraction, frangible	L fra(n)g-
153. fug	'flee, flight' (12)	refuge, fugitive, fugue	L fug-
154. -ful	'full of X' (5)	peaceful, powerful, skillful	OE full
155. fuse, fund	'pour, melt, blend' (4, 12)	fuse, confuse, diffuse, effusive, infuse, profuse	L fund-
156. gam	'marriage, sexual union' (6)	bigamy, gamete, monogamy, polygamy	G gam(o)-
157. gen(er), gn, gon, germ(in)	'birth, origin' (5)	general, generate, gender, genesis, genius, germ, gonad, benign, malign, germinate	*gen-
158. geo	'earth' (11)	geodesic, geology, geometry, apogee, George	G ge(o)-
159. ges(t), ger	'carry, bring, offer' (5)	gesture, gestation, digest, congest, ingest, suggest	L ger-
160. glos, glot	'tongue, speech' (4)	gloss, glossary, glottis, epiglottis, polyglot	G glossa/glotta
161. gn, gnos, gnor	'to know' (4)	cognition, incognito, recognize, agnostic, ignore	*gno-, G. gnos-
162. grad, gress	'step, go' (5)	grade, gradation, gradual, graduate, degrade, agressive	L grad-
163. graph, gram	'make lines, write, record' (4)	agraphia, autograph, telegraph, biography, grammar	G graph-
164. grat	'thankful, pleased, kind' (8)	grateful, gratify, gratis, gratitude, congratulate, grace	L grat-
165. grav	'heavy, serious' (10)	aggravate, gravity	L grav-
166. greg	'flock, gather' (8)	gregarious, aggregate, congregation, egregious	L greg-
167. gyn, gynec	'woman, female' (11)	androgynous, gynarchy, gynocracy, misogynist	G gun-, gunaik-
168. hab, hib	'to have, hold' (11)	inhibit, exhibit, habitable	L hab-
169. hetero-	'other' (7)	heterosexual, heteronym, heteromorphic	G heter(o)-
170. -hood	'state of, condition of' (5)	childhood, womanhood, priesthood	OE hōd
171. hol(o)-	'whole, entire' (5)	holocaust, hologram, holarthritic	G. hol(o)
172. hom(o), homeo	'same' (6)	homogeneous, homomorphic, homonym	G hom(o)-
173. heli	'sun' (7)	heliotrope, parahelion, helioscope	G heli(o)-

174.	**hem, em**	'blood' (3)	hemoglobin, hemophilia, hemoptysis, anemia	G haim-
175.	**hemi-**	'half' (5)	hemisphere, hemicirle, hemistich	G hemi-
176.	**hend**	'seize' (7)	apprehend, comprehend, prehensile	L (pre)hend-
177.	**her, heir**	'heir' (10)	inherit, inheritance, hereditary, heir	L her-
178.	**hes, her**	'stick, hold back' (2)	adhere, coherent, incoherent, inherent, cohesive	L haer-
179.	**hon**	'worthy' (10)	honor, honorable, dishonor, honesty	L honos
180.	**hor**	'shudder' (7)	abhor, horrible, horror	Lat. horr-
181.	**hum**	'damp, wet' (11)	humid, humidity	L hum-
182.	**hyd(r)**	'water' (11)	dehydrate, hydrant, hydrate, hydraulic, hydrogen	G hudr(o)-
183.	**hyper-**	'over, to excess' (5)	hyperactive, hypersensitive	G hyper-
184.	**hypo-**	'under, slightly' (5)	hypotactic, hypoglossal, hypotoxic	G hypo-
185.	**-ia**	'condition' (5)	personalia; amnesia, paranoia	G/L -ia
186.	**iatr**	'treat (medically)' (3)	iatrogenic, geriatric, psychiatry, pediatric, podiatry	G iatr(o)-
187.	**-ic**	'having the property X' (5)	alcoholic, naturalistic, romantic; atheistic	G -ik(o)-, L -ic-
188.	**idio**	'particular' (7)	idiom, idiolect, idiot, *idiosyncratic*	G idi(o)-
189.	**-ify, fy**	'to cause to (be) X' (5)	purify, sanctify, verify, satisfy, liquefy	L fac-
190.	**in-**	'in, into, within' (5)	inaugurate, inchoate	L in-
191.	**in-**	'negative' (5)	indiscreet, ineffectual, incredible, illegible	*n-
192.	**infra-**	'below, underneath' (5)	infra-red, infrastructure	L infra-
193.	**inter-**	'between, among' (5)	interchange, interpose, intersect, interloper	L inter-
194.	**intra-**	'inside' (5)	intracity, intramural, intracellular	L intra-
195.	**is-, iso-**	'equal' (5)	*isochrony, isosceles, isotope*	G is(o)-
196.	**-ish**	'to become like X' (5)	churlish, boyish, peckish, stylish	Gmc. -ish
197.	**-ism**	'doctrinal system' (5)	communism, realism, romanticism	G -ism(o)-/-isma
198.	**isol, insul**	'island' (11)	isolate, insular, insulate, peninsula	L insul-
199.	**-ist**	'one connected with' (5)	socialist, perfectionist, dentist, pugilist	G -ist-
200.	**-ity**	'state, quality' (5)	agility, diversity, actuality	L -ita-, Fr -ité
201.	**-ive**	'characterized by' (5)	abusive, contradictive, retrospective	L -iv-
202.	**-ize**	'to cause to be X' (5)	popularize, legalize, plagiarize, miniaturize	G -iz-
203.	**jac(t)**	'throw, lay, lie' (2)	ejaculate, adjacent, reject, inject, eject, project	L iac-
204.	**jug, jung**	'join' (2)	jugate, conjugal, conjugate, jugular, juncture	L iu(n)g-
205.	**journ**	'day' (9)	journal, sojourn, journey	L diurn-

	MORPHEME	MEANING	EXAMPLES	SOURCE
206.	**kine, cine**	'move' (5)	*kinetic, kinesics, kinesiology,* telekinesis, *cinema*	G kine-
207.	**lab**	'take, seize' (5)	epilepsy, narcolepsy, prolepsis, syllable, astrolabe	G lab-, lep-
208.	**lat**	'carry' (6)	correlate, elated, legislate, relate, translate	L lat(us)
209.	**lat**	'hidden' (10)	latent, latebra	L lat-
210.	**leg, lect**	'choose, gather, read' (4)	legion, elegance, sacrilege, elect, select, neglect	L leg-
211.	**leg**	'law, charge' (4)	legal, legislate, allege, delegate, legitimate, privilege	L leg-
212.	**leg, log**	'speak, write, read, reason' (4)	logo, logic, apology, eulogy, prolog(ue), prolegomenon	G log(o)-, leg-
213.	**-less**	'without, free from' (5)	forms adjective from noun, as in faultless, keyless	OE less
214.	**-let**	'diminutive' (5)	hamlet, gauntlet, leaflet, driblet	Fr. -(l)ette
215.	**lev, lieve**	'light, rise' (2)	levity, levitate, lever, elevate, alleviate, leavening, relieve	L lev-
216.	**liber**	'free' (9)	liberty, liberate, deliberate	L liber-
217.	**lig**	'bind' (2)	ligature, ligament, oblige, religion	L lig-
218.	**liqu**	'fluid' (9)	liquidate, liquid, liquor	L liqu-
219.	**liter**	'letter' (9)	illiterate, literature, alliteration	L liter-
220.	**lith**	'stone' (11)	lithograph, lithosphere, monolith	G lith-
221.	**loc**	'place' (2)	locus, local, locative, locomotion, allocate	L loc-
222.	**loqu, locu**	'speak' (4)	locution, circumlocution, loquacious, colloquial	L loqu-
223.	**lud**	'play' (9)	allude, delude, elude, interlude, prelude, ludicrous	L lud-
224.	**lumin**	'light' (12)	illuminate, lumen, luminous	L lumen
225.	**-ly**	'appropriate, befitting' (5)	friendly, timely, shapely, fatherly	OE -lic(e)
226.	**macro-**	'large, broad scale' (5)	macroeconomics, macroclimatology	G makr(o)-
227.	**mag(n), maj**	'great, large' (10)	magnanimous, magnify, maximum, major, majority	L mag-, mai-
228.	**mal(e)-**	'bad ill, evil, wrong' (5, 8)	dismal, malodorous, malaise, malaria, malevolent	L mal(e)-
229.	**mand**	'order' (9)	mandatory, command, reprimand.	L mand-
230.	**mani**	'intense desire' (6)	bibliomania, mania, maniac, megalomania	G mani-
231.	**mar**	'sea' (9)	marine, submarine, mariner, marinara, ultramarine	L mar(in)-
232.	**mater, metr**	'mother, womb, surrounding substance' (6)	material, matter, maternal, matron, matrix; matrimony; metropolis, Demeter	L mater, G meter
233.	**medi**	'middle' (10)	mediocre, media, medieval, Mediterranean	L medi-

234.	**men, mon, mn**	'think, remind, warn' (3)	mentor, dementia, monitor, reminisce; mnemonic	*men-
235.	**-ment**	'condition of being X' (5)	advancement, treatment, abandonment	L -ment-
236.	**memor**	'recall' (9)	memorize, memorial, memorable, memory	L memor-
237.	**merc**	'pay, trade, sell' (7)	mercantile, mercenary, mercy, commercial	L merc-
238.	**mero-**	'part, partial' (5)	merocracy, meroblastic, meronymy	G mer(o)
239.	**merg, mers**	'dip, plunge' (9)	emerge, merge, merger, submerge, immerse	L merg-
240.	**meta-**	'transcending, changed' (5)	metaphysics, metamorphosis	G meta-
241.	**meter**	'measure' (10)	metric, metrics, metronome, perimeter, symmetrical	G metr(o)-
242.	**micro-**	'tiny, small scale' (5)	microorganism, microscope	G mikr(o)-
243.	**mid-**	'middle' (5)	midwinter, midlands, midnight, middling	OE midd
244.	**migr**	'wander' (6)	emigrate, immigrate, migrate, transmigration	L migr-
245.	**min**	'little, least' (10)	diminish, diminutive, minor, minority, minuscular	L min-
246.	**mis-**	'badly, wrongly' (5)	misspent, miscalculate, mislead	OE mis
247.	**misc**	'mix' (9)	promiscuous, miscellaneous, mixture	L misc-
248.	**miso**	'hate' (6)	misanthrope, misogamy, misogyny	G mis-
249.	**mit, mis**	'send, go' (5)	admit, emit, omit, transmit, admission, promise, missive	L mitt-
250.	**mob, mot, mov**	'move' (5)	motion, motor, promote, remote, emotion, mob, move	L mov-
251.	**mod**	'moderate, measure' (8)	mode, model, accommodate, commode, modal	L mod-
252.	**mono**	'one' (7)	monochrome, monogamy, monograph, monologue	G mon(o)-
253.	**morph**	'form' (10)	amorphous, morphology, morphogenesis	G morph-
254.	**mort**	'death' (11)	immortal, mortal, mortgage, mortify, mortuary	L mort-
255.	**multi-**	'many' (5)	multifaceted, multivalent, multiform	L mult-
256.	**mun**	'common, public, gift' (8)	communion, communism, community, immune	L mun-
257.	**mus**	'one of the muses' (9)	music, muse, museum	G mous-
258.	**mut**	'change' (9)	mutate, immutable, mutant	L mut-
259.	**nat, nasc**	'be born' (9)	natural, native, innate, nascent	L nasc-, nat-
260.	**nav, naut**	'sail, swim, boat' (9)	naval, navy, aeronaut, aquanaut, nautical	L nav-, naut-
261.	**nec(ro), noc(s)**	'death, harmful' (11)	internecine, pernicious; nectar, nectarine, *necrophilia*	*nek-
262.	**neg**	'not, no' (7)	negate, neglect, renegade, renege	L neg-
263.	**neo-**	'new, recent' (5)	neonatal, neolithic, neotype	G ne(o)-
264.	**-ness**	'state, condition' (5)	bitterness, fairness, idleness	OE -ness

	MORPHEME	MEANING	EXAMPLES	SOURCE
265.	**nom**	'law, system' (8)	*autonomous, anomie,* economy, antinomy	G nom(o)-
266.	**nom, onom, onym**	'name' (4)	ignominy; anonymous, antonym, homonym, onomastic	*(o)nomen
267.	**non-**	'not' (5)	nonsense, non-resident, non-intervention	L non-
268.	**nub-**	'to marry' (6)	connubial, nubile, nuptials	L nub-
269.	**nunc**	'speak' (8)	annunciate, enunciate, pronunciation, renunciation	L nunti-
270.	**ob-**	'inverse, facing' (5)	object, occur, obverse, opposite,	L ob-
271.	**-oid**	'having the shape of, resembling' (5)	humanoid, asteroid, tabloid, *anthropoid*	G oeid-
272.	**oligo-**	'few' (5)	oligarchy, oligotrophic	G olig(o)
273.	**omni-**	'all' (5)	omnipotent, omniscient, omnidirectional	L omni-
274.	**op(t,s)**	'eye, sight, look at' (3)	presbyopia, amblyopia, myopia, optical, optometry	G op(t)-
275.	**oper**	'work, creation' (7)	opera, operate, operand, opus	L opus, oper-
276.	**ordin**	'order' (7)	ordinal, ordain, extraordinary, subordinate	L ordin-
277.	**ortho**	'straight' (10)	orthography, orthodontist, orthopedics	G orth(o)-
278.	**-ory**	'connected with' (5)	obligatory, inflammatory, dormitory	L -ori-
279.	**os, or**	'mouth, speak' (4)	adore, oral, oratory, peroration, osculate	L os, or-
280.	**-ose, -ous**	'full of, abounding in' (5)	verbose, morose, jocose, glorious, vicious	L -os-
281.	**pac**	'bind, agreement, peace' (8)	pact, compact, impact, *pace,* pacific, pacifism	L pac-
282.	**palp**	'touch, feel' (3)	palpate, palpitate, palpable	L palp-
283.	**pan, panta**	'all, all embracing' (7)	panacea, pandemonium, panorama, panoply	G pan-
284.	**par**	'beget, produce' (6)	parent, vivaparous, repertory, parade	L par-[1]
285.	**par**	'show' (7)	apparition, appear, transparent	L par-[2]
286.	**par, por**	'part, share, equality' (6)	compare, disparate, parity, parse, impart, portion	L pars, part-
287.	**para-**	'beside, along with' (5)	paramedic, parallel	G para-
288.	**pass**	'spread out, go' (6)	pass, compass, encompass, passport, surpass, impasse	L pass-
289.	**past, pan**	'food, dough, bread' (9)	companion, pannier, pantry, repast	L pan-
290.	**pater**	'father, sponsor' (6)	paternal, patrimony; patriarch	*pater
291.	**path(et)**	'feel, suffer, illness' (3)	apathy, allopathy, electropathy, hydropathy, empathy	G path(o)-
292.	**pati, pass**	'suffer, endure' (7)	patience, impatient, impassive, passion, impassionate	L pat-

293.	**ped, paed**	'child, training, education' (6)	pediatric, encyclopædia, orthopedics, pedagogy	G paid-
294.	**ped, pod, pus**	'foot' (3)	biped, centipede, expedite, impede; podium, octopus	*ped-, *pod-
295.	**pel**	'push' (9)	compel, dispel, expel, propel, repel, compulsory	L pell-
296.	**pen(i)(t), pun**	'punishment' (8)	penal, penalty, penitent, penitentiary, repent, punish	L poen-
297.	**pend, pond, pens**	'weigh, hang, ponder' (7)	append, depend, pendulum, preponderate, pensive	L pend-
298.	**per-**	'through, thoroughly' (5)	perspire, pernicious, pervade	L per-
299.	**peri-**	'around, nearby' (5)	perimeter, peristomatic	G peri-
300.	**pet**	'go, seek' (6)	appetite, compete, competent, impetuous, impetus	L pet-
301.	**phag**	'eat' (9)	anthropophagous, dysphagia, necrophagous	G phag(o)-
302.	**phan, phen, fan**	'show, appear' (2)	phantom, sycophant, phenomenon, fancy, fantasy	G phan-
303.	**phil**	'love' (6)	Anglophile, bibliophile, philanthropy, philology	G phil(o)-
304.	**phob**	'fear' (11)	phobia, arachnophobia, hydrophobia	G phob(o)-
305.	**phon**	'speech, sound' (4)	phonetic, microphone, telephone	G phon-
306.	**phot, phos**	'light' (7)	photography, photosynthesis, phototropism, phosphorus	G phos, phot(o)-
307.	**phys, phu**	'nature, growth, plant, tribe' (11)	metaphysics, physics, physician, physicist, neophyte, phylum, *phylogeny*; *euphuism*	G phu-
308.	**ple(c), ply**	'fold, tangle' (10)	complex, accomplice, complicate, complicity	L plec-
309.	**plen, pleo, pleth**	'abundance' (3)	plenty, complete; pleonasm, plethora	*ple-
310.	**pol(is)(it)**	'city, state' (8)	acropolis, cosmopolitan, police, policy, political	G poli-
311.	**poly-**	'many' (5)	polychromatic, polyangular, polygamy	G polu-
312.	**pon, pos**	'place, put' (5)	component, composite, deposit, expose, impose, oppose	L pon-
313.	**popul**	'people' (3)	depopulate, people, population, popular	L popul-
314.	**port**	'carry' (6)	deport, export, import, portly, purport, rapport	L port-
315.	**post, poster**	'after, behind' (10)	post-mortem, postpone, post-script, posterior	L post-
316.	**pot, poss**	'be able, powerful' (9)	potent, omnipotent, potential, possible, possess	L pot-, posse
317.	**prag**	'do' (9)	practical, pragmatic, pragmatics	G prag-
318.	**pre-, pro-**	'before, in front of' (5)	preconceive, preposition, progress, professor	L prae-, pro-
319.	**prec**	'entreat, pray' (8)	deprecate, precarious, imprecate, imprecation	L prec-
320.	**prec**	'worth, value' (9)	appreciate, depreciate, precious, preciosity	L preti-
321.	**prim**	'first, foremost' (10)	primal, primary, primate, prime, primer, primeval	L prim-

MORPHEME	MEANING	EXAMPLES	SOURCE
322. **princ**	'ruler' (5)	prince, principle, principal, principle ['take first']	L prim- + cap-
323. **priv**	'secret, not public' (5)	private, deprive, privy	L priv-
324. **prob, prov**	'test, find good' (9)	probable, probe, probation, prove, approve, probity	L prob-
325. **prol**	'offspring' (6)	proletariat, prolific, proliferate	L prole-
326. **proto-**	'first, chief' (5)	proto-organism, protoplasm, prototype	G prot(o)-
327. **pseudo-**	'false, deceptive' (5)	pseudonym, pseudo-prophet, pseudo-archaic	G pseud(o)-
328. **psych**	'spirit, soul, mind' (3)	psyche, psychology, psychedelic, psychiatry, psychic	G psukh(o)-
329. **publ**	'people' (5)	republican, publicity, publish	L public(us)
330. **pud**	'feel shame, cast off' (6)	impudent, pudendum, repudiate	L pud-
331. **pung(t)**	'point, prick' (11)	expunge, punctuation, puncture	L pung-
332. **put**	'cut, reckon, consider' (7)	amputate, deputy, dispute, repute, reputation	L put-
333. **pyr**	'fire, fever' (3)	antipyretic, pyre, pyretic, pyrite, pyromania	G pur-
334. **ques, quer**	'ask, seek' (4)	question, request, exquisite, query, conquer, acquire	L quaes-
335. **rat**	'reckon, reason' (8)	rational, ration, ratio, ratify	L ratio
336. **re-**	'anew, again, back' (5)	regenerate, rehearse, restore, reward	L re-
337. **re**	'thing' (5)	real, reality, realize, republic, reify, rebus	L re(s)
338. **reg, roy**	'straight, lead, rule, king' (8)	regal, regent, regicide, regimen, region, regular, royal	L reg-
339. **retro-**	'backwards, back' (5)	retrogression, retrospection	L retro
340. **rig**	'stiff, rigor, rigid' (5)	rigid, rigor	L rig-
341. **rrh, rh**	'flow, stream, measured motion' (5)	catarrh, diarrhea, gonorrhea, hemorrhage	G rhe-
342. **riv**	'river, shore, stream' (6)	arrive, river	L ripa
343. **riv**	'stream, run' (6)	derive, rival, rivulet	L riv-
344. **rog**	'ask, take away' (6)	abrogate, arrogant, arrogatory, interrogate, prerogative	L rog-
345. **rupt**	'burst, become unsound' (7)	abrupt, bankrupt, corrupt, disrupt, erupt, interrupt	L rupt-
346. **salv**	'safe, healthy' (9)	salvation, salvage, salute, salutation	L salv-
347. **sat, satis**	'satisfy' (9)	insatiable, sate, saturate, satisfy	L sat-
348. **scand**	'to leap, to climb' (7)	transcend, scansion, ascend, scandal	*skand

#	Root	Meaning	Examples	Source
349.	sci	'know, discern' (8)	science, conscience, conscious, prescience	L sci-
350.	scrib	'write' (4)	scribe, proscribe, prescribe, describe, ascribe	L scrib-
351.	se-, sed-	'apart' (5)	separate, select, sedition, seduce	L se(d)
352.	sec, seg	'cut, split' (6)	segment, dissect, insect, sect, section, secant, sex	L sec(are)
353.	sed	'sit, stay' (5)	sedate, sedentary, sediment, supersede, assiduous	L sed-
354.	sal, s(a)ul(t)	'jump' (9)	salient, assail, assault, somersault, exult, insult	L sal(t)-
355.	sim, simil, sem, sembl	'similar, same, one' (5)	resemble, semblance, dissemble, simple, simplex, assimilate, facsimile, simile, sempiternal	L sem-, sim-
356.	semi-	'half, partly' (5)	semicolon, semifinal, semi-annual	L semi-
357.	sen(t,s)	'feel, agree, think' (3)	assent, consent, dissent, presentiment, resent	L sent-
358.	sequ, secut	'follow' (5)	sequel, sequester, subsequent, consequence, prosecute	L sequ-
359.	ser(t)	'put, arrange, write, speak' (4)	series, serial, assert, desert, dissertation, exert	L ser-
360.	-ship	'state, condition' (5)	dictatorship, trusteeship, workmanship	OE scipe
361.	soci	'companion' (5)	social, society, socialism, sociable, associate	L soci-
362.	sol	'alone, single' (7)	desolate, sole, soliloquy, solipsism, solitary, solitude	L sol-[1]
363.	sol	'sun' (11)	parasol, solar, solarium, solstice	L sol-[2]
364.	sol, hol	'whole' (7)	solid, consolidate, solder; catholic, holistic, holocaust	*sol-
365.	solv	'loosen, unbind' (7)	solve, solvent, insolvent, absolve, dissolve, resolve	L solv-
366.	some	'-like, apt to' (5)	cumbersome, awesome, bothersome	OE sum
367.	son	'sound' (8)	sonorous, consonant, dissonant, sonata, sonnet	L son-
368.	soph	'wise' (8)	philosophy, sophist, sophisticated, sophomore	G soph(o)-
369.	spec, skep, scop, speci	'look, see' (3)	specious, species, speculum, spectator, aspect	L spec-
370.	sper, spor	'scatter, seed' (6)	sperm, spore, sporadic, diaspora	G spor-, sper-
371.	spond	'pledge' (5)	sponsor, correspond, respond, despondent; spondee	*spond-
372.	spir	'breathe, animate' (3)	aspiration, conspire, expire, inspire, perspire	L spir-
373.	sta	'stay, stand, make firm' (2)	state, statue, armistice, substitute, apostasy	*sta-
374.	sti(n)g	'to stick, quench,urge' (7)	distinct, extinguish, instigate, instinct	L stin(g)-
375.	struct	'build' (9)	construct, obstruct, instruct, superstructure	L stru-
376.	sub-	'under, below' (5)	subdivision, subtraction, subtitle	L sub-
377.	super-	'over, above' (5)	supernatural, supererogatory, superman	L super-

	MORPHEME	MEANING	EXAMPLES	SOURCE
378.	sur-	'over, above, beyond' (5)	surtax, surrealistic	L super-
379.	syn-	'with, together' (5)	synthetic, synchronic	G syn-
380.	tac(s,t)	'order, arrange' (7)	tactics, syntax, syntactic, taxidermy, taxonomy	G tak-
381.	tag(t), tang	'touch, feel' (3)	contagious, contiguous, contact, intact, tangible	L ta(n)g-
382.	tec(hn)	'build, skill' (7)	polytechnic, technical, technique, technology	G tekhn(o)-
383.	ten, tain	'hold, maintain' (7)	tenant, tenement, tenet, tenure, sustenance, tenable	L ten-
384.	ten(d)	'stretch, thin' (2)	attend, tend, extend, intend, intense, ostensible	L tend-
385.	temp	'measure' (5)	temper, temperature, tempered	L temper-
386.	ter	'frighten' (4)	deter, determine, terror	L terr-
387.	termin	'limit' (4)	terminate, indeterminate, terminus, terminal	L termin-
388.	thanat	'death' (11)	euthanasia, thanatophobia, thanatologist	G thanat(o)-
389.	the	'place, put' (2)	theme, thesis, anathema, apothecary, hypothesis	G the-
390.	theo	'god' (2)	theism, atheism, pantheism, theology, theocracy	G the(o)-
391.	therm	'heat' (9)	thermal, thermodynamics, hypothermia	G therm(o)-
392.	tom, tm	'cut' (7)	anatomy, atom, dichotomy, entomology, epitome, tmesis	G tom(o)-, tm-
393.	top	'place' (4)	topic, topology, topography, toponomy, isotope	G top(o)-
394.	tor(t)	'twist' (10)	contortion, distort, extortion, retort, torturous, torture	L tort-
395.	tract	'drag, pull' (6)	tractable, traction, tractor, attract, abstract, contract	L tract-
396.	trib	'give, pay' (4)	tribute, contribute, tributary, distribute, attribute	L tribu-
397.	trop	'turn' (10)	tropic, trope, entropy	G trop(o)-
398.	tu(i)t	'watch, instruct' (4)	tutor, tutelage, intuition, tuition	L tu-
399.	tum	'swollen' (10)	contumely, detumescence, intumescence, tumor	L tum-
400.	trans-	'across, surpassing' (5)	transalpine, transoceanic, transhuman	L trans-
401.	tri-	'three' (5)	triangle, tridimensional	G tri-
402.	ultra-	'beyond, extreme' (5)	ultraliberal, ultramodest, ultraviolet	L ultra-
403.	un-	'not' (5)	unclean, uneven, unmindful, unbearable, uncouth	OE un-
404.	un-	'opposite, reverse' (5)	untie, unlock, uncoil	OE on- < *anti-
405.	uni-	'one' (5)	uni-sex, unidirectional, univocal	L un-
406.	uter, hyster	'womb, hysteria' (6)	uterus; hysterectomy, hysteria, hysterogenic	L uter, G huster-

407.	vac, van	'empty' (10)	vacant, vacation, evacuate, vacuous, vanish, evanescent	L vac-, van-
408.	val	'strong, useful' (9)	valid, valor, value, equivalent, convalescence	L val-
409.	ven	'come, bring, happen' (5)	adventure, circumvent, convent, convention, event	L ven-
410.	ver	'true' (8)	veracity, verdict, verify, verisimilitude, veritable	L ver-
411.	ver, vers, vor	'turn, roll' (10)	adverse, controversy, converse, vertigo, vortex	L vers-, vert-
412.	via, voy	'way, road' (5)	deviate, impervious, obviate, obvious, trivial, voyage	L via
413.	vice-	'in place of, instead' (5)	vice-consul, vice-president, viceroy	L vice-
414.	vic(t), vinc	'conquer' (9)	evict, victory, convince, invincible	L vinc-
415.	**vid, vis, id, eid, oid**	'see' (3)	evident, provide, video, *vide*, advise, television, visit; android, *eidetic, kaleidoscope,* idol, idyll	*weid, *woid, *wid-
416.	vir	'male, man' (6)	triumvirate, virago, virile, virtue, virtually	L vir-
417.	viv	'alive' (4)	vivisection, vivacious, vivid, revive	L viv-
418.	voc, vok	'speak, call' (4)	vocal, vocabulary, advocate, vociferous, vocation	L voc-
419.	volv	'turn, roll' (7)	evolve, devolve, involve, revolve, revolt, voluble	L volv-
420.	-y	'full of, characterized by' (5)	mighty, moody, healthy	OE -ig
421.	xen	'foreign, strange' (8)	xenophile, xenophobe, xenon	G xen(o)-
422.	zo	'animal' (11)	protozoan, spermatozoa, zoo, zoology	G zo(o)-

Index